Martyn Forrester was born in Guernsey in 1952 and educated in Canada, Guernsey and at the University of Exeter. After reading *Robinson Crusoe* at the age of seven he became interested in survival; in more recent years he has undertaken military 'Arduous Training' on Exmoor and an advanced survival course in Cumbria. His interests include hill-walking and skiing.

Martyn Forrester lives in London with his wife, Evie, and their daughter, Louise.

Martyn Forrester

Survival

a complete guide to staying alive

SPHERE BOOKS LIMITED

A SPHERE BOOK

First published in Great Britain by
Sphere Books Ltd 1987
Reprinted 1989

Reproduced, printed and bound in Great Britain by
Cox & Wyman Ltd, Reading

ISBN 0 7221 3588 2

Sphere Books Ltd
A Division of
Macdonald & Co (Publishers) Ltd
27 Wrights Lane, London W8 5TZ
A member of Maxwell Pergamon Publishing Corporation plc

To Team Miller and Team Leather, for pulling me through three tough months in 1981.

And to Akker, who died in the South Atlantic on 19 May 1982, for inspiration that still lives.

Those Himalayas of the mind
Are not so easily possessed:
There's more than precipice and storm
Between you and your Everest.

C. Day Lewis

Contents

Publisher's note

This book contains information which can be invaluable in dealing with a sudden emergency, in the wilderness or elsewhere, when knowledge of fundamental survival rules and techniques could save a person's life.

It incorporates 'state of the art' theories and teaching on survival, and the manuscript has been checked by some of the world's leading authorities on the subject.

But the book is not absolute. It cannot be. In any survival crisis, the variables are so many, so unpredictable and often so subjective, that neither the publisher, the author nor the experts who inspected the manuscript can claim that all the techniques in this book will guarantee you survival.

Some of the techniques and instructions may be inappropriate for persons suffering from certain physical conditions or handicaps. Misuse of the information could cause serious personal injury or damage to property, for which the publisher, the author and the manuscript reviewers disclaim any liability.

It is against the law in many countries or areas to kill certain animals or pick certain natural vegetation – or even to build open fires. Such laws are necessary, and vital for the preservation of wildlife. But when it comes to a genuine survival situation, there is unlikely to be a court anywhere in the world that would convict a person of doing what is necessary to stay alive.

Acknowledgements

Many organizations and individuals helped me during the preparation of this book, and I would like to register my gratitude to them.

My thanks, first and foremost, to the people whose ordeals make up *Survival*. Without them, and what they did to survive, no such book could have been written. To those who have lent me their scrapbooks, notebooks, cuttings and time – Steve Callahan and Dougal Robertson in particular – my special thanks.

Researching the stories was no small undertaking. I would like to thank the editors and staff of the following magazines and newspapers:

Alaska: *News* (Ketchikan); *Empire* (Juneau); *Sentinel* (Sitka).

Oregon: *Enterprise-Courier* (Oregon City); *Oregonian* (Portland); the *Dalles Chronicle*.

California: *San Francisco Chronicle; Tahoe Tribune; Tribune* (Oakland); *Los Angeles Times; Christian Science Monitor; Herald-Examiner* (Los Angeles).

New York: *New York Times; Reporter-Dispatch* (White Plains).

Colorado: *Rocky Mountain News; Denver Post*.

Idaho: *The Press* (Coeur d'Alene); *News* (Kellogg).

Maine: *Sentinel* (Waterville); *Times Record* (Brunswick).

The research task would not have been possible without the patient help of the staff of the British Library at Colindale and the British Museum.

Grateful thanks to the executors of the estate of C. Day Lewis for permission to quote from *Collected Poems*, 1954, published jointly by Jonathan Cape and Hogarth Press. Thanks for kind permission to reproduce certain extracts to Houghton Mifflin (*Adrift* by Steven Callahan), John Clare (*Hostage* by Chris Cramer and Sim Harris), Collins (*And I Alone Survived* by Lauren Elder), Granada (*Survive the Savage Sea* by Dougal Robertson) and George Allen and Unwin (*Almost Too Late* by Elmo Wortman).

Several experts agreed to vet the finished manuscript for inaccuracies, and I am indebted to them for their unstinting help. They are:

Dr Ray Adie, former Director of the British Antarctic Survey.

Dr John Barker, clinical psychologist with special interests in the psychology of survival.

Dr Carl Hallam, surgeon formerly with the Royal Marines.

Nick Steven, managing director of Survival Aids Ltd.

Phil Pennefather, chief instructor at Survival Aids Ltd, with special interests in mountain and jungle survival.

Peter Moor, instructor at Survival Aids Ltd, with special interest in hot-weather survival.

Sgt Roger Allen, formerly survival instructor with the Coldstream Guards, for access to his notes.

Squadron Leader A. J. Gibson, officer commanding the Royal Air Force School of Combat Survival and Rescue, Plymouth for advice on relevant chapters.

Others who have helped me in many other ways include:

Sgt Paul Leadbeater, for access to his notes, and for moral support over and above the call of duty during some very cold and wet days in Cumbria.

Steve Hitchman, for help with map-reading.

Scott Stewart, for help with nutrition.

Trevor Hek, for physical threats when I nearly gave up!

Nancy Rizzardi of the Federal Aviation Administration in Washington.

Dick and Diane Greenbank for water supplies at critical moments.

Last, but absolutely not least, Simon Firth.

Who
survives?

1 Introduction

On 30 April 1980 a group of Arab terrorists, armed with machine-guns, shot their way into the Iranian Embassy in London and took twenty-six men and women hostage. The siege was to continue for six more horrifying days, coming to an abrupt and bloody end when members of the élite Special Air Service stormed the building in broad daylight. All but one of the terrorists were killed.

One of the hostages, a thirty-eight-year-old Iranian who was medical adviser at the Embassy, was taken immediately to an intensive care unit. He had been shot six times by the terrorists as the SAS rushed the building. Two of the bullets struck him in the back, one passing through his lungs and the other within half an inch of his heart; two other bullets shattered his left hand; another went straight through his left leg and the sixth embedded itself in his right hip.

According to doctors, Ahmed Dadgar had only a 5 per cent chance of surviving. They told his English girlfriend that he would almost certainly die.

'But he seems so alert,' she protested. 'He says he can feel no pain.'

'His mind is strong, but his body is almost dead,' the doctors told her. 'He just *thinks* he's alive . . .'

But, within a few weeks, Ahmed Dadgar had confounded the doctors by making an almost miraculous recovery, and was transferred to a private hospital ward.

His battle to survive, and his victory, are not unique. In *Survival* you will meet many such men, women and families, who were confronted with disaster but who wanted to live, and *thought* they could, and did. They were all quite ordinary people, inequipped and untrained, who displayed courage, humour, resourcefulness and more, in quite extraordinary doses. They were not especially prepared for what happened to them but, without exception, when the odds were stacked against them, they rose simply and unpretentiously to quite heroic levels in order to survive. All they were armed with was an admirable common attribute – which this book salutes – a fierce, unquenchable, no-compromise will to live, a steadfast refusal just to give up and die. I think you'll enjoy meeting them.

In the sort of crises that this book talks about, some people have come through unscathed, while others have not. Some have actually been strengthened by their ordeals, while others have been crushed. You will discover that, for the survivors you will meet, the extreme external conditions seem to be matched by an inward strength and detachment – so that, even in the midst of the most desperate life-or-death struggle, there remains a centre of calm. There will be situations, of course, when no amount of composure will stop a person from being killed – but many more times, as you will see, when it is a person's determination and inward attitude that enable him or her to prevail against seemingly impossible conditions and obstacles.

The stories you are about to read should be inspiring examples of just what *can* be accomplished when the chips are down. Above all else, they should prove to you the validity of the single most important rule that anyone could ever teach you about the business of staying alive: *you'll survive if you think you can.*

So important is this rule, in fact, and so fundamental to the whole book, that I'll repeat it at once: you'll survive if you think you can.

Remember this rule, and *Survival* will be a book that can get you out of virtually any situation that threatens to kill you, more or less in one piece.

The book starts with a comprehensive 'how to' section

which incorporates the very latest in survival teaching and techniques, by the world's leading authorities. Everything from signalling to converting your urine to drinking water, and from cooking worms to building snow caves.

Thereafter, each survival story is accompanied by its own particular 'how to' section, telling you what to do in special circumstances, how to do it, and when to do it – whether you've crash-landed in the Sierra Nevada, you're being held hostage by a terrorist, or you're adrift in a life-raft. Taken together, the stories and instructional sections will tell you how to protect your body, and how to protect your mind. By giving you an understanding of the necessities of life, and by showing you how to meet them in every possible terrain and climate, they should help you to believe that survival is possible. By showing you that it is not necessary to discuss every conceivable survival situation because it is, in fact, your attitude of mind that matters, I hope that this book will let you see that you will indeed survive, if you think you can.

Survival is, in short, a book designed to help you stay alive. If it doesn't help you in any other way, you can always use it to sit on (and therefore to insulate you from the ground). You can tear out the pages and stuff them inside your shirt as an extra protective layer. Or you can just use it as fuel for a fire. In a survival situation, you might just find that that alone made the cost of this book the best investment you've ever made!

Who needs a book on survival?

You could be forgiven for finding it amazing that in this day and age people still get into the scrapes they do. This is, after all, the age of satellite navigation, CB radio, electronic location transmitters, and other sophisticated means of pinpointing people within seconds of a disaster and rescuing them: if you get into trouble, technology will save you.

No, it won't.

Conventional radio transmitters still cannot broadcast through mountains. The electronic location transmitter has reduced, but not eliminated, the time required for search and rescue – even in America, if an aircraft goes down at night or in the early evening, it may not be possible to begin the search until daylight. There have been cases when search and rescue teams knew exactly where a downed aircraft was located, but still could not reach it for a number of days because of storms, wind or turbulence in the area.

You might think that plane crashes aren't a good example because they happen so rarely. In fact, out of all the statistics I could give you in this Introduction to prove that an astonishing number of people find themselves in survival situations each year, here is just one: a recent US National Transportation Board survey analysed plane crashes that were caused by snowy weather, in a four-year period, in the USA alone. The number of crashes was, incredibly, 262. Think about it. Consider, too, that in winter conditions the weather at the crash site can be a more serious threat to survival than the impact itself.

Every month, there is a major natural or man-made disaster somewhere in the world. You could be caught in an earthquake, a flood, a bush fire, a hotel fire. Even if you stay at home, you can be trapped in a crowded lift or a burning building, or be the person who figures in those all-too-familiar winter headlines about walkers lost on moors, or motorists trapped in blizzards.

Few of us, of course, deliberately seek out such dangers. But all of us, often with very little warning, could find ourselves pushed to the very limits of our endurance – and beyond.

If you ski, you could face a sudden white-out on a strange mountain, or worse, an avalanche; if you sail, you can never discount the possibility of shipwreck (and if you do, you shouldn't be sailing); if you go fishing, or backpacking, or swimming, or drive into the national parks for a picnic or to visit relations at Christmas in snowy conditions, you run the risk that, one day, 'It' could happen to you.

Death, I am afraid to say, is a great democrat. Or, as the survival skills instructor said to my class: 'Death is God's way of saying you should have done survival training . . .'

The people in this book – why were they chosen?

Experts will tell you that the urge to survive is one of the strongest of all animal instincts. Self-preservation, it's called. We kid ourselves, as a result, that, if confronted by a disaster that threatened our lives, we could readily summon this will to live, and pull ourselves through.

Why is it then, when a yacht sinks in mid-ocean, or a plane crashes in the Peruvian jungle or Canadian wilderness, or a car breaks down in a blizzard on a lonely mountain road, that one person or group survives, and another perishes?

It's not just a question of training. Certainly, when the mind is numbed by cold or injury, survival training can, and will, turn emergency procedures into reflex actions and protective measures into second nature.

It's not just a question of equipment, either. In most circumstances, the right equipment will greatly improve your chances of survival. (In some situations, you will certainly not survive without it – with the best will in the world, if you're reading this page in the nude, in the Arctic, at –40°C, in a 50 m.p.h. wind, I don't rate your chances of getting through another two paragraphs before you're dead.)

The unpalatable truth seems to be that, in reality, very few of us have the basic determination to survive. Most of us would simply give up, and die. What we need are examples: people who can show us just what can be achieved if we – literally – put our minds to it; people who were able to carry on when the limits of training and equipment (usually none) had been exceeded . . . and lived through it. The people in

7

this book, with all the familiar supports knocked away, refused to give in.

So, enter Lauren Elder, the Wortmans, the Kriegers, Larry Shannon, Juliane Koepcke, George Owens, the Robertsons, Anna Conrad, the Cossanos, Ron Flory, Larry Ritchey, John Vihtelic, Steve Callahan and Martin Hartwell – fourteen remarkable men, women and families, and not a professional explorer, adventurer, soldier or mountaineer amongst them.

As you read about them, you might ask whether they can be said to have any – or no – characteristics in common. It is a difficult question to answer. I am sure, however, that survival depends more upon personality than upon the particular danger, weather, terrain, or nature of the emergency. Whether fear will lead to panic or act as a spur to greater sharpness, whether fatigue will overcome the person or leave him or her able to take the necessary action to survive, whether or not they have frost-bitten feet – all are, to a large extent, dependent more on the individual than on the conditions. I have not the slightest doubt that Anna Conrad could survive a jungle plane crash with as much courage and grit as she survived an avalanche, and it wouldn't surprise me to hear that the Wortman or Robertson families had survived a three-month ordeal on the moon.

It seems, however, that the main qualities important to survival are:

1 An ability to make up your mind.

2 An ability to improvise.

3 An ability to live with yourself – some people can't stand being alone, they have to be entertained. Others can take care of themselves and make a good thing out of a bad one.

4 An ability to adapt to the situation and make the best of it – some people can't change themselves, no matter how much their stubbornness costs.

5 An ability to keep cool, calm and collected.

6 An ability to hope for the best, but to prepare for the worst.

7 An abundance of patience – some people must do everything right now; others are able to wait until they have a surer chance.

8 An ability simply to take it – few people know how much they can really take, but expecting things to be tough or unpleasant helps all of us to be prepared to face the worst that can happen.

9 A knowledge of where your special fears and anxieties come from. All of us had accidents, scares and worries when we were children which still bother us. Under survival conditions, these may cause trouble – but if you know where they come from, you can do something to control them.

10 A sense of humour; the ability not to take life too seriously; seeing the funny side of things, even in the middle of a major disaster. At the very least, surely someone in your party can remember a joke? Keeping your own and other people's spirits up can help keep you alive.

11 An ability to set goals. Philosophically, life is made up of setting one goal after another and taking the trip in between. Hundreds of accounts of those who have come through survival crises with flying colours reveal that the survivor has set some type of goal: it may have been just to live, or it may have been a combination of staying alive and accomplishing something else.

The goal-setting process is vital to giving meaning and purpose to staying alive, no matter how much readjustment is necessary as you go along. Yet, tragically, many people have survived tremendously difficult ordeals only to die just after being rescued.

Their main goal, it seems, was to be rescued – they failed to look beyond that goal and establish others. They simply relaxed and gave up too soon.

12 Last, but certainly by no means least, an ability to 'walk in parks' – to see the beauty of nature. To see, like Lauren Elder, a tiny wild flower and think 'how brave it was to bloom in this harsh land'. To see, like Larry Shannon, sun on the snow that 'glittered like diamonds'. Or to watch, like Steve Callahan, the antics of a dorado fish, and be 'profoundly moved'.

As you read about their experiences, you might like to consider, too, some of the factors common to all disaster. Factors such as the total disruption, often sudden, unexpected and beyond one's control, of everything that is familiar – together, perhaps, with the loss of loved ones and material possessions.

How would *you* cope – physically *and* mentally? Imagine that your daily routine is not only impossible, but irrelevant: is it so surprising, then, that so many victims just wander around aimlessly in a state of shock, not even taking the trouble to protect themselves from further damage or look for water or food, until they simply drop to the ground and curl up and die?

I have often asked myself if I could cope as well as the survivors in this book did, in the situations that they faced. Perhaps you will ask yourself the same question – especially as, after reading *Survival*, you'll actually know how to handle those situations. If you do, please don't sit in judgement on the survivors: that is not why their stories have been presented. In fact, I can tell you right now that just about everybody in this book committed what the experts would call 'mistakes'. But by golly, they lived.

Now, before the main 'how to' section of survival techniques – indeed, to show you why such a section might be helpful at all – here is the story of a very remarkable American, Lauren Elder. If ever anyone survived because they thought they could, it was her.

2 Lauren Elder's story

Lauren Elder had been the illustrator for *The American Book of the Dead*. An exhibition of her paintings had just opened at the Civic Art Center in Walnut Creek, California. But, with no other major successes after six years of trying to earn her living as an artist, Lauren Elder had at last set aside a day on which to sit down and decide her future.

The appointed watershed day was Monday 26 April 1976. Lauren had been indoors for ten days, recovering from a bout of dysentery that she had contracted during a recent tour of Mexico with her boyfriend, Jim. But already something had happened which threatened to delay her big decision for another twenty-four hours: Jay Fuller, her boyfriend's partner in the veterinary practice in Oakland, California, had telephoned to say that he was flying over the Sierra Nevada mountains to visit Death Valley. Did Lauren want to go, too?

Eventually, she agreed. 'I remember thinking that I could move through a lifetime making little decisions and never get to the big ones,' she wrote, looking back on that day. She picked up a pencil, and scrawled in large letters across a sheet of paper: *I want to make a bold gesture with my life*.

Jay arranged to pick her up at eleven o'clock, with his girlfriend, Jean Noller. Lauren was to provide a picnic lunch for them all. She hurriedly gathered together half a leftover quiche, peanut butter, cream cheese and jam for sandwiches, and lots of tangerines.

Feeling that this was to be a glamorous 'dress-up' day, Lauren put on a cotton shirt, a top she had bought in

Mexico, a smart wool suit, thick socks and stylish boots with two-inch heels. Then Jay was knocking at the door. Lauren grabbed the paper bag of lunch, her Nikon camera and, as an afterthought, a jacket, a silk scarf and a cap – a cotton First World War flying-ace type, complete with ear-flaps. Who knows? she thought – it might come in handy.

Jay Fuller was thirty-six and divorced. His ten-year-old daughter, Carla, lived with him. He was no stranger to the outdoors – he sailed, flew planes, rode motorcycles and went hiking. His girlfriend, Jean, reminded Lauren of the sleek, blonde, wholesome girls to be seen everywhere on the beaches of Southern California. She guessed that Jean was twenty-one or twenty-two.

They drove to Oakland airport, where Jay had chartered a small red and white Cessna 182. Lauren sat in the back. As they took off and flew inland, the salt ponds that edge into San Francisco looked like big and beautiful geometric shapes, sulphurous yellow against deep carmine. The Cessna flew south-east, over the low-lying Coast Range and into the Central Valley. Jay announced that after Fresno they would be crossing the mountains.

'How high will we be going?' Jean asked.

'High,' said Jay. 'We'll be crossing north of Mount Whitney, and that's over 14,000 feet.'

At about one o'clock, after an hour in the air, the Cessna flew over the foothills of the Sierra Nevada. The terrain was wooded and empty; higher and wilder than any Lauren had ever seen. There were no cabins and no roads. Even lower down, there was snow in all the valleys.

Soon they had climbed above the tree-line. Below, there was nothing but rock, grey and glinting in the afternoon sun. It got colder inside the plane, and Lauren pulled on her cotton cap. Jean giggled.

Jay said that they would cross the mountains at Kearsarge Pass. Ahead was a towering granite wall, one great ridge of grey rock, with only a few low points. One of them was Kearsarge Pass.

'There it is,' Jay shouted. 'Wait for the jolt as we clear the summit. We'll drop with the air currents.'

Lauren saw the wall of rock coming close – terrifyingly close. But the plane didn't climb. It simply smashed into the mountain, tearing and scraping. Then everything was profoundly still.

Lauren felt no pain, but she had a deep gash on her right leg. White bone and sinew glistened beneath the parted layers of flesh. As she climbed from the wreckage of the Cessna, she felt the air strike her lungs, achingly cold and sharp.

Jay had suffered a head wound, and his face was caked with dried blood. 'Help me get Jean out,' he said, moving slowly and awkwardly, as if in a trance.

The plane had failed to clear the mountain by only fifteen feet and the wreckage was resting on a steep slope of rubble. Its nose pointed uphill and its propeller was twisted. The tail section had been partially ripped away. Lauren and Jay pulled the unconscious girl from the wreckage, but there was no level ground where they could lie her down. Every rock had to be tested to see if it offered a solid footing.

'I thought: this is it. We have crashed on the mountain-top. We can't go back and do it again. There is no second chance.'

Lauren thought her mouth was full of gravel but when she spat it out, she was surprised to see white fragments: not gravel, but bits of broken teeth. Then, inside her left forearm, she felt something move that should not be moving.

They dressed Jean in her anorak, and Lauren's socks and boots. The girl groaned and opened her eyes, her body jerking spasmodically.

'We got her on the ground,' Lauren recalled later in hospital, 'but she was very strong and unruly . . . sort of moaning and whining. Just anguished sounds. Nothing so defined as a scream. She was really unconscious.'

Lauren and Jay tried to move Jean back into the plane. But they could not lift her, let alone carry her. Even though

13

Jay was, by now, doubled up with stomach pains, Lauren sent him to radio for help, while she tried to stop Jean from jerking herself any further down the slope.

Lauren listened while Jay sent a Mayday call, but somehow she knew it was futile. When he at last stumbled back, he said he had activated the ELT in the tail of the Cessna. It had its own power source, and would send signals to help rescuers reach them.

They weighed things up. Jay was not required to file a flight plan, so had not done so. According to Jay's watch, which had stopped, the plane had crashed at 2.15. Carla, his daughter, would get home at about three o'clock, but would not expect him back until dinner-time. Jay was not even sure that she knew he was flying that day. Jim would not expect Lauren home until about six – and she had no idea how long it would be before he became concerned enough to raise the alarm.

Jay wasn't interested in such calculations – he was looking for a comfortable place to lie down. But Lauren wanted a plan. It seemed the right thing to do. She decided to look for landmarks. 'I'm climbing to the top,' she told Jay.

Lauren's body had felt numb since the crash, but now pain began to invade it – her injured left arm throbbed badly, and her right thigh was ballooning just above the knee. Her tongue hurt, too. Lauren opened a bottle of beer that had survived the crash, and took a long swig.

Her wounded leg made climbing difficult, but she persevered until she reached the summit, fifteen feet away. The sight at first overwhelmed her. Instead of the forested mountain ranges that she had expected to see, there was just a sickening drop, thousands of feet to the desert below. Then she realized she was looking down on Owens Valley, an area she had visited three years before. She was overjoyed. They weren't lost: all they had to do was get down there. 'Jay,' she announced, 'I'm going to try to hike out . . .'

'Go ahead,' Jay said, the tone of his voice still non-committal.

Lauren set off. She reckoned there was plenty of time to reach the desert floor before dark. Almost vertical at the top, the slope became concave lower down. So the beginning of her trek would be in snow, with just a crust of ice to support her.

Lowering herself carefully over the side of the mountain, Lauren kicked a toehold in the ice first with one boot, then with the other, and punched holes in the ice with her fists. Her left arm was working without any problem. After just six feet or so she lifted her head to check her progress, and her body felt suddenly weak. She knew she had made a terrible mistake in attempting to climb down; it hadn't looked anything like so steep from above. If she slipped, there was nothing to break her fall for hundreds of feet. For an instant she was paralysed. Then she took a deep breath and slowly began to haul herself up again. A chunk of ice came away in her hand. She clawed at a small ice ledge to try to get a grip, and could no longer feel the ice in her bare hands. Don't panic, Lauren told herself over and over. Don't panic. At last, she clambered over the top and lay fighting for breath, totally drained of energy. She was bitterly disappointed, but in a way relieved: she had made a mistake, and it had not been fatal. When she started back towards the plane, Jay watched her progress with his now customary indifference.

There was no chance for Jean now. She had disappeared from view, and Lauren was too weak to help her without Jay.

'Why didn't we make it over the mountain-top?' Lauren asked him.

'I should have circled,' Jay said, 'should have made another approach to gain altitude. It was so stupid.' Then his head slumped again, and he moaned.

Lauren thought about lighting a fire, but couldn't find any matches.

'The plane's cigarette-lighter?' Jay suggested.

They collected everything they thought would burn – maps, the paper bag that the picnic lunch was packed in, the cardboard from the beer cartons. Everything except the plane's log: Lauren put that in a safe place inside the aircraft.

The paper would not ignite at first. Then Jay soaked it in petrol that was dripping from an underwing valve, and it burst into flames. They settled back to enjoy the warmth, but the flames soon died down.

'Throw some petrol on it,' Jay said.

Lauren crawled under the wing and filled a beer bottle from the leaking valve. The petrol made the fire burn fiercely, but they would need more containers to catch the remaining fuel before the tank emptied. Jay drained another bottle of beer, but the fire went out before Lauren could fill it up. If the idea was to work, they would have to keep the bottles rotating. Lauren tried to get Jay to help her, but it was obvious to her from his indifference that their survival was firmly in her hands.

Lauren could afford to sit back for just a few minutes between journeys, and enjoy the warmth of the fire. When darkness fell there was no moon; the only light came from the fire. Out of contact with the fire's heat, their backs were beginning to freeze.

They both realized that Jean could not survive the onslaught of the cold. Lauren reached for Jay's hand. It, too, was cold, and she began to rub it. She needed to feel close to him, to know that they were in this together.

'Can we promise that we'll see this through together?' she asked him.

'Sure,' came the reply. 'We'll make it.'

Lauren lost count of the number of trips she made backwards and forwards between the fire and the petrol valve on the wing. She wanted to give up, but knew she couldn't – the only way to get off the mountain was to keep feeding the fire.

Jay complained again about bad stomach pains. His speech was slurred. Lauren fought back the temptation to tell him that it was taking all her effort just to manage her own body's problems, without having to listen to his complaints.

Probably through carelessness born of fatigue, petrol suddenly splashed on to Lauren's face. Engulfed in flames, she dropped the bottle and raised her arms. She smelt her hair burning, felt her cheeks being singed. She slapped frantically at the flames. Jay heaved himself up to help, and together they extinguished the flames. Then Lauren picked up the bottle, and went for more petrol.

During one of her rests, Lauren sat down on a rock. It felt unbelievably good – it was warm. She told Jay, and began piling up large stones that they could set fire to and produce some sort of radiator.

It was now five or six hours since they had started the fire. Jay had moved very little in that time, although he made a brief effort to help Lauren build her radiator. By the time there were a score of rocks in the pile, the wind had increased, whipping up whirlpools of flame into the dark sky. There were four or five more hours of cold night still to get through. Just think of the next trip for fuel, Lauren told herself. The next step, the next rock. No more. She handed Jay a full bottle of petrol and went back under the wing for another. Jay's job was to build up the flames so that Lauren could see what she was doing, but she suddenly noticed that the light was dimming. Shouting at Jay, she rushed back with her full bottle and poured it over the dying fire. It sizzled, then went out. Lauren climbed back into the cockpit of the Cessna and activated the cigarette-lighter. Nothing happened. The aircraft's battery had gone flat.

Now their only heat source was the hot rocks. To keep the stones warmer for longer, they would have to get them out of the wind, into the tail of the plane. Getting no response from Jay, Lauren started to grope in the dark for the stones. She smelt flesh singeing as her fingers closed round one, and felt the pain. But somehow she held on. Her left arm was of little use now, but still she managed to get several stones into the plane. Then she curled up next to

17

them, out of the wind, and enjoyed their radiated warmth.

She called Jay to join her. There was no answer. When she called again, he laboriously dragged himself over to the plane, between the front seats and over the back seat, so that he came down next to Lauren. The first thing she noticed was that one of his shoes was missing.

'Forget it,' Jay said irritably, tossing and turning in an attempt to get comfortable. The whole plane rocked with the motion. Ignoring the jabs and prods from Jay's elbows and knees, Lauren began to rub his legs and blow on his hands, trying to warm him up. She nagged him constantly to keep his hood pulled over his head, his shirt over his face, his hands tucked somewhere warm.

Silently, Lauren carried out a formal dialogue. Keep moving your toes, she would tell herself. Then she would obediently wiggle her toes and think about nothing.

'We must stay awake,' she said out loud. Jay grunted. 'They must know about us by now,' Lauren said, trying to start a conversation. 'They won't take off in the dark, but the search planes will come at daybreak.'

(In fact, the Federal Aviation Authority issued an alert for the missing Cessna at 2.24 a.m., and at 3.48 a.m. the Air Rescue Centre in Illinois issued a search mission number for the aircraft. Jim Fizdale had gone over to Jay's house at nine o'clock the previous evening, to look after Carla when it was clear that the picnic party was overdue. Later, he started making enquiries by telephone, and eventually he raised the alarm.)

The rocks in the plane had begun to cool; Lauren knew that the next few hours would be the most difficult. But at least she was wedged down beneath Jay in the tail section; the injured pilot was exposed to the open cockpit.

'Come on, sun,' Jay moaned again and again. 'I'm so cold.' Then he threw back his head into the swirling snow and howled – a terrible sound that was a mixture of pain and rage and fear. He began to thrash about again, more heavily this time.

'I've got to get out of here . . .' he groaned, ' . . . got to do something.'

18

'There's nothing we can do,' Lauren protested.

Jay was quiet for a while, then he said, 'I can't feel anything . . .' He began to hammer his hands against the sides of the plane, and cried out. He thrashed about so wildly that Lauren began to pummel him with her fists to make him stop, but to no avail. Eventually she withdrew – mentally as well as physically – squeezing herself down as far as possible into the tail section. It cannot get worse, Lauren thought. It can only get better.

It was several minutes before Jay calmed down. Lauren lay very still, fearful of jogging him into another bout of struggling. Jay's trouser legs had ridden up during his paroxysms, exposing his calves. When Lauren thought it was safe to make a move, she pulled the material down. Her wrist brushed against his leg. It felt cold – frighteningly cold. She reached up and touched his arm. The flesh was frozen solid. She turned him gently, and the dead pilot rolled away from her, his eyes open and staring, the wind ruffling his snow-powdered hair in the first light of day.

There was nothing Lauren could do but to curl up and wait. She started to wonder what her body would look like when the rescuers arrived. Huddled in a foetal position, frozen and grotesque? The thought disturbed her. It seemed such a waste. What she was imagining was tantamount to suicide.

'My mother's brother had died in a small plane when the wings iced over,' Lauren wrote later. 'I didn't want her to go through that again. And I had so much left to do. I had hardly even begun. There were so many places I had not been, so many people I had not met, so much work to be done. I had not laughed enough or learned enough or felt enough. I had not borne a child. No, I said to myself. Not yet. Not now.'

Lauren began to work Jay's socks off his feet, and put them on. Then she was suddenly aware of a sound that was even louder than the noise of the wind. She climbed out of the tail section just in time to see a plane flying over a mountain ridge to the south. Jumping around and waving her arms, Lauren shouted at the top of her voice. But the plane flew gradually out of sight, its pilot oblivious of the drama below.

Loath to get back into the aircraft beside Jay's body, Lauren checked the tree-line below her to the west, wondering if that offered a possible escape route. There would be protection down there from the wind, but it would be a long trek, and her chances of being spotted from the air would be greatly reduced. So her only way out was via the steep eastern slope – the one she had failed to descend earlier.

She climbed to the summit of the ridge and sheltered behind a huge outcrop of granite. As the first sunlight of the day began to warm her aching, frozen body, she noticed for the first time that there were other outcrops of granite, zig-zagging down the eastern slope. Linking them together in her mind in a ragged kind of pattern, she reckoned that by moving on all fours she could punch through the ice crust with her hands and feet, and descend. If the worst came to the worst, she could always go back up again.

Lauren had no way of knowing whether the alarm had been raised at home. No aircraft had come looking for the wrecked plane – but did that just mean they were searching in the wrong area, and would work their way towards her? What if Jim and Carla had simply decided to wait another day before alerting the authorities? Could she handle another night on the freezing mountain?

Slowly she eased herself over the edge. The ice was thicker and harder than it had been the night before. The hole she punched with her foot supported her weight. It took just half a dozen movements to reach the first rock. Her fatigue of the previous evening had lifted. Now she felt revitalized, full of fresh hope.

After an hour or so of punching through the ice and clinging on, using her painful left arm as well as her right, Lauren sensed that the incline was lessening. The slope was shallow enough for her to slide down the ice. She whooped with excitement as she glided down from rock to rock, spinning, glissading, sometimes even turning in circles. She was aware of the sound of her own laughter, echoing down the silent pass.

By mid-morning she had travelled about a third of the way down the snow-field. Soon she was able to stand up and side-step down, heading for an expanse of ochre-coloured rock which funnelled into a dry, rock-filled stream bed. It was only when she stopped for a rest, that she scanned the mountain and saw a row of cedarwood houses curving along a ridge opposite her. Scarcely able to contain her exhilaration, she rushed towards the settlement. On the balcony of the highest house, a man with long, fair hair stood with his arms outstretched, a white robe billowing around him, a large black cross hanging around his neck.

Lauren called out to him. 'I've been in a plane crash! I need help!'

But the man did not reply; did not even move. It was not a man, but a statue – of the sort erected in the Alps to mark the spot where someone died. Then Lauren reached the first of the cedarwood houses and blinked hard. There were no houses. There was no statue. Only rocks. The detour had cost her a lot in terms of time and strength. With another half-mile left before she even reached the base of the snow-field, Lauren turned and started down once more.

There was a dry stream bed at the lowest point in the canyon where two mountain ridges came together. But the ridges meshed at several points, sending the stream bed through a series of sharp turns, and Lauren turned corner after corner only to find another one ahead.

The sun was high in the sky, and hot. To relieve her thirst, Lauren would scoop up a handful of snow from the shade of a rock, sometimes waiting for it to melt, but more often putting it straight in her mouth.

At one point, she noticed a tiny, fragile wild flower. 'For a minute I stood looking at it, trying to understand what there was about it that so moved me. How brave it was to bloom in this harsh land. Had I not come along, no one would have ever seen it. The thought occupied me as I trudged on.'

She encountered more and more scrubby sagebrush, which scratched her legs and tugged at her skirt. Rounding yet another bend, she found herself standing at the top of a dry waterfall that fell, straight down, to the canyon floor a hundred feet below. She was trapped.

'I waited for a few minutes,' Lauren later wrote, 'and then I did the only thing I could think of. "Help!" I yelled, at the top of my voice . . . "Please, somebody, help me." '

Eventually she calmed down, and lay on her stomach to check the descent. What appeared at first glance to be smooth granite all the way down was, in fact, a pitted and cracked surface, offering fingerholds and toeholds, with a series of narrow ledges every ten to twenty feet.

Taking off her boots, she tucked Jay's socks inside and let them drop over the edge down the first ledge. Then she lowered herself over the edge, and started to feel her way down.

She collapsed on to the first ledge with a sigh of relief. Then she realized that her position was now even more precarious than ever: she wouldn't have the strength or skill to climb back up; she was committed to the dangerous descent. A strange feeling came over her. It was a feeling almost of invincibility, as if nothing could go wrong. 'Something was happening between my body and the face of the dry waterfall. They seemed to understand each other.'

Further down, she was helped by a fallen tree that had lodged itself along the side of the gorge and the ledge below, making a natural staircase. She scrambled down it and into a pile of snow. The next ledge down was the widest, with a hollow depression in the middle of it, filled with water more than three feet deep. Lauren took off her clothes, bundled them together with her boots, and dropped them over the side. Then she half-sat in a wet trough in the cliff face and slid down, landing with a splash in the water-filled hollow. The water was wonderfully cool. She bathed her wounds in it, and washed off most of the dust, sweat, blood and grime that covered her body. Suddenly, she saw a glint of light at the top of the cliff: along the southern rim of the canyon was a row of houses, with two cars parked just beyond. Sunlight was reflecting off them. 'Finally, I thought, it has really happened.'

Lauren dressed quickly and started to climb up the snow-covered slope. When she was within a few yards of the first house, a man and a woman came out to meet her.

'I need your help,' she said.

But the couple said and did nothing. It took Lauren a while to realize why. Then it came to her: they weren't there. Again, she was the victim of her own imaginings.

By the position of the sun she guessed it was two o'clock before she half-climbed, half-fell, back to the ledge. To reach the desert floor by sunset, she would have to speed up. But, as she dropped her boots over the ledge and started another descent, she became aware that her strength was failing as her earlier energy failed. Then she reached too far to one foothold and ended up spread-eagled against the cliff face, unable to move.

Lauren could feel the sweat break out on her body. Her grip was loosening. There was only one thing to do, and, with a huge effort, she lunged for the ledge she had just left and pulled herself back to safety. She lay on the ledge trembling with exhaustion, a flap of skin hanging from a toe of her left foot where she had caught it on the granite. Gradually she forced herself to calm down. After a while, she was ready to try again, and levered herself over the edge. She reached the next ledge without incident, and then there was only one to go. After that, just a drop of fifteen feet and she was on the canyon floor. She landed in a snow drift that had piled up against the cliff.

Lauren searched for a stick that would help her to walk, then staggered on. Soon she heard the sound of rushing water and found that the dry stream bed had filled. She limped to it and sat on a stone. Her boots were split open and useless. Pulling them off, she left them behind. From now on, she decided, she would travel in the water.

As the shadows in the canyon lengthened, Lauren knew that she would have to move faster if she was to avoid another freezing night out in the open. For a while the only noises were her own breathing and her slipping, sliding progress through the water. Then, above these, she heard a louder roar, that got even louder and more furious as she moved forward. The stream plummeted in a fifty-foot waterfall that threw up a fine drizzle of icy mist. To the right a wall of granite reared a hundred feet; to the left, a gradual slope of sand, loose rock and scrubby bush rose above the waterfall. It was her only way out. With a final burst of energy, Lauren struck out determinedly for the top. When she reached it, she was rewarded with a beautiful sight: the rest of her journey was going to be a gentle descent to the desert floor. I'm going to make it, was her immediate thought. Later, in hospital, she admitted to having felt 'kind of tickled to get to the bottom'. She launched herself down the slope and, almost at once, came across a path. 'There, in the middle of it, was a dried-out ball of horse manure. I kicked at it. That's what it was: genuine, 100 per cent horse manure. "Praise the Lord." I began to cry for the first time, and I could not stop the tears . . .' But, cruelly, she began to have visions again. Rocks and trees became young men in pick-up trucks. She chased them, begging for help. For almost an hour, she wandered around the desert, wasting energy, getting nowhere. Then, as a deep twilight fell over the valley, lights began to blink on. At last, Lauren had some point of reference. In the distance, she could see a long strand of lights: a highway. She told herself to ignore everything but the lights. After walking for hours, she stumbled on to the highway, and very soon afterwards arrived in the small country town of Independence. At a junction with another road she found a small motel, with a neon sign that announced: NO VACANCY. Lauren rang the bell and watched as a teenage boy left his chair in front of a television set. He opened the door.

'I've been in a plane crash,' Lauren said. 'I've walked a

very great distance and I'm tired. Do you have somewhere I can rest?'

The youth looked at Lauren's tattered clothes and bare, bloodied legs. 'Sorry,' came the unbelievable reply. 'Like the sign says, we're full.' He gave directions to another motel.

Dumbfounded by the youth's reaction to her plight, and with her feet aching from the gravel and broken glass by the roadside, Lauren hobbled on to the next motel. The sign said VACANCY. A man opened the door. He, too, examined her warily. Lauren was desperate to convince him that she was sane. 'But then the words tumbled out . . . I told him about the plane crash . . . if he could just lend me enough money to make a phone call . . .'

'I'm sorry, miss,' he replied, 'I have only one room left, and it's reserved . . . There's a Baptist minister across the street. He has a trailer – he sometimes lets people stay there for nothing.'

By now too tired to think, and numbed by her injuries and the devastating reception the town was giving her, Lauren limped away. The minister's house was in darkness; not wanting to disturb him, she crossed to an old-fashioned-looking hotel. The old man who greeted her listened to Lauren's story without seeming to understand. But at last he reached for a room key, and was just about to hand it over when the door burst open and a deputy strode in.

'That's her,' man behind him said. 'That's the one . . . says she's been in a plane crash.'

'Is your name Elder?' the policeman asked simply. When Lauren nodded he said, 'We've been looking for you . . . Let me help you.'

Lauren was taken immediately to South Inyo Hospital in Lone Pine. A doctor stitched up the gash in her leg, and gently but thoroughly cleansed her bleeding feet, where the sand and rocks had worn away most of the skin on the soles. The radius bone of her left wrist was fractured; the arm was swollen and ugly.

A helicopter landed the next morning near the crashed

25

Cessna. Jean's body was found some forty yards from the plane. According to the coroner, she had died of craniocerebral trauma and hypothermia, her severe head injuries having caused extensive brain damage.

Jay's body was where Lauren had left it. The cause of his death was haemoperitoneum and hypothermia. A massive amount of blood was found in his abdominal cavity; given the extent of his injuries, Jay had borne his pain very well.

As word spread of what had happened, the townspeople of Independence began to visit Lauren in hospital. A sheriff's deputy explained to her that the notorious Charles Manson had been brought to Independence and held in the town gaol for two months before his trial in Los Angeles for the Tate – La Bianca murders. Two of the Manson 'family's' women had hung around the gaol and, ever since, the townspeople had been wary of strangers – especially wild, dishevelled-looking women who descended on them in the middle of the night.

It has been calculated that Lauren Elder climbed down from 13,460 feet to 4,000 feet, a distance of at least ten miles. Then she walked a further ten miles across the desert.

The area is described in a guidebook as 'some of the most rugged country in the High Sierra'. In such terrain, an experienced and well-equipped hiker might expect to cover fifteen miles a day – on a clear trail. Lauren covered twenty miles, in not much more than twelve hours.

From her hospital bed in Lone Pine, she had this to say of her ordeal: 'I thought, well, I've got two choices. I can either resign myself as gracefully as possible to freezing to death, or I can see it through. I was just not going to cash in my chips this time around . . .

'I just had a real strong focus. I had unfinished business with friends and family. I just wasn't ready yet . . .'

No one could deny that on 26 April 1976, Lauren Elder had indeed made a bold gesture with her life.

Survival techniques

The book is devoted to the business of getting you out of a disaster, more or less in one piece.

It has nothing to do with a lot of people's preconception of survival – living off the land like Japanese soldiers left behind in the jungle, or being Swiss Family Robinson. That is either pure bushcraft or primitive self-sufficiency – skills which, once mastered, are no longer survival, but day-to-day living.

As far as this book is concerned, *survival is really nothing more than managing your body and your mind in an unusual or hostile environment*. There are certain golden rules of survival, and many hundreds of techniques that will help you to obey those rules. You have read about a woman who managed her body and mind successfully, in the face of the most appalling adversity. But Lauren Elder's actions were intuitive rather than trained: in case you're not so lucky, the next section of the book teaches you what to do, when, and how.

3 Emergency procedures

Every emergency is different, and so is every person involved in one. But there *is* a two-stage sequence of drills that can save you in just about every survivable situation. Study it, say it aloud to yourself, write it down. Do whatever you have to in order to carve it into your memory, so that under the stress of disaster you won't be one of the victims who are running around like headless chickens. *You* are not a casualty – you're a survivor.

Immediate actions:

Away from danger – friends – first aid – stores.

1 *Away from danger*. Move yourself from any further danger.

2 *Friends*. Move other people away from any further danger.

3 *First aid*. Check yourself and others for injury: apply first aid if necessary.

4 *Stores*. Move essential stores, especially water and food, away from danger.

Secondary actions:

Protection – relaxation – evaluation – location – water – food (My personal mnemonic for remembering this is: Percy Riggs Eats Limes With Figs!)

1 *Protection.* If you are not injured, there are only four more dangers of any immediate threat to your life: panic, cold, heat and dryness. Your body – and your mind – must be protected against them.

2 *Relaxation.* This is mostly the mental part of the protective process.

3 *Evaluation.* Making an inventory of skills and materials. Making decisions about staying put or travelling.

4 *Location.* Preparation of signals. Travelling if necessary.

5 *Water.* Without which survival is measured in days.

6 *Food.* Without which survival is measured in weeks – though your mental and physical performance will be severely impaired.

It is hardest to maintain rational behaviour and correct action during the first thirty seconds after an emergency – or after you have actually acknowledged that there is an emergency. Stay calm for this period, and your chances of survival are much increased. Your best weapon is probably a sense of humour: look on the occasion as a great opportunity to practise everything you've learned about survival; or an opportunity, when it's all over, to make money by selling your story. At the very least, you can look forward to contacting me – I'll buy the lunch!

First aid

This section gives a basic list of emergency medical problems (and their treatments) that might confront you as a survivor, but in no way is it a substitute for a good first-aid course. Enrol on one at the earliest opportunity.

There will, however, be two major differences between what you will learn on your first-aid course and the sort of emergency measures you will need to apply in a survival situation. First aid is geared to relatively short-term treatment to stabilize an injury until professional help arrives. Under survival conditions, you will not know how long it will be until you can get professional treatment. And you may have to use – or misuse – the injured part of your body to deal with higher priorities, like shelter-building or signalling. When that happens, as it did to Lauren Elder, Juliane Koepcke and a lot of others, you'll have to bite the bullet and just get on with it.

Depression

The first illness that you are likely to encounter is a mental one: depression. That's because whatever affects you physically also affects you mentally, and whatever affects you mentally will ultimately affect you physically. After a disaster you may be cold, hungry, thirsty, lonely, in pain, exhausted or bereaved – and any one of these can be enough to produce depression. Treat it seriously.

Treatment

- Realize that you are depressed, and do anything, literally anything, to get yourself out of the condition. Build a shelter. Light a fire. Organize a means of signalling. Anything. The longer you do nothing, the worse the depression will become and the more damaging it will be to your morale and well-being.

- Try looking on the bright side of your predicament. Consider that here in the wilderness, or on your life-raft, there are no overdrafts, no gas bills, no insurance salesmen phoning you. Make a mental list of things you dread or hate, and try to enjoy your time away from them.

- Consider how well adapted man is to the predicament you are in. You have hands and a brain to get yourself out of trouble. You can eat anything that a rat can eat, and more. Humans can survive very well on an all-meat diet, a vegetarian diet, or a combination of the two. You'll be OK!

Major injuries

As far as we are concerned, here is the definition of a major injury: it bleeds.

In any medical emergency, check for breathing, bleeding and shock, in that order. Your first-aid course will teach you how. If the casualty is breathing all right, but also bleeding rather a lot, here's what to do.

Treatment

Wipe the wound thoroughly and try to spot the bleeding points. Try direct pressure on these points and bind up the wound. If the dressing doesn't soak itself with blood, leave it for twenty-four hours – then tease out the packing and expose the wound to nature's finest healing agent: the air.

- If it's still bleeding, try the process again.

- Still blood everywhere? Pinch each bleeding point and tie it off: do *not* stitch the wound. Don't worry if it's an artery that needs to be tied off – it will survive.

- Once the bleeding has stopped, inspect the rest of the wound and clean it if necessary. Dead tissue and any pieces of fat present should be cut away, and foreign bodies picked out carefully. (Live tissue bleeds gently; dead tissue doesn't.) Don't be squeamish about any of this: a wound only hurts at its edges; you can cut away inside without any pain.

- Never sew up a wound. It must be allowed to heal from the inside outwards. Leave it open to the air and bear in mind that sunlight destroys bacteria. Even deep, penetrating wounds should be opened right up and allowed to heal from the inside outwards: one of the major causes of gangrene amongst the Argentinian forces in the Falklands conflict of 1982 was the immediate stitching of deep wounds by inexperienced medics.

Fractures

Any fracture is a serious problem in a survival crisis, because it might prevent you from dealing with priorities such as shelter-building.

Prevention is better than cure, so always be careful. Suppose you happen to locate a sheep, for example, and have decided you're going to eat it. If you try to jump on the animal from a wall, the chances are very high that you will break your wrist – the commonest fracture of all. Sheep have lightning-quick reflexes, unless they are asleep. So in this particular case, why not just wait until nightfall, when the sheep is asleep, and attend to the matter then?

Treatment

Simple fractures must be set. First, compare the damaged limb with the undamaged one, to make sure it is fractured. If you think it is, immobilize it with two splints.

In the case of a broken wrist, if you are brave enough, there is a painful and chancy way to reset it. Tie the fingers of the damaged hand to a tree and lean back with your body weight until you feel the broken bones jump back into position. Then bind on the splints. Like any other fracture, it will be very painful for a day or two, but after three weeks – all being well – the fracture should have healed.

Minor injuries

Blisters, splinters, small cuts – no seemingly insignificant injury should be neglected. In a survival situation small infected injuries can soon lead to major problems. You're unlikely to have antibiotics handy, so great care must be taken to ensure there is no infection: do this by licking even the smallest nick or scratch with your tongue to wipe away the bacteria. The golden rule is: keep yourself clean. Not only is it hygienic to wash yourself as carefully as possible – and a great morale booster – but it also means that in the course of doing so you can check your body minutely for any signs of minor injury.

33

- If you find any splinters, try placing the affected area of skin in firm contact with the top of a bottle or jar that's partly filled with hot water. The action of the air cooling and contracting will suck the exposed flesh into the top of the container, and this ought to squeeze the affected area sufficiently to start the splinter moving. If this trick doesn't work, remove the splinter immediately by any means you can. Enlarge the wound so that it can heal from the inside outwards.

- Blisters should be pricked from the side and the fluid removed. Then let them dry.

- Clean the area around the injury by washing or licking – whatever you can manage to reduce the population of bacteria around the site and give the body a better chance to repair the damage.

- Now keep the cleaned wound exposed to the air – but watch it for infection. If it goes red and becomes infected with pus, remove the pus and go through the cleansing process all over again. Keep the surface dry after cleaning – bacteria cannot move over a dry surface.

Lice and ticks

The human body contains an average of 5,000 c.c. of blood. Lice multiply in great numbers and need blood for breeding. Each louse sucks one c.c. of blood per day. You don't need a calculator to tell you that in a remarkably short space of time lice can kill you – especially if you are debilitated in the first place. Ticks are also bloodsuckers.

Treatment

Lice look like pinhead-sized wood lice. Inspect your body – especially the creases in your skin – and your clothing as often as you can. Get rid of every single one you find.

Ticks are about the size of a pea, and they are easy to detect. Get rid of them by pulling, but beware: they bite, and the mandibles can break off and be left in your skin. Treat the mandibles the same as you would a splinter.

Frostbite

Frostbite can occur at any time in cold weather. Wind chill factor is important here, because wind alters the temperature very quickly and dramatically: if the temperature is 5°F above zero, for example, it only takes a wind of 15 m.p.h. to produce a wind chill factor of − 25 °F. When the temperature is this low, your flesh can freeze in sixty seconds. Any exposed part of the body – usually the fingers, nose, ears and toes – can easily get frostbitten. Just as there are first, second and third degree burns, there are three degrees of frostbite.

First degree: the flesh is white or blue, waxy/frosty-looking and fairly pliable. Fingers are stiff and numb. After re-warming, the skin may peel or blister.

Second degree: the flesh is rather mushy, like semi-frozen ice cream. When thawed, it blisters and may turn black. The skin may peel off.

Third degree: frozen solid. Whatever you do, be careful – the frozen parts are so brittle they can easily snap off! When thawed, the skin blisters badly. The victim may well lose the damaged part.

Treatment

● Discover frostbite quickly before there is much chance of damage. Check for it every three to five minutes by wiggling your toes and crinkling up your face – if any area is numb, thaw it and protect from further frostbite by covering it up.

● The best way to thaw minor frostbite is in warm water. But you must be in a place where your entire body can stay warm before the thawing process is started: if you are cold, there will not be an adequate blood supply to the damaged area after it has thawed. Continue thawing for at least thirty minutes, even though there will be considerable pain.

● If no warm water is available, use armpits, a stomach or crotch as a heat source. Using a fire is dangerous: the frozen area will be so numb that it could be burnt before the victim realizes it.

Wind chill factor

The reading on the thermometer does not necessarily indicate how cold you are likely to feel. In a stiff wind, for example, a still-air temperature of 32 °F (freezing point) will feel considerably colder than freezing. This is called the wind chill factor.

Here are a few examples of the difference that wind chill can make to temperature – and bear in mind that at any effective temperature (the combination of thermometer reading and wind velocity) below – 20°F, there is a danger of exposed flesh freezing within one minute. At an effective temperature below – 70°F, exposed flesh will freeze within thirty seconds.

Still-air reading	In 15 m.p.h. wind this feels like	In 30 m.p.h. wind this feels like	In 40 m.p.h. wind this feels like
°F	°F	°F	°F
30	10	0	– 5
20	– 5	–20	–22
10	–15	–30	–38
0	–35	–50	–53
–10	–48	–65	–68
–20	–60	–80	–85
–30	–70	–95	–100

There is an old wives' tale about rubbing frostbitten areas with snow. Forget it. Never, ever, massage a frostbitten area with snow or anything, even warm hands – it will only lead to further tissue damage. With frozen fingers and toes, get the circulation going by just moving the limb up and down.

Do not take alcohol. Do not smoke – tobacco constricts the blood vessels and limits the flow of blood (and body heat) to the frostbitten area.

After thawing, bandage the affected area loosely (it's going to swell).

Third degree frostbite should not be treated unless you are sure that rescue is more than a few days away, or if you don't plan to move anywhere and have plenty of stocks of water, food and firewood. You can walk on frozen feet for a whole day without causing any further damage, and you may need that mobility to get you to a safer or better location.

If a frostbitten limb thaws and then refreezes, it creates an automatic case of gangrene. What is more, the agony of thawing feet may be more than you can bear without pain-suppressing drugs; certainly, you won't be able to walk on them for at least six weeks.

A final word on frostbite: if the frostbitten area turns black, shrivels up and looks as though it will fall off, do not try any sort of amputation yourself. After your rescue, make sure the doctor knows what to do, too – even after three to six weeks, life can still return to a frostbitten limb.

Snow or sun blindness

If you don't have protective sunglasses or goggles, you must improvise some at once. Snow and sun blindness are very painful conditions, which can totally incapacitate you – and make your survival much less likely.

Use a handkerchief, scarf or some article of clothing, tied over your face, with tiny slits for each eye. Or use adhesive tape or mud, even blood, over your regular spectacles, so that just a small peep-hole is left through each lens. You can also darken the area around your eyes with charcoal, soot or mud, or, if your hair is long enough, comb it forwards over your face.

The symptoms of snow and sun blindness are the same.

Your eyes will begin to feel as though they are full of sand. Then they start to burn and suddenly things become hazy. The pain increases horrendously, until finally you can no longer see and the pain is unbearable. Blindness will probably start eight to twelve hours after exposure and will last from three to five days. Prevention is definitely better than cure!

Treatment

Put a bandage over both eyes to block out all light absolutely. Any light at all will aggravate the burning and watering of your inflamed eyes and also cause headaches and bad vision. You will now be incapacitated for up to a week.

A final word on first aid. Pain can be one of the biggest enemies to survival. The body does not like pain and functions reluctantly when it is present. But, as the stories about Lauren Elder and others illustrate, the human spirit is a remarkable thing. You can use your mind to trick your body into obedience. Simply tell the affected part to stop bothering you: if it wants to hurt, then that is its business and nothing to do with you. Dissociate yourself completely and callously from the problem and you'll be surprised at how quickly it can disappear.

4 Protecting your body

Man is a 'homeotherm' – that is, we try to maintain a constant body temperature irrespective of the temperature of our surroundings. The body consists of an inner 'hot' core, surrounded by a cool outer shell. The core consists of the brain and other vital organs (such as the heart, lungs, liver and kidneys) contained within the skull, chest and abdomen. The shell is what is left: the skin, fat, muscle and limbs – in effect a buffer zone between the core and the outside world, protecting the organs of the body which are necessary for survival from any catastrophic change in temperature.

The maintenance of proper internal body temperature is the most important factor in determining your survival. Even in extreme cold or heat, your core temperature will seldom vary more than two degrees either side of 98.6 °F, with the shell just a few degrees cooler. If your core temperature rises above 109 °F or falls below 84 °F, you will die.

Protection against cold

Your body generates both energy and heat as it burns fuel. When you start to shiver, your body is telling you that it is losing heat faster than it is being replaced. The shivering reflex exercises many muscles, increasing heat production by burning more fuel. If the temperature at the core of your body drops even a few degrees, you're in trouble. Shivering alone will not warm you up again. Under survival

39

conditions, your only hope is to prevent hypothermia happening in the first place by reducing heat loss. In other words, you need a shelter, fire, insulation and more clothing.

Your body has a thermostat located in a small piece of nerve tissue at the base of the brain, which controls the production or dissipation of heat and monitors all parts of the body in order to maintain a constant temperature. When the body starts to go into hypothermia, the body thermostat responds by ordering heat to be drawn from the extremities into the core. Your hands and feet will start to stiffen. As the body core temperature drops, the body also draws heat from the head. When this happens, circulation slows down and the victim doesn't get the oxygen or sugar the brain needs – the sugar the brain ordinarily feeds on is being burned to produce heat. As the brain begins to slow down, the body stops shivering and irrational behaviour begins. That is a sure danger sign – and one you are not likely to recognize, because the biggest danger of hypothermia is that it takes away your will to help yourself. You stop shivering and you stop worrying. You are dying, in fact, and you couldn't care less.

At this point, your body loses its ability to reheat itself. Even if you have a sleeping bag to crawl into, you will continue to cool off. Your only hope is by adding heat – from a fire, hot drinks, or another human body. Indeed, one of the most effective ways of re-warming a hypothermia victim is to put them in a sleeping bag with another person whose body temperature is still normal. Both bodies need to be stripped for adequate heat transfer to take place and it is worth noting that for some strange reason of chemistry, this heat transfer is 5 per cent more effective if the two people are of the opposite sex.

To understand how to prevent hypothermia, it is important to understand the mechanics of heat loss. Heat leaves the body by four basic means:

1 *Evaporation*. Moisture and heat leave the body when we perspire and breathe. If your lungs were laid out on the ground, they would cover an area the size of a tennis court. That's the area that has to be re-warmed every time you take in a cold breath!

2 *Radiation*. When the body is warmer than the outside temperature, heat leaves the body in particles or waves. (When the outside air is warmer, heat radiates into your body.)

3 *Conduction*. Body heat flows into objects in actual contact with the body (clothing, air, or water). In a very cold environment, air and water are the most dangerous conductors.

4 *Convection*. Moving air (the wind, for example) transports heat away from the body.

The body loses heat by all four of these means. Insulation with proper clothing and shelter is crucial. If the body is wet, or bare skin is exposed to the wind and cold, heat is lost at a very rapid rate.

The main priorities in a cold, wet and windy survival situation are therefore first, *to get out of the wind – it can kill you*, and, second, *to stay dry*. After that:

- Put on extra clothing (if you have any) before you start to shiver.

- Don't sit on or lean against rocks or metal – you will lose heat very rapidly through conduction.

- Light a fire at the first hint of a chill; if possible, get more than one fire going, so you can heat yourself from more than one side.

- Drink as much hot fluid as you can. If you have spare food, use it to refuel and keep your body furnace going – eating little and often, rather than all at once.

- Do not take alcohol: it short-circuits the automatic reflex that is requisitioning all your blood for your vital organs. Blood rushes to your face, hands and feet and your core temperature will drop.

- Don't work harder in the rain or snow than you have to. Try not to work up a sweat.

- If you are alone and you start shivering, stop what you're doing. This might be the last symptom of hypothermia that you'll be able to recognize. Get out of the rain or snow, build a fire, try to dry your clothes and your body.

- Don't eat snow. It not only takes body heat to melt the stuff, but it cools the body from the inside, cooling the vital organs in the body core.

- Don't do any vigorous exercise. The increase in circulation will take too much heat to the periphery of the body, which is where it is lost.

- Check, re-check, then check again that you're not losing heat through evaporation, radiation, conduction or convection.

Shelter

Because of the danger to life posed by extreme cold, shelter is second in importance only to first aid in a survival crisis in mountains and cold regions. In fact, shelter can be considered a type of preventive first aid.

'Shelter' refers to anything that extends the body's comfort or safety. Therefore, all clothing as well as enclosed structures – vehicles, natural shelters, improvised shelters – should be considered.

Clothing

When your plane crashes in the Alps or you get hopelessly lost in winter conditions, here is what you will ideally be wearing: not one thick item, but several lightweight layers of clothing to trap warm air – and in increasing sizes, to avoid compression of the under-layers. Then, when inactivity or falling temperatures bring about a need for more warmth, simply add more layers. As activity increases or temperatures rise, such layers may be removed to keep you comfortable.

The ideal layers would be:

- Thermal underwear, preferably made of polypropylene. This material draws moisture away from the body, thus reducing chilling caused by the cooling of body sweat after exercise.

- Two pairs of socks – polypropylene first, then wool. Two pairs help prevent blisters.

- Another layer of wool or fibre-pile clothes.

- An outer shell, which must be windproof and waterproof.

- Woollen mitts (Dachstein mitts are best), with Gore-Tex over-mitts.

- Good boots, with Gore-Tex gaiters.

- The head is a very important area. At 40 °F, the uncovered head loses up to 50 per cent of the heat the body is producing. And this jumps to a staggering 75 per cent at 5 °F. Headgear should be selected to allow it to be rolled down over the ears when necessary.

That is the theory, but, needless to say, it is not people who are well equipped and clothed who find themselves in trouble in the wilderness. Frequently, they are people who planned for a pleasant day in pleasant conditions, only to have conditions suddenly change. With inadequate clothing at their disposal, they are in serious trouble. If this happens to you, just remember to protect your body core. The key word is *insulation*. You can improvise some insulation with dry plant material. Heather, pine needles, dry grass, leaves, whatever you can find – stuff them between layers of clothing. It is impossible to have too much insulation: as a rule of thumb, stop stuffing your clothes when you closely resemble the Michelin Man! Vehicle upholstery may be ripped open to get at the stuffing. Seat covering or car headlining may be cut and sewn into improvised extra layers of clothing, using a needle made from wire. When cold threatens, nothing is too sacred, too precious or too valuable to be used for your protection. Yet, all too often, people have been found – dead – after blizzards and snow storms with all the material to hand that would almost certainly have saved them – if only they had known how – (or dared) to use it. I can safely say that if all that stood between me and hypothermia was a suitcase full of da Vincis, I'd have the *Mona Lisa* down my trousers faster than you could even say 'protective layer'! If you ever find yourself up against it in such circumstances, try to remember that your survival will almost certainly depend, in part at least, on your own sense of self-worth.

Hyperthermia

At the other extreme of the quick-acting dangers is heat: we've all seen what happens to a car when it overheats. Your body has an excellent cooling system, capable of keeping your temperature stabilized in even the hottest desert – you just have to be careful not to overtax it.

Your body heats itself by movement, using food as fuel. It cools itself by perspiring, breathing and radiating. But if you work so hard that most of your sweat is running off rather than evaporating, your temperature will begin to rise. As this happens, the body's heat-regulating system in the brain shuts down and your body stops sweating. Your skin flushes and becomes dry. Before long, you will have collapsed with classic heatstroke. You obviously cannot treat your own heatstroke. Instead, you must make sure your temperature does not get too high in the first place.

- If you're stuck in the desert, or anywhere in the heat, it is absolutely imperative that you get out of the sun. Just as if it were extremely cold, find shelter. Get into the shade of a tree, some bushes, a rock – anything, as long as it's near by. In the middle of the day or even two or three hours before sunset, your chances of making it to shelter more than two miles away are almost nil.

- If you have a stranded vehicle in the middle of the desert, with no natural source of shade, get into it, or under it. In a car, leave the doors open – but don't forget to turn the interior lights off. If the problem is that your car is stuck in the sand, do not use the radio or any other car accessory that will drain the battery – when the temperature outside has dropped enough for you to try to dig the car out, you don't want to find yourself with a flat battery.

- Your absolute distance limit in the heat of the day is 500 yards. If this doesn't sound much, consider this: in 120 °F of heat, walking one mile is equivalent to running hard on the spot for twenty minutes in a sauna!

- Don't exert yourself physically until nightfall.

- The sand under a vehicle will be hot until it has cooled down in the shade for a while. If you don't have a shovel, improvise one, scooping out the sand to a depth of three to five inches. The deeper you go, the cooler the sand will be.

- Stay away from the engine, exhaust and transmission, all of which will still be hot. If you have a blanket in the car, make a kind of tent by draping it over the shady side of the car. This will keep shade longer than if you were just under the car.

- Do not take all your clothes off. This is not St Tropez, and no time to start trying to top up your tan. You'd only sweat more without your clothes on. You would therefore *feel* cooler. But just think about where the

45

sweat is coming from. You can't afford to lose any precious water from your body. Only discard clothes that don't allow your body to breathe – such as leather coats, or nylon jackets.

Although heatstroke is the most dangerous form of hyperthermia, heat can also cause other problems unless you do something to avoid them. Heat cramps are painful and disabling, and can occur even when your body temperature is normal. What happens when you sweat is that you lose not only water, but essential body salts as well – called electrolytes, because when dissolved in water they form the conductive medium for electrical nerve impulses. Even if you're drinking plenty of water, the lack of food or salt input can cause a change in electrolytic balance, and your muscles, in turn, might start to cramp. Avoid cramps the same way you would heatstroke – by not exerting yourself.

Dehydration

Dehydration is no respecter of climates: you can become dehydrated in the middle of an Arctic winter just the same as in the middle of the day in the Sahara.

Physical exertion produces sweat, even in the cold. The vapour clouds we can see when we exhale in cold weather are exactly that – vapour clouds: precious moisture, leaking from our bodies. The cold makes us urinate more, too, which means more fluid lost. Be warned that if your urine gets darker each time, it is a sure sign that your body liquids are concentrating.

Thirst is a very unreliable indicator of dehydration. The problem is that just a few sips of liquid might quench your thirst, without improving your internal water deficit. Or you may not even notice your thirst because there is too much else going on that needs your urgent attention. In general, however, a moderate to severe sensation of thirst is indicative that you need more water.

Further symptoms of dehydration that can easily go unnoticed are a vague feeling of discomfort, a slow-down in movement, redness in the face, impatience, loss of appetite, increased pulse and breathing rate.

After losing about 5 per cent of your body weight through dehydration, you will be struck by waves of nausea which, in fact, destroy your desire to drink. If you vomit, you'll lose even more precious fluid. It's a vicious circle. Soon you will experience dizziness, a severe headache, shortness of breath, tingling in your fingers and toes, and a dry mouth, slurred speech and an inability to walk. Dehydration at this level is extremely dangerous. You must prevent it.

Water may be scarce in a survival situation. There is little you can do to stop yourself from losing as much as four pints of water a day from urination, bowel movements and breathing. But you *can* reduce your losses in other areas. The golden rule is: *unless you have lots of water available, eat as little as possible and ration your sweat.*

Besides protecting your mind from panic, protecting your body from hypothermia, hyperthermia and dehydration will be the most vital factor in your survival. Just keep thinking of your body as a machine running on limited fuel, coolant and lubricant and you'll be OK.

Protective procedures

Hypothermia, hyperthermia and dehydration are killers. You must protect yourself from them as quickly as possible. The golden rule is: *choose the shelter that will get you out of the weather most quickly*.

If you have to *build* a shelter, choose the smallest, easiest, and most effective one that can be made with the materials available. Above all, conserve your energy when building it: no need for elegant log cabins when a simple lean-to will do.

There are two types of shelter: ready-made and improvised. The most obvious ready-made shelters in many about smoke. Don't make your lean-to more elaborate than you have to. Don't waste energy. All you need is a pole long enough to stretch between two trees, and two other poles with forked ends. Now for a simple bit of physics that will save you hours of lashing the poles in position: just hold the first pole against the trees at the right height, rest one forked pole against one end of it, and the other forked pole at the other. The structure will support itself. You now have the basic framework for your roof. Thatch it with branches, foliage, moss, earth, snow – anything – but preferably fir boughs, laid like tiles on a roof, starting with the bottom row and working upwards. Lay the boughs upside down, and with the undersides of the leaves or needles uppermost. Insulate the floor as much as you can with leaves, dead pine needles and more boughs. Then drive two sticks into the ground, about three feet from the lean-to entrance and at a right-angle away from it. Use them as a prop for two or three large logs, piled one on top of the other – the reflector for your fire. Build the fire against the reflector, and you're in business.

When heavy snow falls in coniferous forests, there is not much drifting and the snow stays light, powdery and uniformly deep. Natural shelters are built at the base of thick evergreens with low branches, in the form of a 'well' in the deep snow at the base of the tree trunk. If you need a winter shelter fast, this kind is unbeatable.

It is impossible to exaggerate the importance of insulation: 70 per cent of your body heat can be lost to the cold surface beneath you. You will need bedding that is a good foot thick between you and the ground; the smaller the boughs, the more comfortable your bed. But be careful that your insulation does not creep out towards the fire – being warm is one thing, being incinerated is quite another!

How to build a snow cave

1 Choose a big drift of packed snow. The best location for a snow cave is in a drift with a fairly steep face – greater than 30°. This will ensure that there is sufficient depth

of snow and that it can be easily disposed of down the slope. It also ensures that the shelter can be built reasonably quickly and that the snow is likely to be in good condition for cutting.

2 Mark your cave site, to prevent anyone falling on top of you while you're digging.

3 Probe first for trees or other obstacles, then dig. Although the final entrance should be small, it is best, for ease of working, to make this larger to start off with and fill it in later. Dig a deep slot into the drift, high and wide enough to allow you to work upright. Remove loose snow with a plastic bag or anorak, if you don't have a shovel.

4 Excavate the snow on either side of the slot to create an open living area. For the maximum insulation and structural stability, the walls and ceiling should be at least two feet thick.

5 You'll find that your biggest problem while digging is getting wet – it's hard work and the effort will make you work up quite a sweat. Only dry clothing will keep you warm during the night ahead. What's more, there is always the danger of wet clothing freezing. So strip off while you're digging.

6 About eighteen inches above the floor of the cave, shape a bed platform. Even if you are claustrophobic, don't build a palace. The smaller the area to be heated the better, although it should be big enough to undress in and manoeuvre yourself into your sleeping gear.

7 A single candle will provide ample heat; in fact it may be too hot, and make the roof drip or sag. You can cut down on dripping by making the roof as dome-shaped as possible and by glazing the inner surfaces with the candle flame. If any drips develop, dab on a handful of snow.

8 Insulate your bed with boughs or anything to hand. Cut a ventilation hole in the roof and another in the block of snow or ice used as a door. Check from time to time to make sure they are still clear, especially if you're using a candle, stove or lamp.

9 Reduce the entrance to a size which will allow access by crawling. Your pack, a sack or plastic bag filled with snow or a block of snow or ice all make excellent doors.

10 Take your digging tool inside, in case you have to dig your way out.

11 If it is freezing hard, wrap your boots inside a plastic bag (if you have one) and take them into your sleeping bag (if you have one).

12 Brush off all particles of snow clinging to clothing before entering the shelter or they will melt and wet you. For the same reason, if you're cooking, avoid having liquids simmering or boiling.

13 If you leave the cave at night, be sure to leave a light on to guide you back.

Often there will not be sufficient snow to enable the survivor to carve out a snow cave. Even limited amounts of snow, however, mean an Eskimo *quinzhee*, or snow heap, can be thrown up – as long as the air temperature is 20 °F or less.

1 Mark off a circle in the snow between eight and ten feet in diameter. Thoroughly stir the snow in this area down to ground level.

2 Place a pole (about seven feet in length) upright in the centre of the circle. From the centre, lay another long pole to extend beyond the edge of the circle. This will indicate where to start digging later.

3 Pile the stirred-up snow – and any more you might need – within the circle, into a cone-shaped heap, with just the

top of the upright pole showing. Leave the pile undisturbed for at least two hours and make no attempt to pack the snow down. The snow will settle naturally as recrystallization takes place.

4 When the pile is firm, scrape off the apex of the cone to form a dome shape. Locate the tip of the horizontal pole and tunnel along it until you reach the vertical one.

5 Begin hollowing out the interior. The thickness of the walls should taper from about ten inches at the base to about six inches at the apex. A thin stick may be used as a probe to check wall thickness as you progress.

6 Be sure that the shelter rests directly on the ground: in extremely cold environments the earth will actually serve as a source of heat.

7 Keep the entrance small – no bigger than is necessary to let in the largest member of the party. It may be closed with packs, a snow-block, or fabric. If possible, cover the floor with a thick layer of insulation – boughs, stuffing from car seats, or whatever is available.

8 Cut a small two-inch hole near the apex for ventilation. The interior walls should be kept carefully curved – smooth them with a gloved hand to allow any melting snow to trickle down.

Happiness is a warm bum – building a fire

As Lauren Elder will testify, there is one simple act that can do more for your morale and peace of mind in a survival situation than any other: building a fire.

A decent fire not only protects your body from lethal temperatures, it protects your mind, too. Those hot, dancing flames will imbue you with a sense of well-being and drive away the loneliness and the fear. So build a fire as soon as your shelter is ready. In fact, I like to build a fire the moment my shelter has a makeshift roof – then, if darkness overtakes me, at least I know I'll have some shelter *and* a fire, rather than just a well-built shelter but no fire.

survival situations are vehicles – cars, boats and planes. Vehicles offer excellent protection from water and wind, but once their engines are dead they are hard to heat and cool and offer little in the way of insulation. So if your car is stuck in a snow drift, for example, and you know that the outside temperature is well below zero, you would be better off digging a snow cave. Snow caves generally don't get below 30 °F, as snow is an excellent insulator. Even without a sleeping bag, when it's extremely cold outside, you can be relatively snug inside – but be ready for two or three hours of hard work!

Another means of escaping the wind in snow two feet or more deep is to dig a snow trench. Even if you can't cover it over, it will protect you from the brunt of the wind. If the snow conditions are right, you might be able to cut blocks that you can lean together to form an A-frame roof. Otherwise, cover the trench with a good foot of fir boughs, and pile on a layer of snow. After climbing in, fill the entrance with snow, wreckage, more boughs – anything. Try to make the trench airtight, with a small air vent poked through. Then light your candle, if you have one, and relax.

Ready-made shelters include barns, ruins, wilderness cabins (nobody will mind you breaking in), bridges, culverts (but beware of flash flooding), caves and rock overhangs (but stay as near the entrance as you can), hollow trees and logs (check out for other occupants first!).

There are an almost infinite number of ways to improvise a shelter which can be modified to suit the weather, terrain – or personal taste. One of the simplest and most versatile of all shelters is the lean-to. With your bare hands you can build a decent lean-to, which will give you dry, roomy accommodation that can be heated with a fire. A lean-to is essentially a steeply sloping roof that extends to the ground – steep enough (60°) to shed rain, high enough to let you sit comfortably, and wide enough to let you stretch out parallel to the entrance if you are alone, or from front to back if you are sharing. Build it so that you are protected from the wind and so that you can light a fire in front without worrying

Anyway, the message is: don't wait. The colder, wetter or more scared you become, the harder it will be to light that fire.

You will need tinder (material, such as paper, that is very easy to burn), kindling (twigs and the like, small enough to be burned by the tinder: don't put on anything too large, too soon), fuel (a whole range of larger pieces of wood and other materials, up to big log size) and a lighter.

Fires don't burn solids, they burn gases. It would be a bit ludicrous to try to light a big log with a single match, wouldn't it? (as I remarked to someone I once saw trying to do just that!) To vaporize large logs, you need a lot of heat – heat generated from the kindling and tinder. Remember, you *build* a fire. Keep this principle in mind and you shouldn't go wrong.

The golden rule of building a fire is: there are no short-cuts. Make your first effort a success – you might only have one match. First, as Mrs Beeton would say, catch your kindling and fuel. Lots of it. More than you would think necessary. Work out how many branches and logs you think your fire will burn – and double it. Then add a few more logs for luck. As you gather your kindling, store it inside your shelter in case it starts to rain or snow. Stack all the larger pieces well within arm's reach when you're lying in your shelter. I can promise you, leaving the warmth of your fire to get at your pile of logs is purgatory.

Now drive two stakes into the ground behind the fire and at an angle away from it. Pile two or three big logs against it, one on top of the other, as your fire reflector. If your shelter is a lean-to, try to make your reflector about six feet long.

Lay two long, thick logs parallel to each other, and about eighteen inches apart, in front of your shelter. As your fire burns, you can make it spread between the logs until it's heating the whole length of your body. Or, if there are some rocks near by (don't waste energy trying to carry really big, heavy ones) or large stones (not from a riverbed – if they are at all wet, they might explode), make a ring of them to contain your fire. If the fire goes out for any reason and you cannot relight it at once, you can always bring the hot stones into your shelter with you for extra warmth. One good variation is to lay stones in the shape of a keyhole: then, if you need embers for cooking, you can just channel them into the opposite section. Another good idea is to build your fire on a platform of thin logs. Not only will this reflect heat back up into the fire and help it to get going more quickly, but on snowy ground it will prevent it from simply sinking without trace!

You can now start to build your fire. The actual architecture of the fire depends on your needs and personal taste. The basic way of starting nearly all wood fires is the 'teepee' – although it does have a tendency to collapse and will need rearranging. Build a little teepee of thin, delicate twigs around your tinder. When there is sufficient heat add more, and bigger, twigs. Another proven method is to find three pieces of dry bark, place one piece on the ground, drier side up, and put your tinder on top. Lean the other two pieces of bark together over the top, like a steeple, and light the tinder inside. Gradually add kindling and blow on the flames if necessary.

The 'log cabin' is easier to build, more stable and requires less looking after than either method. Make it by laying a log on each side of a tinder and kindling teepee. Put two more logs across the ends of the first two and continue upwards in the same way, adding as many levels as you want. It's best to slant the 'walls' inwards slightly as you go up and to lay a flat log 'roof' across the top.

A variation is the 'grid' or 'cross-gate' type – really a log cabin with whole rows of logs, rather than just two per level. It has the advantage of producing a large bed of hot coals, as opposed to the log cabin's rather hollow blaze, with few coals at the centre.

The best source of heat for lighting your fire is from a lighter or matches. There are other more exotic methods of lighting fires but, under emergency conditions when you need them most, you can guarantee they won't work! If you don't have a lighter or matches, however, it is certainly worth trying any of the following:

- A camera lens (no need to remove it from the camera – simply open the back of the equipment and keep the shutter open).

- A convex lens will set tinder smouldering if the sun is strong enough. Two wristwatch glasses sealed together with clay/chewing-gum/tree sap, with the enclosed space being filled with water, is theoretically sound. Any single spectacle lens can be tried, as can a gun-sight lens, the magnifying glass on a Silva compass or a binocular lens.

- Concave mirrors will also work. These can be mirrors from car headlights, plane landing sights, even a shaving mirror – the larger the better.

- A piece of steel struck hard against a flint or stone.

- Potassium permanganate from your first-aid or survival kit. Place a small pile of the crystals on dry leaves or paper, add a few drops of anti-freeze from your vehicle radiator and screw it up into a ball. After a few seconds the bundle will burst into flames.

- If you are stranded with a vehicle, use the battery. Cover the rest of the engine with anything, from floor mats to coats – anything to stop a fire starting with so much petrol vapour in the air. Then, either touch two spanners (or anything similar) across the terminals to produce a spark, or, preferably, lead wires away from the terminals and clear of the vehicle, so that sparks can be produced out in the open. Any wire can be used, including barbed-wire fencing, but you will have to make sure it is insulated from contact with the body of the vehicle or that it naturally hoops clear. Don't overdo this technique unless it is more important that you have a fire than a battery in good condition!

- Don't overlook the cigarette-lighter that might be in your car or plane!

- *Fire drill and bow.* This method of lighting a fire without matches looks a bit like a bow and arrow, with the bow string twisted once round the arrow so that backwards and forwards motions of the bow produce a fast-turning arrow. The drill head is pressed down into a bowl cut in a wood board, and pressure applied at the other end of the arrow with a palm piece – another block of wood with a bowl to accept the drill end, which fits into the palm of the hand.

- The drill needs to be well rounded at the palm-piece end, and pointed at the other. It should be about a foot long, and an inch thick. Try to make the drill and the base board of the same wood. As you move the bow backwards and forwards, smoke will begin to rise almost immediately from the junction between the drill and the fire board. A deep brown to black powder will begin to accumulate in the bowl of the fire board, around the point of the drill.

- Don't get too excited. This is the easy bit. It's turning this hot powder into a flame that's the hard bit. What you have to do is watch for a coal to ignite in the charred dust in the bowl – quickly stop drilling and tip this coal into a little tinder nest. Wave the nest around in your cupped hands, and pray.

- *Fire thong.* Use a strip of dry rattan, preferably about a quarter of an inch thick and about two feet long, and a dry stick. Split one end of the stick and wedge it open with a small stone or another stick. Then rest one end off the ground. Jam a small wad of tinder in the split, leaving enough room to insert the thong behind it. Kneel astride the stick to brace it, and work the thong back and forth.

- *Gunpowder.* Extract the powder from a cartridge or bullet. Prepare a sheltered pile of kindling and wood. Place the powder at the base of the pile. Take two rocks and sprinkle a little powder on one of them. Then grind the two rocks together immediately above the powder at the base of the pile. This will ignite the powder on the rock and, in turn, the larger amount of powder and kindling wood. Or, strike flint or rock against steel so that a spark falls on the powder.

● *Fire saw*. This method of fire-lighting is commonly used in the jungle. Use split bamboo or other soft wood as a rub stick and the dry sheath of the coconut flower as a wood base. A good tinder is the fluffy brown covering of the apiang palm and the dry material found at the base of coconut leaves.

There are many materials which can be used as tinder. Excellent natural tinders, the first three of which will burn whether wet or dry, are: birch bark, resin shavings, pitch shavings (a common tinder in coniferous forests known as 'Indian Kerosene', formed when conifers are injured and 'bleed'), cedar bark, dry tree moss, dry pine needles, dry leaves, rotten wood, the nests of birds, rats, mice or termites, dead bamboo, bats' droppings (powdery dry), fine down from the breasts of birds, dry grass – and, if you're really stuck, your own hair! Good man-made tinders, the first three of which will burn whether wet or dry, are: candle stubs, insect repellent, magnesium shavings, cotton wool, scorched cloth, charred rope, lint from dressings, photographic film, petrol- or oil-soaked sand or earth, oily rags, paper, paper money and teased fabric.

Don't feel restricted to wood as a fuel for your fire. If dry animal dung, a spare tyre, mats or petrol from your car are all you have, then use them. Whatever you use, remember to conserve your energy when collecting it. Don't waste energy by breaking up branches into convenient log-sized pieces – just feed them into the fire a bit at a time instead.

5 Protecting your mind

We have met the enemy and they is us . . . – Pogo Possum

As a victim of misfortune, it is easy to feel depressed and sorry for yourself: thoughts turn to the unfairness of the situation, and feelings of hopelessness begin to creep into your mind. It is vital that you resist, however, for if you cease to believe in your eventual rescue, you will shortly lose the will to live. Remember that survival is a state of mind and your life may very well depend on it. You'll survive if you think you can.

Pain, cold, thirst, hunger, fatigue, boredom, loneliness and fear are all enemies of survival, because they can sap your morale so quickly. Everyone has experienced such feelings, but few have known them to the extent that they have threatened survival. In the survival crisis, the feelings of pain, cold, hunger and so on are no different from those experienced elsewhere – they are just more severe and more dangerous. With these feelings, as with fear, the more you know about them and their effects on you, the better you will be able to control them, rather than letting them control you.

The most important thing to remember is that what affects someone physically, also affects them mentally – and whatever affects them mentally will ultimately affect them physically. Realization of this fact alone should have tremendous impact on your ability to cope with stress – especially if you add to it the thought that even if all the other priorities have been taken care of, if an individual lacks the will to live or the ability to cope with the situation mentally because of his or her physical condition, then all is lost. Remember, although this book contains many ideas about techniques for coping with environmental extremes, it is the ability to cope with ourselves that is ultimately more important.

Pain is nature's way of making you pay attention to something that is wrong with you. But nature can be made to hold off pain, if you are too busy doing something else to pay attention to the injury right away. Pain may go unnoticed if you tell it to go away and leave you alone, or if your mind is preoccupied with plans for survival. On the other hand, once you give in to it, pain will weaken the drive to survive. It will get the better of you if you let it, even if the pain isn't serious or prolonged. So keep your hopes up, and keep busy!

Cold lowers your ability to think, and your ability to think about anything but getting warm again. It sneaks up on you, takes you over before you really notice. Before you know it, you are finding it hard to move – you want to sleep, you want to forget your goal until tomorrow. The trouble is, your goal is survival, today. Tomorrow will be too late.

Thirst, even when not extreme, can also dull your mind. But as with pain and cold, thirst too can be endured if the will to survive is strong enough.

Hunger is dangerous because of the effects it can have on the mind, primarily in lessening your ability for rational thought. Both thirst and hunger increase a person's susceptibility to the debilitating effects of cold, pain and fear.

Fatigue, even in moderate amounts, can substantially reduce mental ability. It can make you careless and make it more and more easy not to care what happens to you. The confused notion that fatigue and energy expenditure are related may be responsible for many deaths in survival situations: certainly, there is a real danger of over-exertion, but fatigue comes too from hopelessness, lack of a goal, dissatisfaction, frustration or boredom. Fatigue may simply represent an escape from a problem which has become too difficult. Recognize fatigue for the danger that it is, and be ready to overcome it.

Boredom and loneliness are two of the toughest enemies of survival, mainly because they are so unexpected. When nothing happens, when something is expected but doesn't work out, when rescue doesn't come, when you must stay alone, these feelings can overwhelm you. Try to amuse yourself. Do useful projects. Make a map of the area. Clean your shelter. Get more wood. Improve your signals. Make up a game. Sing songs. Make up crosswords. Play chess in your head. Talk to yourself. Make plans for the future. Do *anything*, absolutely anything, you can think of to stave them off.

Fear is a very normal reaction any time your life is threatened. It may ruin your chances, or may actually improve them. There is no advantage in avoiding fear by denying the existence of danger – but don't invent dangers that don't exist. Keep trying to replace the unknown with the known. Enjoy, and make use of, the heightened powers brought on by the biological response to fear – but don't ever give in to panic. There is always something that can be done to improve your lot – so do it.

Factors increasing fear are mainly helplessness and hopelessness. Factors decreasing it are confidence in yourself, in your equipment, in your training, and concentration on the job to be done. How a person will react to fear depends more on character than on circumstances. It isn't always the physically strong or happy-go-lucky types who most effectively handle fear – timid or anxious people may respond more coolly under stress, and so have a better chance of survival. Though fear affects different people in different ways under different circumstances, the physiological response is always the same. Be ready for it.

The nervous system responds massively and very quickly to stress. The heart beats faster, adrenalin flows into the body and there is a change in the flow of the digestive juices. Psychologically, the person becomes hyper-vigilant, on the look-out for further danger. Facial expression changes – the eyes become wider and the lip comes up from the teeth. Emotionally, the person becomes detached from normal processes – as if feelings were in free-fall – but what happens next depends on the course of events.

When people are under stress they rarely panic – so don't go against the general trend yourself! Panic only tends to come on when people are trapped and there is a time limit, or space restriction, on their escape.

People have different ways of coping with fear. Some convince themselves that the terrifying events are simply not happening to them. Some resort to hysterical joking. Some displace fear by occupying themselves with various tasks. Do not stick around the scene of danger, however, out of bravado. It has been shown that people may be able to cope with one shock, perhaps two, but by the third or fourth major incident you will be pushed past your limits into a state of immobile terror.

When you are confronted by fear, the best advice is for you to keep busy somehow – but not by making a physiological inventory of your injuries and ailments! Be positive! If you start hyperventilating (breathing too fast and deeply with fright), breathe into a paper bag if you have one, or hold your breath.

Relaxation

Remember the most important thing anybody's ever going to tell you about survival? You'll survive if you think you can. In 99 per cent of disasters and emergencies, surviving is a battle in the mind. It's not really a battle that you can be taught to win, but the example set by the people in this book should go a long way towards providing inspiration and hope. So remember what they went through, and remember: you'll survive if you think you can. Here are the techniques that will help you win the mental battle.

1 *Sit down*. The moment you have carried out the immediate action drill, and have taken shelter, sit down. If your only problem is that you are lost, sit down. If you're in a lift that has jammed, sit down.

It's very difficult to panic when you're sitting down. It's even harder to give in to it and start running if you're not standing up. Tie your shoe-laces together if panic starts to grip you – it will be even more difficult to run away!

If you're sitting down, you present less body area to the elements and so the risk of hypothermia is reduced. You use less precious energy. The terrain will also look different from a sitting position – perhaps it won't seem so hostile. And, just by being in a seated, or more foetal, position, you'll feel more relaxed and soothed, and able to think more clearly. If you still have a desperate need to do something, now is the time to build yourself another fire.

2 *Calm yourself*. While you're sitting down, look around you. Try to feel the serenity and beauty of the landscape. Even if you're not usually that way inclined, say a prayer. Breathe gently and with control. As you breathe out, say aloud: 'Calm . . .' Keep doing it, until you are calm.

Think of a time or a place where you have been warm and contented. Relax with this image, instructing each part of your body to respond to it now as it did then. Imagine the tension and anxiety floating away. Gradually breathe more deeply, and each time you breathe out, still say: 'Calm . . .'

3 *Now think*. Be prepared to take responsibility for what happens to you, including your inner feelings – they, too, are under your control. Your survival is in your hands.

Make some positive statements to yourself, such as: 'I know I can make it', or: 'This situation will not frighten me', or: 'I'll survive if I think I can', or: 'It's not the end of the world', or: 'There's nothing either good or bad, but thinking makes it so', or: 'Not one moment of worry will make things any better'.

If you prefer, you can make a strongly negative 'positive' statement. Choose yourself a target, and say: 'They will not get at me,' or: 'I'm damned if that bastard in data processing is going to grind me down. I'll handle this all right. That'll show him.' When you find a statement that you like the sound of, latch on to it. It is now your password, your mantra. Say it as often as you like.

At about this time, the three fears – of the unknown, of discomfort, of your own weaknesses – will start creeping up on you. Be ready for them. Pick them off one by one. Face them rationally, and head-on. What frightens you? The dark? Wild animals? Strange people creeping up on you at night? Being alone? Being hungry? Recognize that these fears are so common they have even been put in those three categories. It's not just you that's afraid. Everyone is. If rationalizing doesn't work, try reciting your mantra a few more times.

Now use your imagination to conjure up an image of the sort of person who might handle this situation well. John Wayne? Rambo? Clare Francis? Lauren Bacall? An SAS trooper? Whoever you think would do well. Now imagine that person acting properly in your position. Visualize them going through the immediate action drill, and coping from now on. How do they do it? What do they look like? Cool and calm? Quietly efficient? Ruthlessly professional? With much dash and style? Whatever it is, do it yourself. You've got your model, just follow it. You've already visualized them coping. Just copy their fine example, and start formulating a plan to get yourself out of the mess you are in.

Evaluation

There are three separate aspects of this part of the response sequence:

(a) general consideration;
(b) whether to stay put or to travel;
(c) taking stock of skills and materials.

The time to evaluate is when you've got your feet up, relaxing. Easily, calmly, systematically, weigh the situation up. How serious is it: How many people are injured? How extensive are their injuries? How close is civilization? Will people come looking for you? What's the weather like? What's the terrain like?

Now is the time you'll wish you'd actually done a survival course. If you've successfully weathered such storms before, you will be more likely to cope with this one. Competence in outdoor skills and experience in dealing with simulated survival situations will foster confidence and calm, and you'll be better equipped to evaluate appropriately, dispassionately and effectively.

Don't worry if you haven't done a survival course. All is not lost.

Before deciding whether to travel or stay put, make an inventory of the skills and materials available which could aid your survival. What is available to make your life more comfortable? Your aim should be to remain as alert as possible – what is going to help you do that? Is anyone a doctor or nurse, or otherwise specially trained? What stores have you salvaged, and what do people have in their pockets or among their belongings? Ordinary items can be modified or used in imaginative ways – items like keys, key rings, shoe-laces, cameras, cosmetic mirrors, lipsticks and combs.

Keys can become fishing lures. Sharpened by rubbing on a rough stone surface, they can also be used as cutting tools or scrapers.

Key rings can provide the wire or metal parts for trap triggers, snares or holders for cooking utensils.

Coins can be sharpened and used as cutters. Small ones can become fishing lures.

Lipstick can be used to prevent chapped lips or as a sunburn preventive, or even as a soothing treatment for minor scratches and abrasions. It can also be used as a direction marker, or for writing messages.

Combs are an excellent morale booster – there's nothing like tidy hair for making you feel good (apart from brushing your teeth). The teeth of combs can be sharpened, broken off, and used as sewing needles. And don't forget to make a comb and paper instrument to while away the time around the fire!

Material, if it's not needed for anything else, can be unravelled for thread.

Webbing belts can be unravelled to produce yards of strong cord. Belt buckles can become tools. Leather belts can be cut to produce yards of leather thong.

The list is endless (especially if you have a vehicle), and is limited only by your own needs and imagination.

6 To stay or to go?

This is the question that must be considered very carefully, particularly if you are the sole survivor of a crashed or stranded vehicle. Unfortunately, there are no golden rules – just good reasons for staying or going. You'll have to weigh up the pros and cons and make the final decision yourself.

Survivors have a strong urge to move when confronted by discomfort, fear of the unknown, their own weaknesses, or even embarrassment about being lost in the first place. The experts call it 'get home-itis.' If at all possible, however, make yourself stay put. If you are with a vehicle, you are a bigger target for searchers. What is more, if the searchers know what vehicle you are in, they will take into account the limitations of that vehicle when trying to guess your position. If they guess right, you should be there.

If you are on foot, trying to walk to safety could result in injury – especially if you are anxious or depressed and are not concentrating on where or how you walk. There is also a good chance that you might walk out of the main search area!

In a survival situation you will need all the energy you've got. So don't waste it on travelling unless you are certain that no one will be looking for you, you know exactly where you are going and how to get there, and you also know you can make it without exhausting yourself.

At the most, move only a few hundred yards if that will get you up to a ridge line or hill-top, where you and your signals might be more visible.

Six good reasons for staying

1 People will come looking for an aircraft, boat or car which is known to be overdue – and, to start with, they will be looking for the vehicle, not the occupants.

2 A vehicle is much larger than a person, and therefore easier to spot.

3 Wreckage can provide shelter – against wind, wet, heat and moderate cold (but remember, metal is not an efficient shelter against extreme cold).

4 Materials for making distress signals are more readily available from a wrecked or stranded vehicle.

5 A vehicle, particularly an aircraft, might be carrying water, food and first aid supplies, as well as clothing.

6 Weather conditions, or the terrain, might make travelling so difficult or dangerous that it should only be undertaken when there is absolutely no chance of rescue.

Five good reasons for going

1 No one knows your whereabouts, and there is no chance that you will be missed for a long time.

2 The place where you are stranded makes it unlikely that you will be spotted – for example, jungle or dense forest.

3 There has been no sign of a search-party after several days.

4 Search aircraft or search-parties have been spotted, but they have not responded to your distress signals, and several days have elapsed since they were seen.

5 To stay with the wreckage might be more dangerous than to leave it – you might be at high altitude, or in a precarious position.

If your decision is to go, leave a clear message, which is

easily visible, telling searchers your name, the date, the time, what supplies you are taking with you, what you are wearing, the direction in which you are heading, and any other information you feel is important. If you have nothing to write with, draw arrows on the ground, or mark trees to indicate your direction of travel.

The decision to travel through wild, unpopulated regions under survival conditions should be made only after much thought. Evaluating whether your chances for survival are better if you move on or stay put will be among the most important calculations you will have to make. Although your instinct may be to rush off, that could be very much against your best interests. Rescuers are more likely to spot the wreckage of your vehicle before they will locate someone amid vast acres of wilderness.

Crossing unfamiliar terrain leaves you open to unpredict-able dangers and increases the risk of injury or exhaustion. Unless you feel strongly that there is something to be gained by travelling, you would probably do better to remain in one place. Establish a base, and deal with the priorities of survival, as you see them, from one location.

Generally, the only exception to remaining *in situ* is in tropical rain forest. Habitation there normally only occurs along waterways, and the survivor would have to travel to, and then along, such waterways until help was found. Also, visibility from the air is almost nil in dense vegetation, and search aircraft would not be able to see the survivor, nor the majority of ground-to-air signals.

There may be other situations where it is necessary to travel, however. A hiker or traveller who has left no indications of route or plans, and for whom a search is not likely to be started, may have to travel in order to survive.

In most temperate areas, travel – if it must be undertaken – ought not to follow streams. The old idea that streams will sooner or later lead to civilization is simply not true. The only definite fact is that streams are always located in the lowest part of the terrain, and are usually choked with vegetation. Following a stream places survivors in tangled vegetation where it is almost impossible to see or hear them. The stream itself may well flow into swamps, marshes, or simply further into the wilderness.

If possible, select a route that keeps to high ground – but this does not mean going from summit to summit in mountainous terrain! Try to travel well above drainage patterns, on ground that provides a view of the surroundings and increases the chances of being seen by searchers on foot or in the air.

If your decision is to travel, head for the nearest point where rescue is likely. Set a pace that can be maintained for long periods. Generally, this means a pace that seems too slow to begin with. As fatigue sets in, the pace will probably be about right. There is no rush!

Before doing anything, however, make a plan. Delegate to various members of the group those tasks that must be accomplished. Be sure everyone has something to do and can feel useful. Don't try to do everything yourself. If you are the only person in the group trained in survival – or the only person who has read this book – let this be known and assume leadership, right from the outset. A leaderless group wastes energy and resources.

Unless the plan is shown to be wrong conclusively, stick to it. Don't go back to the drawing-board as soon as things don't work as well as you had planned and don't jump from plan to plan – this also wastes precious time and energy.

General rules for travel

● Travel for a set period of time, then rest a few minutes. When resting, keep facing the direction in which you are travelling, or mark your direction by a pointer of some kind.

● Take the easy way up slopes, at a slant and zig-zagging, instead of wasting your energy in a straight-up climb. As a rule of thumb, you should be able to whistle as you walk. If you can't, you're out of breath! Try to go round obstacles rather than through or over them. Detour round swamps, mud flats and heavy brush thickets. Go round ravines and gullies rather than climbing down and then up again. Whenever you do make such a detour, be sure to back-sight to your last identifiable landmark to re-establish your course.

● When travelling in a party, keep together and adjust the pace to that of the slowest person. Put one of the stronger people at the rear of the party to help anyone who lags behind.

● In poor visibility and during storms, make camp while there is still light and wait for better conditions before resuming travel. Get shelters up and fires lit before darkness falls.

● When crossing streams, carry a pole and probe the stream bottom for holes. Always face the current, so that your legs are not made to buckle under you.

● Avoid swamps if possible. If not, step on clumps of grass and exposed roots. If you do get mired in the mud, simply lie flat on your stomach and swim out of trouble. In quicksand, throw yourself flat on your back if you find yourself sinking. If you are carrying a pole, put it underneath your shoulders for extra support, then pull your legs out of the sand and roll or crawl back to firmer footing.

● In some areas, such as lowland jungles, rivers will offer the easiest and surest route to civilization. When using a raft, however, travel only by day and stay out of rough water. At the slightest hint of trouble, head for shore.

Measuring the width of a river

If you need to gauge the width of a river or ravine, then here's how to do it:

1 Choose a prominent object on the opposite bank like a tree or boulder, and position yourself directly opposite it.

2 Estimate the approximate half-width of the river and pace off that distance in either direction along the river-bank. Count your paces.

3 Mark the point where you stop with a stick or stone, and continue pacing along the bank.

4 When you have walked the same number of paces as you did in step 2, stop, and mark that point, too.

5 Now turn and walk directly away from the bank at an angle of 90° to the river. Continue walking until the object on the opposite bank and the first marker are both directly in line. Stop.

6 The distance between your second marker and your present position equals the width of the river or gorge.

Signals

Once protected from injury and the elements, your next consideration must be your location: where you are, where you should be and how you're going to get from one to the other – or whether you're simply going to stay put, and try to attract attention to your position.

If you are in trouble and need help, you have to ask for it. You need signals – things that effectively make you bigger and more noticeable. All signals fall into one of three categories: sight, sound or electronic. Sight signals are designed to attract the eyes of the searchers, by providing contrast in the form of colour, shape or movement – preferably all three. Sound signals should be more than just your own voice. The ultimate aim of any signal is to make you stand out from your background. The golden rule is: *Make a fuss!*

● If you don't have flares or electronic devices, prepare a

signal fire – you need lots of smoke during daylight, lots of flame at night.

- The signal mirror is one of the most effective daytime signals. It is quite common for mirror flashes to be seen twenty-five miles away. Commercial signalling mirrors (heliographs) are available, but it is easy enough to improvise your own. Point the mirror at the sun and flash the reflected spot on a nearby object. Then raise the mirror to your eye level and reach out as far as you can with your free hand, which should be open with the palm facing you, and making a V between an extended thumb and fingers. Catch the spot of light in the V, and turn your whole body and the mirror together, keeping the spot of light in the V until the target aircraft or whatever is also in the V. The reflected sun will be bang on target; wobbling the mirror slightly will cause the brilliant reflected light to flash on and off.

- You can stand out by making so much smoke that your signal couldn't possibly be mistaken for an ordinary campfire. One method is to pile green or wet leaves, or evergreen boughs, on to your fire when you hear planes or other signs of rescuers.

- Another technique is to build what is known as a Canadian smoke generator. Make a tripod of six-foot poles, with cross-pieces about halfway up. All bindings should be wire, if possible. Place green sticks on the cross-pieces to form a platform; on this, build a fire in the usual way – tinder, kindling and fuel – but don't light it. Then thatch the tripod above the level of the platform with evergreen boughs as you would a lean-to shelter, butt upwards, to shed any rain. When you want to use your signal, simply put a match to the tinder, and the fire will produce a dense cloud of white smoke very quickly.

- You can create contrast by using shadows and geometric shapes. Straight lines are uncommon in nature, and stand a good chance of being noticed from the air. Rocks laid out in a straight line might do the job, or shallow trenches, or turf cut out and turned over. Tramp out straight lines or a big SOS in the snow. Prepare banners and flags if you have the materials to spare.

Rescue is not a one-way affair. Simply sitting down and waiting to be found is almost as useless as running off in the grip of panic. You need to know what your rescuers are likely to do to find you, so that you can help them. Search and rescue professionals know that the first six hours of a search are the most critical. People without survival training or knowledge will have got themselves into such a mess by then that the chances of a successful rescue are drastically reduced. This means that the professionals will be trying to find you quickly – so you, in turn, must start thinking about attracting attention to yourself as soon as you think the alarm has been raised.

7 Water

Drinking water is essential to survival. Even with no physical activity, you can last an absolute maximum of ten days without it. It has been estimated that an average adult will lose two pints of water per day sitting in a room doing absolutely nothing – just through respiration and perspiration. With a lot of activity, you will need a gallon of water per day, in the winter as well as summer.

If water is plentiful, drink as much as you can. Carry water in your stomach rather than in a canteen. There is no advantage in rationing your water supply (except, perhaps, a psychological one). A sip every few hours is not going to do you any good, other than to moisten your lips and mouth. Satisfy your thirst if you can, and then ration your sweat. Remember that it is the water in your body which will save your life, not the water in your canteen or container. Bear in mind also, however, that the human being cannot store water like a camel, and your body will get rid of any excess by urination.

In winter, you are unlikely to find a source of running water. You will have to rely on snow and ice – but try to melt it first. If you are cold or haven't eaten, the intake of ice or snow greatly increases your chances of going down with hypothermia (see chapter 4). Your body has to use its heat to melt the snow or ice; if you have absolutely no alternative but to eat it, let it melt in your mouth before swallowing. Remember, if you find a stream or river that isn't frozen over, be careful not to fall in – hypothermia is a quicker killer than dehydration!

To melt snow, pack it into small balls and put it over a low heat – if the flame is too hot, the snow can actually scorch. Water made from snow and ice will taste very flat. You can add a tiny pinch of salt to improve the taste, or aerate it by pouring from container to container. (If you don't have a container, you can make one by folding birch bark or waxed paper.)

If you are in the desert and you find a source of water, stay with it. If you find water anywhere, in fact, regardless of how unpalatable it looks, it is better to drink it than to lie down next to it and die of dehydration. Almost any water is better than no water.

If the water does look bad, pull a piece of cloth tight over your mouth and put your face down in the water and suck. Better still, if you have the materials, filter the water through a sock (or a length of bamboo, with grass stuffed into one end as a stopper) which has six alternate layers of charcoal and sand – then boil it for at least two minutes. The danger signs in water are: lack of insect life; absence of animals or animal tracks; and a white coating on the rocks or ground around the water. One interesting test for the freshness of water is to wiggle your finger in your ear and pull out a bit of wax. Drop this into the water: if the water is fresh, the wax will settle to the bottom. If the water is questionable, the wax will form an oily sheen on the surface.

If there are bugs and insects, you're lucky – you have a rich supply of protein on tap. Try to avoid high-alkaline water, which gives the rocks and ground around it a white coating. But if that's all there is, go ahead and drink it. Sip a small amount, let it settle, then drink another small amount. Don't gulp down a lot, or you'll vomit, and so lose valuable body fluids. Muddy water is perfectly drinkable, if you strain it first or let it settle overnight. In many arid, semi-desert areas, most of the water you find will be a watering-hole for cattle. You can also drink water in which you find cow manure – just brush the manure away and drink.

If you're unable to find water on the surface, try digging down in a dry stream bed at the outer sweep of a bend, or under banks in low spots. If you don't find water within two feet, however, stop digging and try elsewhere. In areas abundant in granite rock, look over the hillsides for green grass. Dig a ditch at the base of the greenest area and wait for the water to seep in. In low forests, along the seashore and in river plains, the water table is close to the surface. Very little digging usually yields a good supply of water. Along the seashore, water can be found in the dunes above the beach or even on the beach itself. Look in the hollows between dunes for visible water, and dig if the sand seems moist. If there are no dunes, scoop holes in the sand a few yards above the high-tide mark. Both fresh and salt water may be present, but the fresh water will float on the salt water, and can be scooped off very carefully. The water may be brackish, but can be filtered to improve the taste.

Under no circumstances must you drink sea water. Its salt concentration is so high that body fluids must be drawn to eliminate it. Eventually your kidneys will simply pack up. Avoid even rinsing your mouth out with it, because the temptation to swallow a little may be more than you can bear – and next you will swallow more, and more and more.

Don't drink urine or blood, either – they, too, have a high concentration of salts, with the same effect as drinking sea water. And don't drink petrol, anti-freeze, alcohol, after-shave lotion or any other such liquid which under normal circumstances you would never think of touching. You shouldn't drink water which tastes salty or soapy or – if you get it from a plant – which looks milky (unless you know it's definitely safe, as you would with, say, coconut milk). Any of these undrinkable fluids, however, can be used in a solar still (described below).

If you are unsuccessful in your search for ground or run-off water, or if you do not have time to purify questionable water, a water-yielding plant may be the best source. Many plants with fleshy leaves or stems store drinkable water. Trying them is the way to find out. Climbing vines found in tropical forests yield a very large amount of fluid – but make sure it is clear, not milky. To get the fluid, cut lengths of vines, roots or branches, and hold them vertically above your mouth. Make sure the lengths (of about one yard) are actually cut off from the rest of the plant, or an airlock will prevent any flow. Even in arid areas, tree branches or roots – on or near the surface – may also give you a reasonable supply of fluid.

Don't neglect your need for water in cold conditions. You may not feel thirsty, and it is easy to convince yourself that you only need a little water in a cold climate. But you need to keep your intake at an adequate level, so force yourself to drink water under cold climatic conditions – even if you think you don't need it.

Don't eat any food if you have a supply of less than two pints of water per day. If you have more at your disposal, then you can eat carbohydrate foods, such as biscuits and sweets. Proteins, such as meat, fish, shellfish, beans and cheese, use up a lot of water in digestion. Don't eat them unless you have *plenty* of water.

Sources of water

Rain is an obvious source of water, but you'll need something to collect it in. Scrape a depression in the ground as a catchment area, and line it with a waterproof coat, plastic sheet or large leaves. If you're desperate for water, use your clothes to soak up the rain, and wring them out into a container. You can also collect rainwater from a sloping tree trunk by twisting a piece of clothing or cloth around the trunk and leading the end down into a container.

Even in arid areas, considerable amounts of dew can form at night on rocks, exposed metal surfaces, and vegetation. Dragging a cotton shirt or cloth through foliage first thing in the morning can produce a lot of moisture, which can then be wrung out into a container. Tying a plastic bag around a leafy branch can often yield as much as half a pint of dew.

Cliffs sometimes show seepage on the actual face, or at

the bottom. Isolated clumps of vegetation or patches of moss may also indicate seepages. Caves, particularly limestone caves which are formed by running water, sometimes contain streams or pools.

You can harvest water from birch sap, especially in the early spring. Make a knife slash on the bark in the shape of a V; the sap will trickle out – delicious!

Solar still

In deserts and very dry areas, water may be present in the ground. If you have a piece of plastic sheeting, you can rig up a very effective still to produce water by condensation.

Dig a hole about three feet across and three feet deep (or bigger, depending on the size of plastic sheet you have available – but remember not to over-exert yourself). At the bottom of the hole, in the centre, place your bucket, cup, or improvised container. Place around it any vegetation you can find – sliced up, or shredded, or broken, to expose as much juice as possible. Pour over the vegetation any polluted fluid you have available – urine, blood, milky sap, radiator water, sea water (even better to place it in a shallow container, so that no liquid at all is wasted). Now cover the hole with a large plastic sheet, allowing it to sag down into the hole until it is just a few inches from the container, yet not touching the sides of the hole or the vegetation. Put a small stone wrapped in cloth (to prevent it from heating up and burning through the plastic) in the centre of the sheet, so that it keeps a taut, inverted cone shape. If you have a length of rubber tubing, put it into the container and lead it out under one edge of the sheet. Now anchor the edges of the sheet with rocks and sand or earth, to create a system as near watertight as possible.

The sun's heat raises the temperature of the air and earth under the plastic sheet until the air becomes saturated with vapour, which condenses in tiny drops on the cooler underside of the plastic and slowly runs down the sloping surface, dripping off into the container. Solar stills produce about half as much water between 4 p.m. and 8 a.m. as they do during the daylight hours. The reason they produce some water at night is that, after sundown, the plastic cools rapidly while the temperature of the soil remains relatively high, and so water vapour continues to condense.

A solar still should produce at least a pint of water in twenty-four hours, and maybe more. If you have more plastic, make more stills. You will find that your still may also become a possible source of food: the water container attracts snakes and small animals, which slide under the plastic and then cannot climb out again.

You may have few choices for the site of a solar still. But the best locations for digging the pit are in a river bed (whether or not there is surface moisture), where there are signs of moisture, or where there is any vegetation – even if the growth appears dry or dead. If you're digging in a river bed, the best site is at the edge of an outer swing. If none of the favoured sites is available, select the lowest area (water percolates downwards) with the least forbidding impediments (such as rocky ground). Clay soil holds more moisture than sandy soil – dig in a clay soil if you can. Any site you choose *must be free of shade*: the still only functions when exposed to the sun.

If the dimensions of your plastic sheet mean that you have to dig a trench rather than a hole for your solar still, make sure the trench lies east–west, to get maximum exposure to the sun. If you have no plastic sheet, there is another effective means of purifying water by condensation. Scrape a depression in the ground, and fill it with the impure water supply. Drive two stakes about chest-high into the ground, on either side of the hole. The stakes should have forked ends to support another pole between them (or the pole can be tied in position). Over the pole drape a piece of cloth or clothing, as if hanging up washing to dry. Now heat some stones in a fire, and push them into the water-filled depression. The fluid will become steam, which will condense on the cloth. All you have to do then is wring out the cloth into a container.

There are two variations of the solar still: the vegetation still and the urine distillation still.

Vegetation still

A vegetation still will produce a fair amount of water with very little effort on your part, as long as you have a plastic dustbin bag or survival bag handy (clear plastic is best, though coloured ones will do), and some vegetation – the saguaro cactus is perfect.

1 Scoop out a hole with two craters – inner and outer – on a slope or built-up mound of sand or soil.

2 Place the plastic bag over the hole, with the bag opening down the slope.

3 Inside the bag, use a stick or something similar to make a tent over the crater. (Pad the ends of the stick.)

4 Place clean rocks or weights inside the bag around the outer crater rim to hold the plastic tent taut.

5 Fill the inner crater with vegetation. Do not use any plants that you know to be poisonous, and be careful not to have any vegetation touching the outer crater or the plastic.

6 Close the bag tight.

7 As the vegetation warms up, water will condense on the inside of the plastic, and droplets will run down the tent and collect in the outer crater. (It has been shown that the vegetation still works faster and produces more water than the traditional solar still.) From the outer crater, water runs down the trough to a catch pool.

To get water from the bag, scoop a deeper hole just below the catch pool and open the bag just enough to pour the water out.

Make sure you don't drink any water that has been in direct contact with the vegetation, nor any water formed under the vegetation.

Urine distillation still

Urine, blood, radiator water, alcohol and any other unusable fluid can be converted to drinkable water with a urine still. Basically just a version of the old-fashioned whisky still, it will work at any time of the day or night, in any climate. You need roughly the same materials as for a solar still.

1 Dig a hole for the fire.

2 Dig another hole, exactly as for a solar still, about twelve inches away.

3 Between the holes, form some sort of tunnel, big enough to take a radiator hose, or whatever you are going to use to move the steam between the two holes.

4 Set up the second hole as for a solar still, with a plastic cover weighted with a padded stone in the middle, and a catchment container beneath. (A car wing or door or sheet of metal will do just as well as a plastic cover in this particular still.)

5 Build a fire in the first hole. Place urine and other fluids in a flameproof container, and fix it over the fire. You need something like a length of radiator hose or piping to lead the steam from the boiling liquid into the second chamber. You also need some means of guiding the steam into the hose – metal foil is ideal.

6 Light the fire, and prepare to be amazed.

Signs of water

Although some mammals are able to obtain moisture from their food, the majority need water if they are to survive. So if you come across an animal trail that looks well worn and shows fresh signs of use – like browsed leaves or moist droppings – then following it might lead you to water.

All seed-eating birds need a supply of water. Flocks of finches or other birds seen feeding on grass seeds are a sure indication that water is near. Pigeons, especially, will also be found near to a water supply. In the late afternoon, they make their way to water, so you may be able to track down the source.

Some of the more highly organized insect communities need water, and may lead you to their supply – however small it is. Bees require a lot of water – in tropical and subtropical regions, mason bees, which build their hives with mud, are a good sign that water is not far away. If you can find their source of mud, then a little digging should produce a hole of muddy water. Ants too are always near to water. If you see a column entering or leaving a hollow in a tree trunk or fallen log, there is a good chance that you'll find water inside. Test with a dip-stick to see if water is present, then tie a shirt or piece of cloth to the end of the stick, soak it in the water, and either suck it or wring it out.

Remember, you must have water to survive, and at all times you must make every effort to satisfy this need. Your need for water must *always* take precedence over your need for food. If you cannot get the water you require, you must do everything you can to conserve your body water levels. If you are active in a hot climate, the loss through perspiration will be very high. Cut down this loss by making all your movements slow, methodical and totally unrushed. Try to keep in the shade at all times. Keep all your clothes on, even adding some, if available, to reduce water loss through perspiration: *ration sweat, not water*. If there is a breeze, get into a position in the shade that places you in the breeze as well. Travel only if absolutely necessary, and even then, go at night and in the very early morning.

Wipe your face, brow, and the back of your neck with a cloth soaked in sea water, urine, after-shave lotion or any undrinkable fluid or crushed succulent plants that you can spare.

8 Food

Food is last on your list of survival priorities, because it is not a necessity. People have lived well in excess of a month without eating. Even under extremely harsh conditions, there have been several cases of survivors lasting two or three weeks without food. In fact, in most cases the food you ate before the survival crisis will be more important than anything you might forage – so always travel on a full tank!

Unfortunately that doesn't seem to have stopped the experts from writing reams and reams about trapping, snaring, fishing and other methods of food procurement. I am about to do precisely the same, for a very important reason: food may not be a necessity, but it is a very welcome bonus. It's a provider of comfort, warmth, and a sense of well-being, so if your other priorities have been taken care of, it's worth looking for. What's more, just thinking about food and planning how you are going to trap or harvest it can be an invaluable way of taking your mind off your overall dilemma. Looking for food gives you something to do. The most important points to remember are:

- If it moves, eat it.

- Eat in the morning to give you energy for the day, and eat at night to keep your body warm. In between, eat a little (or lots if you have it!) and often.

- Don't eat protein unless you have a lot of water to go with it.

Plants and grubs are likely to be your most important food

supply, for the simple reason that they don't run away. Flesh foods (when you catch them) have better nutritional value. You can eat just about everything that swims, flies, walks, crawls, wriggles or just sits and waits for its prey to float past – everything from worms and caterpillars to rats and seagulls. That's why I recommend putting curry powder in your survival kit: with your eyes closed, you could swear curried rat was curried chicken.

Plants

Plant don'ts

DON'T eat fungi, unless you're an expert. The dangers of wrong identification far outweigh any nutritional advantages.

DON'T eat anything that looks like beans or peas. They are often full of concentrated minerals, and toxic.

DON'T eat bulbs, unless they look, smell and taste like onions or garlic.

DON'T eat plants that look very brightly coloured or simply weird – hairy leaves or stems, spines, thorns, or very shiny leaves.

DON'T eat any plant that irritates your skin when you touch it.

DON'T eat any plant with a milky sap – except for dandelions.

DON'T eat any plant with umbrella-shaped blossoms.

DON'T eat any white, yellow or red berries.

DON'T eat any fruit which is in five sections.

DON'T eat anything that resembles a cucumber, melon, parsnip, dill, parsley, or tomato.

Some plants can ruin your day even though they fit none of the categories above. But you can separate these from the harmless ones by the following simple edibility test. It's time-consuming but effective. Anyway, it's quite useful that the test is so time-consuming, because it staves off boredom.

Plant edibility test

1 Make sure you choose a plant that is in plentiful supply and easy to recognize. There's no point finding out that a plant is edible, if the only sample of it was the one you have eaten, or is easily confused with something else.

2 Select the part of the plant that appears most palatable to you. Check the juice or sap. If the sap is clear, put a drop on your tongue. Wait for ten minutes. If it tastes bitter, produces a numbing sensation on your tongue, lips or mouth, or makes you feel nauseous, reject the plant (but see step six below).

3 If there is no reaction, eat a small piece and wait two hours.

4 If there is still no reaction, eat a little more and wait one hour.

5 If there is still no reaction, eat a little more and wait for a further half-hour. If there is no reaction you may assume it is safe to eat.

6 If the plant tasted bitter, either stand it in cold water overnight or boil it, then try steps 2 to 5 again.

Preparing plants

There is no room in a book of this size to start describing all the world's edible plants and their uses. Here, however, are a few of the commoner types, and how to prepare them.

Dandelion. Eat the whole plant. The root is high in carbohydrate, but bitter, so boil it first. The seeds are edible and high in oil. The leaves taste like slightly bitter lettuce.

Plantain. High in iron and some vitamins. Boil it twice, changing the water. (Remember to drink the water.)

Nettle. Eat the leaves boiled – the smallest, freshest ones are the most nutritious. Nettles are high in iron and vitamins, low in carbohydrate. (You can use the dried stems to make cord.)

Clover. The flowers are high in carbohydrate, the leaves high in protein. The whole plant is edible, raw or boiled.

Dock. The whole plant is edible, but it has a bitter taste, so boil it twice. The seeds are edible, but should be cooked.

Thistle. Edible after the spikes have been removed. Thistle nuts and roots are high in carbohydrates.

Sorrel. The whole plant is edible, raw or cooked.

Goose-grass (cleavers). The whole plant is edible.

Burdock. The roots, leaf stem and flower stem are all edible, but must be peeled first, then boiled.

The inner bark of these trees is high in carbohydrate: willow (eat the twigs, too, in spring – but avoid the outer bark, which contains a sedative), poplar, birch, sycamore, pine (also eat the new shoots) and hawthorn (whose new shoots are delicious). Boil the bark first.

You can eat the roots and fleshy stems of all reeds, rushes and bullrushes – raw or boiled. They are very high in carbohydrates, but fibrous.

Insects and grubs

Insect forms of one kind or another live in practically every conceivable habitat. They are tasty, nutritious, numerous – and everywhere. They are likely to be the most reliable source of animal food in a survival situation, even in the desert. But before you tuck in, learn these four rules:

● Eat only fresh insects.

● Don't eat pupae found in the soil.

● If you're in doubt about any particular insect, apply the plant edibility test.

● Don't eat hairy caterpillars: they sting.

These are the only don'ts. Everything else is fair game. But cook it first, if possible. Roasting is the easiest way, on a thin stick. Cook insects until they are dry.

If you can't bring yourself to eat insects whole, try grinding them into a powder after cooking and mixing them in with any other food, or a drink. Or use them to prepare stock for soups, or to add to stews.

Finding and preparing insects

A fire at night will serve to attract various night-flying insects. A torch or lantern will also attract certain edibles – perhaps all you'll need to keep you in good condition. Discard the wings before eating moths.

Look in the branches and hollow trunks of trees. Turn over stones and debris and tear open hollow logs. Many insects, such as grasshoppers, are best collected at night or early morning while they are still lethargic.

Top of the bill are termites (remove their wings first; termite eggs, too, are a delicacy), beetle grubs or larvae (generally from one to seven inches long, and white or cream-coloured, with a wrinkled body and usually three pairs of short legs), grasshoppers, locusts and crickets (take off the hind legs of these three before eating, to minimize scratchiness when you swallow), smooth caterpillars and various aquatic insects.

Last but definitely not least is the common or garden worm. Pound for pound more value than beef, worms are deliciously noodle-like when boiled, squeezed (to get rid of grit) and boiled again. Save the water for stock. If you can find birds' eggs, a worm omelette is one of the greatest things you'll ever taste (besides possibly a Big Mac with strawberry shake). While you're eating it, you can make plans as to how and where you'll open your first worm omelette chain back home.

To the injured person, what is especially attractive is the fact that insect larvae are slow. Very slow. Even if you're at death's door, you should be able to outrun a grub. Some larvae are almost 50 per cent protein (don't forget to drink lots of water with them). Most are no lower than 30 per cent, whereas good beef is only about 15 per cent. Insects may also have a substantial fat content. The outer covering of adult insects is made of a substance which is indigestible to humans, but all the inner anatomy is easily digested. The rather crunchy outside is just added fibre. Bee and wasp larvae have a pleasant flavour, but they are well defended, so approach them only as a last resort! Slugs and snails are best boiled – but you'll probably want to skim the slimy scum off the top of the water. They can be roasted, too, but it will be a bit like chewing elastic bands.

Insects are probably your easiest source of survival nutrition, as long as two conditions are met: (a) you have adequate drinking water (insects are protein); and (b) you can overcome any feelings of squeamishness you may have about eating them. Hunt them early in the morning, when they are cold and sluggish, and cook them by roasting or frying. For safety's sake, stick with the ones you can more or less identify.

Food that runs away

Just about anything that walks, swims, crawls, slithers or flies is edible. None the less, there are one or two rules about edibility which need to be followed.

- It's safe to eat the flesh of all mammals when it's fresh and unspoiled. The offal or innards of all mammals is edible, too – except the livers of seals or polar bears, which can hold a posionous amount of vitamin A.

- It's safe to eat the flesh of all birds, even sea birds and scavengers. Their eggs are also edible.

- It's safe to eat the flesh of all lizards, snakes, frogs and salamanders – but skin them first. Don't eat toads.

How to catch your supper

The simplest way to catch a small mammal is with a snare. To make a basic one, you'll need a length of springy wire about eighteen inches long. Twist a small 'eye' into one end of it and thread the other end through the eye to form a loop that is just large enough for the head of your prey to pass through. Secure the free end to a stake, or tree root, and position the loop carefully. Choose a heavy-traffic area, and try to funnel the animal into your snare with small twigs pushed into the ground to create barriers. Set a lot of snares!

If you are in an area with lots of squirrels, you can improve your chances of a catch by leaning a pole two or three inches in diameter and about eight feet long against a tree. Put snares every foot or so along the pole, with the nooses uppermost.

Most birds can be caught in a box trap. A ready-made box, or one made in log-cabin fashion from sticks tied together, is rested with one edge on the ground and the other propped up on a short stick. Tie a length of string round this stick, and retreat to your hiding place. When the bird wanders underneath the box to investigate the bait, yank the string and the box will trap it.

Meat-eating or fish-eating birds can be caught with a fish-hook imbedded in a scrap of bait, and tied to an anchor point.

All lizards are edible and pleasant to taste, and they are easily snared with a noose on a long pole. Skin them by slitting down the belly, and then remove the internal organs, and eat them roasted – delicious!

Snakes are very tasty. Kill them before handling. A blow anywhere on their back will immobilize them – but beware the fangs while you're cutting the head off. Don't try to use a forked stick to trap them – they'll wriggle away. An ordinary stick is much better. Bury the head after severing; just so you don't forget where it is and sit on it! Boiled snake falls apart; frying or roasting are better methods. Prepare it by skinning, and remove the entrails simply by running your thumb down through the body cavity.

Here are three easy bird traps. The bigger the bird, the better the traps work. The first two are especially effective for pheasants and quail, and they both appear almost too simple to work – but they do! Try the dunce's cap and V-trench both at once (and several of each), to give the bird more chance of making a fool of itself.

Dunce's cap

1 Find a sheet of paper or very thin bark, about twelve inches square.

2 Find a spot where the birds are roosting, and bait the area well before setting the trap.

3 Push a stick with a sharpened end into the ground and rotate it, until you have a conical-shaped hole about twelve inches deep and six inches wide.

4 Form the paper/bark into the same conical shape, and pin it with a small twig or hawthorn, or seal it with resin.

5 Stick pine resin to the inside surface of the cone. Put bait similar to the advance bait you have been using into the

bottom of the cone, and leave the cone in the depression in the ground.

6 The bird will put its head down into the cone for the bait, and lift it out again wearing a dunce's cap.

V-trench

1 Dig a shallow trench shaped like a wedge, about three feet long. The wedge should slope from ground level down to the end wall, whose depth should be neck height for a pheasant (about eight inches). Looked at from above, the trench should not be an open rectangle. Its top should be V-shaped, with the point of the V above the deepest part of the wedge.

2 Lay a trail of bait (for instance, grass seed, crumbs or raisins) down the wedge.

3 The bird, following the bait, walks down the incline into the narrowed end of the trap, and is then either unable or unwilling to back out.

Water fowl or duck trap

Good siting and setting are essential, but this trap is very effective.

1 Gather three sticks about three feet long and an inch in diameter, and sharpen them at both ends.

2 Drive the sticks into the water in the shape of a triangle. The distance between the stakes will depend on the size of the stone or weight which you are going to use. The stakes should be angled slightly outwards.

3 On top of the stakes, balance a stone weighing about five or six pounds, to which you have tied either a baited hook or a snare.

4 When the water fowl takes the bait it topples the weight from the stakes. Its head is dragged under the water, and it drowns.

Other tricks

- Deadfalls will trap both birds and animals, and the basic principles can be infinitely varied to meet specific conditions. A deadfall consists of a heavy weight, such as a long log, supported by a trigger stick which stands at an angle of about 60°. The bait is tied to the base of the trigger stick – before the trap is set!

- Birds can be trapped with bird lime, which may be any strong adhesive, but is usually made from plant sap – that of the breadfruit tree is good, forming a glutinous substance when exposed to air – or resin (fig sap can be boiled into especially good bird lime). Smear the bird lime on slender sticks which will catch on the bird's wings and prevent it from flying. Study the birds you hope to catch, and work out where the smeared sticks should be placed so that they come into contact with the bird's wings. Heated chewing gum makes a good substitute. One good method is to rig up a tripod of three sticks, smear them with bird lime, and then use insects for bait. Bird lime does not work in cold climates.

- The best way to attract mammals to a trap is to place salt along a trail or at a water hole.

- Squirrels and other mammals which inhabit hollow trees can be pulled out by inserting and twisting a short forked stick. Pin the animal against the side or bottom of the hollow and then twist the stick. The fur and loose skin will twist around the fork and the animal can be pulled out – but keep tension on the stick when you withdraw it.

- A noose fastened to the end of a long pole can be used to snare an animal as it comes out of its burrow – or a bird roosting on a branch.

- You can use smoke to drive animals out of their dens or burrows. Snare, club or net the quarry as it emerges.

- You can bait a hook with a minnow and place it near water to catch gulls, crows and other scavengers.

● Place snares in areas previously used for butchering animals. Use animal entrails for bait. After you have erected traps, snares and barriers to channel the animals into them, sprinkle animal blood or bladder contents in the area – this will help neutralize your scent.

Fishing

Water supports more animal life in a given area than the same area on land. Izaak Walton might not have agreed, but here are the compleat rules for getting your meals from it:

● There are no known poisonous freshwater fish anywhere in the world.

● Only catch the amount of fish that you need – it goes off very quickly.

● Remember that you are not fishing for trophies: a three-inch tiddler is better than nothing.

● All seaweed is edible. Make sure it is fresh. The bright green and red ones are best.

● Most snails are edible, but not very tiny ones. Feed them on identifiably safe vegetation for twenty-four hours to cleanse their intestines.

You can sometimes find fish under the banks of a river. Feel your way along with your hand, and when you come into contact with one, tickle its belly and feel for the gills. Whilst tickling, pinch the gills and flip the fish out of the water. The best place for this activity is underneath the branches of overhanging trees, where the fish are waiting for insects to drop. Allow your hand to reach water temperature before trying it, however, and don't attempt it in warm climes: you're more likely to catch a fingerful of snapping turtle or other undesirable than a nice fat trout.

If possible, always take the bait to be used for fishing from the fish's indigenous waters. When you catch a fish or frog, check its intestines to find out what it has been eating. Small chunks of apple can make good bait. Old rotten bark will provide small grubs – crumble it up and drop it in the water above your hook.

One excellent way of fishing is with a blown-up balloon or condom. Improvise a net (a pair of tights will do), and place it over the inflated balloon. Attach as many baited hooks, on lines of varying lengths, to the net as you like, and tie on an anchor line. As the fish tug on the bait, the bag will be pulled down under the water. Then as its buoyancy reasserts itself, it will pop back up, snatching the fish.

Fish are attracted by light. Flying fish can be landed on a raft by reflecting torch or moonlight on to a sail or shirt, and catching them as they jump. Or reflect moonlight with a mirror on the riverbed – the fish will come and lie over it. Prawns, too, will rise to a light at night and can be scooped up.

Experiment with different lures – feathers, bits of plastic, buttons, coins, bright cloth, fish entrails, slivers of fish flesh, small shells.

You can make sure your line isn't bitten through by attaching the hook to your line with thin wire. You can improvise line by unravelling a sheet of dry canvas, and plaiting the threads. Hooks can be made from bone and wood, as well as bent pins, safety pins or small pen-knives with the blade tied at an angle. Or try a skewer hook – a piece of metal, wood or bone about the size of a small matchstick. Tie the line around it half-way along its length, then lay the skewer along the line. Feed bait over both skewer and line. When the fish takes the bait, jerk the line and the skewer will open out and jam in its stomach.

Even without a line or hook, there are ways to catch fish. You can stun fish in pools and ponds by burning coral or seashells to make lime, and throwing it into the water. Shade attracts many small fish. A lowered sail, sheet or even a shirt may gather fish. Try dangling a piece of fish or bird gut (or a whole bird wing) in the water. Allow the small fish to swallow the gut, then snatch them up out of the water.

Skin frogs before cooking them, as the skins of many species secrete irritating and poisonous fluids. Avoid those marked with yellow and red. Frogs legs are a real delicacy, but there's no reason why you shouldn't eat the whole body. Find them at night by their croaking. Approach slowly. Club them with a stick or snag the larger ones with a hook and line. Kill them by sticking a knife through the spinal cord just behind the head.

Generally speaking, fishing as practised by the survivor has very little to do with the leisurely activity of anglers. It is a tricky business, calling for patience, a highly acute sense of observation, a little skill, and a great deal of ingenuity: sometimes fish are driven only by curiosity, so don't despair if you have no food bait. Dougal Robertson, as you will see in chapter 13, used a bit of cloth hooked on to a spoon made from a food can. (It didn't work!)

If you're on a raft, try leaning over the inflated ring and drawing your hand round the edge of the raft's bottom to collect barnacles. When shelled, these make excellent bait. You can try harpooning scavenger fish, but don't be too ambitious in terms of the size of fish you go for. Robertson used the handle of a paddle to make a harpoon. He carved out the barbs and strengthened the point with two nails. If you have a gaff, you can slide it carefully into the water and pass it under the fish. Immobilize a large fish by forcing your thumb and middle finger into its eyes and cutting off its tail fin. If you have a bucket or bailer on the raft, empty fish entrails slowly over the side inside it. Fish might swim in to get at the offal. If you have a plastic jerrycan-type container, you can make a fish trap by cutting away most of the side opposite the normal filling hole. Dip a line with bait on it into the jerrycan through the normal opening. Then dip the baited jerrycan into the water, holding it by the handle. When a fish swims into it, all you have to do is to lift the trap and tip the fish into the raft.

- Don't eat any fish which is not fresh and which does not look, feel or smell right. In the tropics, fish can putrefy even minutes after death and form dangerous poisons – so make sure you cook it at once.

- If you squeeze a fish and the indentations remain, forget it.

- If the fish's eyes are milky, forget it.

- If the fish doesn't have scales, forget it.

- Don't eat any fish that doesn't look like a fish – this includes fish which are shaped like a box, fish which inflate themselves like a balloon after being caught, fish which look like a pig, with a snout-like mouth or fish which look like a rough stone.

- Don't touch any conical or spindly-shaped shellfish.

- Never eat the offal of fish, even fish which you recognize and know to be safe. As with the livers of polar bears and seals, the liver can kill you. Use it as bait instead.

Cooking

Although food is the least important consideration in most survival situations, it is nevertheless especially important in maintaining a positive attitude and, if nothing else, alleviating boredom. Remember that, unless you have absolutely no means whatsoever of lighting a fire, you *must* cook the food. Boiling is by far the best way, because it preserves natural juices and vitamins. Boil water in a concave rock or bark container by placing clean, hot rocks in the water. Then add the food, cover with large leaves, and cook.

You can make a birch bark container with a bit of fancy origami, ending up with the sort of paper boat you used to make as a child. If this is beyond you, hold the corners in position with hawthorns or split twigs or even resin. The bark will not burn as long as the water is not boiling – so remove the container from the heat as soon as boiling starts.

It's also possible to roast or fry food on rocks with reflected heat, or you can improvise a griddle with a rock over flames. You can roast food by wrapping it in leaves or wet newspaper and burying it under a fire in sand or soft soil. Line a small, shallow pit with leaves, then fill it with food, or wrap food in plant leaves or cloth. Cover the pit with about half an inch of sand or soil and build a fire directly over it.

Roll fish, hedgehogs and other food in mud or clay and roast them in hot coals. There's no need to scale fish or to skin animals – when you remove the clay the scales or skin will peel away with it.

Steaming works particularly well for shellfish. Dig a hole and line it with rocks. Build a fire in the hole and allow it to burn down into ashes and hot coals. Remove the ashes and coals and place the food directly on and between stones. Cover with whole plant leaves, green grass or seaweed, and cover that layer with sand or soft soil. Poke small holes in the dirt, and pour water in to create steam. Plug the holes to prevent the steam escaping. An hour and a half of steaming should be sufficient for most items of small or medium size.

If you're in the tropics and you don't have a fire, you can 'cook' fish by pickling it in lime or lemon juice.

Add salt as a seasoning if you have it to spare, but don't get paranoid about your salt intake as a survivor. Perhaps because sodium and potassium salts are so vital to your body, they are lost from it only under extremely stressful conditions. It is, in fact, very easy to take an overdose of salt, and produce nausea and vomiting. Never take salt tablets unless you have lots of water to go with them. If your body does for any reason tell you that you need salt, I warmly recommend the highly sociable expedient of licking the nearest person!

Survivors'
lessons

9 Lost

I've never been lost, though I will admit to being confused for several weeks . . . – Daniel Boone.

Imagine that you're in the wilderness, and you're lost. It's getting dark. You're scared. Lions, bears, natives, Hell's Angels, Daleks, Mekons: they'll all be coming to get you. Now I'm sorry to have to tell you this, but life just isn't as exciting as that. Being lost is no big deal. At worst, it means a night under the stars. As Christina Dodwell says in *Explorer's Handbook*: '. . . we awoke lost, were lost as we travelled, and stayed lost at night . . . Over the years I have worked on the theory that . . . you are only lost if you fail to find somewhere specific, or don't get there on time.'

So don't panic. Remember that the most dangerous animal in the wilderness is you: your own imagination can wreak more havoc than any of the wild animals you'll never see. If anybody knows where you are (and someone should), you can be sure that they will be concerned about you if you don't show up by nightfall. If you have a survival kit with you (and you should), you really have nothing to worry about.

When you first realize that you are lost, Stop. Find somewhere nice to sit down, and have a think about where you could have gone wrong. If you're lost on a hike, you'll have a map and compass, of course. Get your map out and check it against the landmarks around you. Anything familiar? If not, don't panic. Have a look at all the beautiful and interesting things around you. They must be beautiful and interesting, because otherwise what on earth are you doing hiking through them? The environment is not hostile. It's not out to get you.

Now look at the map again. Do you know where you were a couple of hours ago? If so, find that place on the map. You can't be far from it. If you still can't work out a return route, get a little fire going. If it's cold and miserable, get a big fire going. If it's getting dark, accept that you're going to have the pleasure of a night out, and build a temporary shelter (unless there's a natural one to hand). Eat only a little of your emergency rations – save the rest for tomorrow. Stay put in your camp. Get your signals ready, and mark the direction of sunset on the ground.

In the morning, if you are sure that no one is searching for you, you have a couple of ways of finding yourself back on familiar ground. First, can you hear anything? Perhaps the sound of traffic, or a farmer's barking dog, or a chain-saw. If you can't hear anything, climb a tree and try to get a bearing on a recognizable landmark.

One way to get a bearing, for which you'll need a map and compass, is triangulation – but you have to learn how to do it. Another is zigzagging or otherwise sectoring a search – but be careful always to be able to find your way back to your camp. If you're still lost, you'll have to head in the estimated direction of a road or railway or similar, preferably at right-angles to it, so that you stand the greatest chance of walking into it. One tip: if you're lost in woods and you have encountered a track which then forks (with you at the stem of the Y), then you're probably going deeper into the forest. Retrace your steps.

What do you do if you don't have a compass? If you have a watch, you can determine direction by pointing the hour hand directly towards the sun (or, in cloudy conditions, towards the area of brightest light). Bisect the angle between the hour hand and 1200, and you have south. (The reverse is true in the southern hemisphere.) If your watch is digital, by the way, simply draw a conventional watchface on the ground, with the hands at the correct time, and orient yourself accordingly.

If you don't have a watch, and you don't know if it's morning or afternoon, you can still use the sun to find direction. Push a thin, straight stick into the ground, and mark the tip of its shadow with a small stone or another stick. Wait fifteen to thirty minutes (the longer the better), and mark the tip of the new shadow. Facing the two markers, put your left foot on the first marker, and your right foot on the second. You are now facing south.

When the sun sets and the sky gets dark, stars become efficient compasses. The North Star is the most accurate natural guide available. To find it, first search for the Big Dipper (or Plough), a group of seven stars which look something like a long-handled saucepan, sideways on. The two stars which form the side of the saucepan furthest from the handle are the pointers to the North Star: extend the line formed by them for roughly five times its length, and you will see the North Star.

In the southern hemisphere, a line through the long axis of the Southern Cross points to the South Pole. There is no guiding star above it – only a blank space in the sky so dark by comparison that it is known as the Southern Coalsack. East of the Southern Cross are two very bright stars. By using these and the Southern Cross as guides, you can locate a spot within the Southern Coalsack which is approximately above the South Pole: extend a line along the long axis of the Southern Cross, to the south, and join the two bright stars east of the Cross by a line. Bisect this line with one at right-angles to it. The point at which this line intersects through the Cross is approximately above the South Pole.

If the stars are partly obstructed by trees, fog or mountains, you can still find the general direction by observing any star for movement. To do this, push two sticks into the ground about two feet apart. The stick nearer you should be shorter than the other. Now lie down on the ground and sight along the stick tips on to any star in the sky. Watch closely for movement : if the star dips, it is in the west; if it moves left, it is in the north; if it moves right, it is in the south.

One reasonably accurate method of navigating by the moon is to draw a line to sea level from the two horns of a half-moon. This line will indicate south in the northern hemisphere and north in the southern hemisphere. One inaccurate indicator of direction, if all else fails, is to stand a person (yourself, if you are alone) on a piece of level ground and make them turn very slowly through 360°, pausing about every 45° and attempting to raise their arms straight out and away from their sides. You should resist this movement of their arms. The force of lift, apparently, is strongest when the person is facing the direction of the place where he or she was born!

If you have lost a person from your party, don't leave camp to search for them at night. Sound travels much better than you can: stay up, all night if necessary, banging saucepans, blowing whistles, shouting. And light a big fire.

Calculating time without a watch

The 'shadow stick' method which is used for finding direction can also be used to determine the approximate time of day:

1 After drawing an east–west line, draw an intersecting north–south line. The line to the west indicates the position of the stick's shadow at sunrise (0600 hours, say). The line to the east indicates the shadow position at sunset (1800 hours say). The north–south line indicates shadow position at noon.

2 The shadow of the stick becomes the hour hand of your clock, and you can estimate time using the noon line and the six o'clock lines as guides.

3 The shadow clock is not as exact as a watch – it divides the day into twelve unequal hours, with sunrise always 0600 and sunset always 1800.

4 Twelve o'clock shadow time is always true midday, but spacing of the other hours varies somewhat with location and time of year.

Time at night can be determined by using the Pole Star.
(Remember that you locate the Pole Star by sighting along
the bottom two stars of the 'saucepan'.)

1 Visualize a standard clock face with the Pole Star at its
   centre.

2 Facing directly north, determine what hour of this clock
   the two pointer stars point closest to.

3 Subtract this number from 12. Multiply by 2. Add 11 to
   determine local star time, or 24-hour clock time.

4 Subtract two hours for each full month since 23 March,
   and another four minutes for each remaining day. The
   result is hours and minutes in conventional time.

The Wortmans

'I knew that . . . my son and I would live. I knew also that it was at the fatal expense of my two younger daughters . . .'

Unlike the rest of the state, south-east Alaska has a mild climate. It tends to be wet and misty for most of the year, but subject to sudden, violent storms which crash in from the Pacific. In February 1979 it was hit by the worst weather this century, and became the scene for a quite remarkable story of human endurance.

Elmo Wortman, who was divorced, had come to this corner of Alaska in 1975 with his four children, whose ages ranged from eight to twelve. A former US Marine, carpenter by trade, Wortman had increasing physical problems with his work. A doctor diagnosed ankylosing spondylitis, a rheumatic illness affecting the back, neck, arms and shoulders. The only prescription for this incurable condition was permanent rest.

Hoping, however, that just a few months of rest would make an improvement, Wortman loaded *Home*, the family's thirty-three-foot home-made yacht, with school-books and headed 500 miles north. Isolated from civilization, the Wortman family had almost no money, but harvested food from the beaches, tide-lands and waters. The children loved it, and for Wortman it presented a more dignified way of life than social security and rent subsidies back in Washington State. To create more living space, Wortman built a twelve-by-thirty-three-foot floating cabin which became the family's main living centre.

A disability pension began to arrive, and Wortman was at last able to afford the dental treatment his children needed. He wanted to float the cabin down to southern California, but the children outvoted him: they wanted to go 500 miles even further north, to Alaska. Twenty-one days later they anchored near Craig, Alaska, on the west side of Prince of Wales Island. Margery and Cindy went to high school in

Craig; Randy and Jena Lynn to a school in the small town of Klawak.

Each trip to the dentist, however, meant sailing 180 miles over some of the roughest water in North America, to Prince Rupert in British Columbia, then driving ninety-six miles inland to the surgery – and coming back again. Wortman decided to move the float-house to Port Refugio, which was closer to the facilities of Prince Rupert. Margery went to live with a family in Klawak. Wortman visited her every week, and she spent the weekends at home on the float-house.

At 4 p.m. on 13 February 1979, the Wortmans set sail from Prince Rupert to return to Port Refugio. Jena, the youngest, was by now twelve years old. Randy was fifteen and Cindy sixteen. For the first time that he could remember, Elmo Wortman was spending a crossing on his bunk, feeling strangely weak and ill. It was Jena who was at the wheel when the storm broke that night.

For thirty hours their yacht withstood the battering and whims of 80 m.p.h. winds and massive seas, but near midnight on 14 February they finally ran out of sea-room. Surf was exploding against cliffs just fifty feet away. Wortman started the engine, but the propeller fouled on a loose line. They dropped both anchors, but he knew they could not hold position for long. The next giant swell would pound them on to the cliffs. Randy worked frantically to untie the small plastic dinghy lashed to the cabin roof, while Elmo alerted his daughters. Already up and dressed, they stuffed food and clothing into plastic rubbish bags. Randy launched the dinghy and threw the bags aboard, but the painter suddenly snapped. The dinghy was sucked towards the shore and buried under tons of water.

Randy ran to the wheelhouse and made room for another load of survival supplies by throwing overboard a pile of plastic foam sheets. He hoped the supplies would be washed free as the boat went down.

Elmo Wortman was down below, desperately loading matches into glass bottles, when the boat rolled a full 90°.

He made his way to the hatch, but was instantly flattened by a surge of water from the wheelhouse. When he got to his feet, the water in the cabin was knee-deep. Stuffing one bottle into his pocket and passing the other to Randy, Wortman shouted over the thunder of the surf for the children to quit the wheelhouse. The deck was awash as they made their way to the stern and put their feet over the side.

'Everyone is on their own,' Wortman shouted. 'Grab rocks and pull yourselves out. Don't let the water drag you back or you'll die.'

When they jumped, they were soon split up by violent waves. Wortman felt his boots being wrenched away as he was bowled over by the water. He was slammed against a near-vertical cliff, lifted bodily up its face by a large wave. Desperately he clung to the icy cracks and barnacles, only to be pulled back by the force of receding water. Several times more he was thrown against the cliff and then back into the sea, each time being scraped up the jagged rock-face. At last he managed to hold on and scramble a few feet higher and out of reach of the water. Unable to climb the vertical cliff, Wortman wedged his left knee and arm into a narrow rock crevice and then, more tired than he had ever been, he lost consciousness.

When he came to the next morning, he could not at first make sense of his surroundings, or focus his mind. Then, slowly, he realized that the tide was out, and the wind had lessened. The surf was quieter, and a light coating of snow lay on the rocks around him and in the folds of his jacket. On his left foot was a torn, bloody sock; on the right, nothing. The bare flesh was an unnatural white. Blood ran down into a rock crevice, which seemed to hold gallons of the crimson fluid. He felt for the container of matches. It had gone. He looked again at the steepness of the cliff towering above him, and down at the rocky beach, and then at his frozen, bleeding feet. 'The children were gone. I tried to shout for them. No answer.'

Wortman assumed that the children were dead. 'I

thought it was the end, I thought it was time to go. And I lay down to do just that.' Unzipping his jacket, he exposed his wet clothes to the freezing wind. But even in this frame of mind, the cold was unbearable, and he zipped himself up again. His mind turned to the Bible. He thought of the Sermon on the Mount, the Crucifixion, and of the Book of Revelations, ending with a verse that he spoke aloud: 'Even so, come quickly, Lord Jesus. Amen.'

Unbeknown to him everyone had survived the shipwreck. The children had searched for him far along the beach, but Elmo's position in the crevice hid him from view. Then, on the sweep back, they clambered over the rocks.

'When we found him he was all beat up,' says Cindy. 'I thought he might have hit his head, because he was talking like a child, and saying over and over, "We've got to get some place, we've got to build a camp".'

Elmo was at first unable to walk on his frozen feet. Cindy brought a boot they had found on the beach, and a sweater to wrap round the bare right foot. She and Randy eased their father down the steep rock, and they made their way to their camp, where Jena was waiting. She, too, had lost her boots – and her trousers. Randy had dry matches, and he gathered some driftwood for a fire. Cindy produced a small can of paraffin that had been washed ashore, and they soon had a good fire going. Elmo surrendered the sweater to Jena, telling her to put it on upside down as a substitute pair of trousers. Cindy found a short piece of line to tie the garment round Jena's waist.

Randy and Cindy continued combing the beach for wreckage. They found the orange plastic dinghy, one of the sails, three foam pads and Elmo's other boot. Elmo now directed them as they built a shelter: two long driftwood poles across the top of two large, chest-high rocks, with the sail draped over the top and then arranged as a floor. The opening faced the fire. Further searches of the beach produced six apples and three onions, the boat's sink, a full plastic container of corn oil, a nearly empty jar of orange juice powder, a small amount of cheese spread and a packet of seasoning for spaghetti sauce. Late in the afternoon Randy arrived with a handful of mussels, which Elmo made into a thin stew in the sink. There was a cup of hot broth for everyone, but Elmo, still suffering the effects of the mysterious illness which had started before the storm, could not drink his. Instead, he had a few sips of warm water.

'Our first priority is to work out where we are,' he said to his children that evening, 'and then we have to get out of here quickly.'

During the night, snow which had collected on the sail dripped through, and they slept badly, if at all. Randy spent much of the time outside, tending the fire. At daybreak, Elmo hobbled down the beach and worked out their position. They were near the southern tip of Long Island – to the west, across the Kaigani Strait, was Dall Island; Wortman knew of a cabin in Rose Inlet, which he estimated was no more than twenty-five miles away. From there, they could hitch a boat ride, and be home within an hour. But the steep, rugged beach would make it impossible to walk up Long Island. The dinghy was too small for all of them; their best hope lay in constructing a raft.

The hull of the plastic dinghy was damaged. With a new sense of urgency, they gathered up the foam sheets and broke them into appropriate sizes to plug the various holes and cracks. Elmo loaded it with pieces of salvage that might be helpful in constructing the raft – a rope ladder, lengths of electrical wire and rubber tubing.

Elmo wanted to move round the coast to get out of the cold south-easterly wind. Randy and Jena would paddle the dingy along the coast, while Elmo and Cindy clambered along the cliff-top. The idea of going back into the water was too much for Jena, however, who broke down and cried. She held tightly on to the rock where she was sitting. Cindy told her it was the only way they would get out of there; in the high-heeled shoes they had salvaged, Jena would never make it over the rocks.

Elmo and Cindy walked all day and most of the night without sighting the beached dinghy. Along the nearly vertical face of the shore were three deep inlets that led inland from the sea's edge as far as half a mile. They had to follow the course of each one, picking their way through the rocks and deep snow until their feet were numb. When they could go no further, they built a fire and sat huddled together until dawn. Then they resumed their trek.

Within ten minutes they came across Randy and Jena, camped in a small cove. Dozens of logs for raft-building lay strewn along the shoreline, ranging in size from small poles to giant trunks.

It was now the fourth day since any of them had eaten anything except the apples and a few mussels. Randy dug up several large clams with a stick. Elmo left the fire and made his way along the beach. The wind had shifted to the north, blowing directly down the strait. They would need a south-easterly to get them across to Dall Island, and there hadn't been one of those for two weeks. He came across a large piece of plywood, part of the rear wall of the wheelhouse, with the glass missing from the small window in the centre. Unable to carry it because his feet were hurting so much, Elmo summoned Cindy and Randy.

The children were concerned about their father's weakening condition. They had talked about taking the dinghy to fetch help. Elmo had given no answer. Back at the camp, Jena was sitting shivering by the fire. The cold wind was blowing through the neck opening of the sweater-trousers, and on to her bare thighs. Elmo went down the beach a little way and removed his underpants. When Jena put them on over the sweater, the opening was covered.

At nightfall Cindy again raised the idea of going for help.

'No, we're going to stick together,' Elmo said emphatically. 'As long as we're together, we're OK. We can help one another.' There was no more discussion.

The next morning they rolled two long logs into position on the gravelled tide-flat in front of their camp. The logs were about ten inches in diameter at the thicker end, and twenty-four feet long. Laying them parallel and about four feet apart, they lashed a weathered four-by-four-foot post near the narrow ends with salvaged rubber tubing. Halfway along the logs they fastened a two-by-ten plank, its ends left extending beyond the logs. The dinghy was tied between the logs and behind the plank, with the plywood section of wheelhouse lashed on to create a raised platform at the stern.

As the tide began to turn, they loaded everything on board. The raft floated! Now as soon as the weather changed, they could simply raise a corner of the sail and catch the wind up the Kaigani Strait, towards Rose Inlet. In the meantime, they paddled. All went well for several hours, then the tide peaked and the current flowing up the strait weakened. Soon the tide would turn. Elmo decided they should put ashore on Long Island.

That night they all seemed to sleep well, for the first time since the shipwreck. Elmo woke the others early, and after a quick warm-up next to the fire they boarded the raft again. As they moved further from the camp, the north wind freshened, and the raft was soon caught in the full force of wind and waves. At once, everyone was drenched. Now the cold was intensified by freezing wind chill, and they could make no headway against the strong wind. They had to turn back.

Once ashore, Elmo stood next to the fire, coughing. Breathing in hard to clear the congestion in his sinuses, he suddenly realized what had made him so weak and nauseous. 'Good Lord,' he said, 'I've had 'flu. That's what's been wrong with me the whole time.' The revelation was astounding to him, and uplifting: if the virus had run its course, he would now be starting to get better.

They sat round the fire and discussed their predicament. The unpredictability of the weather made their visits to the dentist very irregular, so no one was likely to report them missing immediately. Certainly, Margery could not be expected to raise the alarm for at least another four days.

'But I don't think she will,' said Cindy. 'We've been late before. And this time we didn't even check out with customs.'

During the night the north wind blew even stronger. By morning there were white horses on the water in the channel. They would have to wait. Elmo noticed that his daughters were weakening, staying closer to the fire. Cindy's salt-soaked jeans had rubbed the skin from both her knees, and her feet were hurting more each day. With Elmo also still having trouble with his feet, it was up to Randy to scour the beach for mussels and firewood. Randy was frustrated by the delays, knowing that the cabin was only about fifteen miles away.

As the sun went down, sea conditions improved in the Kaigani Strait. With the tide rising, Elmo elected to travel at once – even though it meant a night voyage. Cindy and Randy took the oars, sharing the three gloves they had between them. When Cindy began to lose her strength, her hands white, puffy and sore from the constant contact with the water, her father took over as best he could. His rheumatic condition forced him to row by leaning forwards, bending at the waist and then pulling back with his body against the oar. They reached Dall Island just as the tide turned, after paddling for six hours. But they could find no place to beach the raft, and had to spend a sleepless night aboard. At dawn, in the face of a strong north wind which they knew would halt any further progress towards Rose Inlet, they finally went ashore. There they were stranded by the wind for another night and day. Randy spent the time gathering wood at high tide, and digging for clams at low tide. But Jena was becoming increasingly withdrawn, and Cindy disturbingly lethargic. Elmo prayed for a change in the wind.

Late the following afternoon, just as the sun was setting again, the wind suddenly dropped. They loaded the raft and pushed away from the shore. Elmo had not counted on hunger being a factor in their survival. But now the effects on his children were more and more apparent. Even Randy had slowed to a stumbling, plodding pace. They were weakening with every mile.

They were now in the narrowest part of the strait, and the speed of the tidal current began to increase alarmingly. The raft picked up momentum, as though on a swift-flowing river. Thick clouds began to move in from the north. They hugged the coast of Dall Island to keep out of the worst of the wind, but were eventually beaten landwards. They were washed ashore between two forested arms of dark rock. The beach was a shelf of sloping rubble, in the middle of which a single spire of rock reared up. The little inlet, which faced directly north, had collected a layer of more than two feet of snow. As the children soon discovered when they searched, the northern exposure of the site meant that there was little firewood. Staring across the straight, Randy could see the long, open expanse of water beyond the north of Long Island: they must now be very close to Rose Inlet. He joined his father, who was trying to light a fire. Snow was blowing in hard on them, and the fire refused to catch.

Cindy was at the end of her strength. She sat shivering next to Elmo, and when she spoke, she seemed very distant. 'When we were building the raft and waiting in the sun I wasn't afraid at all,' she said softly. 'I thought we could survive on the beach for ever . . . But Daddy, this is bitter . . .'

In the morning Elmo and Randy walked along the shore. No more than a mile or two away, a cluster of small islands sheltered an apparent indentation in the coastline. It had to be Rose Inlet. Elmo decided at once that he and Randy should leave the girls at the camp, and paddle the dinghy to the cabin. Even if no one was there to provide help, or there was no boat, they could raise the alarm on the CB radio that Elmo knew was there.

Randy began freeing the plastic dinghy from the raft while Elmo went to tell the girls. As he said goodbye, he was mindful of the fact that they had no food, and no means of making a fire. He promised they would be back in three hours. As they launched the dinghy into the two-foot waves, Elmo and Randy were almost envious of the girls, curled up under the sail. It certainly seemed more merciful to spare them further misery at sea, in the bitterly cold wind and snow.

When the clouds lifted, they knew that they had made a mistake. The indentation they had seen was not Rose Inlet. But rather than use up extra energy by going back and telling the girls, Elmo decided to press on. They struggled on, arms heavy and lungs burning, occasionally beaching the dinghy to bail it out.

The three hours in which they had promised to return had long since passed. At last, a cluster of small islands which they definitely recognized as those in the mouth of Rose Inlet came into view. The inlet – and the cabin – were now just two more miles away, but night was falling and Randy was exhausted. Taking one objective at a time, Elmo coaxed more effort from his young son's muscles. 'Just to that rock, Randy, you can do that much . . . Now the point on the other side of the channel, just to the point . . .'

Then they could see the grove of trees that hid the cabin. Everything was covered in snow. There was no smoke. Just silence. The cabin, sitting on a small peninsula about fifty feet above the high-water mark, was empty. They found half the inlet covered in sea-ice, which forced them to walk the last mile. At one point, Elmo fell through the ice.

'Randy was just about moving,' Elmo recalls. 'If I slowed, he would slow more. I would take a few steps and I would hear him catching up – I didn't turn, didn't have energy for that – then I would proceed on a few more steps and wait again. Randy had given all he had.'

In the cabin Elmo busied himself immediately with lighting a fire, while Randy investigated the kitchen. The shelves were stocked with beans, rice, flour, macaroni and various tins. On one shelf was the cabin's CB radio. Connecting it to a twelve-volt car battery, Elmo heard a loud snap and saw sparks. Afraid of damaging the set, he decided to wait until daylight. They huddled in the waves of hot air radiating from the stove, but very soon their hands started to hurt and they had to move away. Then total fatigue took over and they both fell into deep sleep.

At daybreak Elmo repaired the radio. On a chart, Randy identified the girls' position as Keg Point. Elmo started to transmit a Mayday message. There was no response. He tried sending on different frequencies, but still with no result. He turned off the set to save the battery.

Elmo and Randy both now had to endure the pain of thawing flesh. The outer edges of Elmo's little fingers were turning black, as well as the tips of the two fingers next to them. His feet, too, were starting to come to life. Randy walked only with difficulty, turning the bottoms of his feet inwards and walking on the outer edges. From time to time he could not stop himself from shouting out with pain.

The next morning Elmo tried transmitting distress signals on every channel on the radio. No answer. By now he found it necessary to support himself on furniture as he walked, and he knew they needed to take drastic measures to save the thawing limbs from infection. They soaked them twice a day for an hour in bowls of steaming water and disinfectant. The effect was agonizing.

As the days blurred together for Elmo and Randy into one long continuum of pain, Jena and Cindy were becoming weaker and weaker. 'We had the sail folded several times,' says Cindy. 'We always had it all the way over us because it was too cold outside. All we had to eat was seaweed, and handfuls of snow that we melted in our fists . . . I never just looked at Jena and realized how sunken her cheeks were or anything, but we knew it was getting pretty bad when we could no longer get up to go to the bathroom.

'We talked food, all food, and any food. It didn't matter what we talked about, as long as it was food.'

On the fifth night after they had split up, it was exceptionally cold. The wind was blowing hard, and Elmo had not slept since his feet thawed on the second day. Randy did not sleep that night either. They both realized, in Elmo's words, that: ' . . .as cold as it was for them, and as miserable as we were with these comforts, the girls couldn't do it out there with no fire, no food . . .' In the numbing cold of that night at Keg Point, the girls resorted to singing to give themselves some comfort.

'But we didn't have enough breath,' Cindy remembers. 'We made it through about three lines of "Amazing Grace" and we just couldn't do it.'

In the morning, Elmo was forced to conclude that the girls must now be dead. 'It was hard to handle. I mentioned we had to get back. Randy said: "Suicide". He said all we could do was crawl out there and die. And he said that wouldn't gain anything. And he was right. We had to write them off.' He hoped and prayed that his daughters had both died on the same night, in their sleep. The worst thing he could imagine was for one of them to wake up and find that the other was dead.

'No inquisition is as merciless as the one honestly applied to self,' Wortman wrote after the ordeal. 'I knew that, barring massive infection in our feet, my son and I would live. I knew also that it was at the fatal expense of my two younger daughters. The guilt we felt was thick and oppressive.'

But the girls had somehow made it through yet another freezing night. Cindy was buoyed up by faith in her father's promise to return. 'I just knew that they would be back, I just knew it.'

'If I had been there alone,' Jena adds, 'I wouldn't be here now, because it's support you need . . . moral support. To have to handle something like that alone . . . you'd be in a loony bin. It's just not possible.'

When the swelling in his limbs reached its maximum, Elmo found it hard to recognize his feet. His ankles looked like dimples in the sides of overstuffed sausages. Finding a surgeon's scalpel in the cabin, he cut away dead pieces of flesh to expose the festering layers to the disinfectant and hot water. He removed nails and nail beds, and sections from the bottom of his right foot. Randy worked at his big toes until bone was exposed.

Meanwhile, although the girls still clung to life, they were

117

losing their grip on reality. Cindy dreamed that the family were on the float-house, getting ready to eat. She talked out loud about it, and Jena yelled at her to stop. Even as she woke, it all seemed terribly real to her. She wanted to cry, but she was too weak. 'I couldn't even sob, because my lungs were so wasted away . . . there weren't any muscles there.' Both girls believed they would be rescued, if not by their father and Randy, then by fishermen when spring came. 'Fishermen use the strait a lot, and we figured that by April there'd be fishing boats going all over,' Jena remembers. 'We'd just flag one of them down and we'd be off. That was only a couple of months later – we thought we could hold out that long.'

At last, on the twelfth day after Elmo and Randy had left the girls at Keg Point, the area had its long-awaited change in the weather. Overnight, the snow and ice melted, the wind turned to the south-east, and it started to rain. Elmo and Randy found an old motor-boat hull down on the beach, made it as seaworthy as they could, and fitted it out with paddles. It still leaked badly, but Elmo planned to bail while Randy rowed. He was determined to go back to Keg Point. 'I wanted to go back to pick up the girls' bodies and bring them with us. It just seemed the decent thing to do.'

Leaving a note for the owners of the cabin, Elmo and Randy took enough food for four days, and two sleeping bags, and departed. It was now three and a half weeks since the shipwreck, and nearly fifteen days since the girls had been left on their own. Cindy had dreamed on the very first night under the sail that Elmo was with them, telling her to take one day at a time. Later, when the rescue promise was not kept, she guessed that Elmo and Randy had made it to an empty cabin, and were too weak to return. 'We've got the easy part,' she told Jena. 'All we have to do is wait.' Cindy continued to have dreams about Randy. She thought he was tending a fire near by. Jena had nightmares about boats sinking at sea and huge waves washing her overboard. Their hair was beginning to fall out, and their gums were receding and sore. Jena often mentioned how much her feet hurt.

Cindy worried that her sister's frostbite was worse than her own.

Elmo and Randy approached from the north to pick up what they were sure would be the bodies of the two sisters. Elmo did not know what condition they would be in: if they had died on the open beach and below the tide-line, shrimps, crabs and other small crustaceans would be feeding on them; if they were above the tide-line, and were uncovered, then it was possible that birds might have pecked their faces, or that other animals had fed on them. Elmo devised a scheme to keep Randy from seeing his sisters in such a mutilated condition. He told him to row over to a rocky point, where they would be able to beach the boat at low tide and repair it.

Elmo walked up the beach with a heavy heart. As he approached the camp site, he could make out the shapes of two bodies under the folds of the sail.

'We didn't hear him coming,' says Jena. 'We were just lying under the sail after eating our last bit of kelp. We were resting – even eating took energy.'

'I had a handful of snow,' adds Cindy, 'and was just settling down when we heard Daddy say: "My babies, I've come back to get my babies." I thought I was hallucinating, but I looked over at Jena and her eyes were just wide open – and so I knew she'd heard it also. And I threw the sail off us . . .'

There was no movement as Elmo approached, no sound. But as he stooped to lift the sail, Cindy seemed to explode out from underneath it. Her eyes were sunken but, in her father's words, 'big and blue and just shining'.

Wortman could not hold back his tears. 'How did you live?' he cried, 'How did you do it?' Then, as he knelt and hugged them to him, he said over and over, 'Oh, my babies! My sweet, lovely, stubborn babies!'

Randy had heard the commotion and was moving up the beach. 'They're still alive, Randy!' he shouted. 'Hurry, bring the boat over here.'

'That was the high point in my life,' says Elmo Wortman.

'And I can't possibly see anything that could surpass it in the future.'

Jena could not stand. As Elmo and Randy carried her to the boat, her legs dragged limply behind, like the limbs of a rag doll. She slumped to a reclining position in the bow of the boat. Elmo removed her clothing. Her emaciated body was covered with a rash and open sores, from below her knees to her shoulders. There was something that she felt compelled to tell her father. 'Cindy and I are really close now,' she said. 'Sometimes, we felt so close that we would just lie with our cheeks together.' Elmo wrapped her in a sleeping bag, and went to help Cindy.

Cindy told her father what had helped them survive. They would recite the Lord's Prayer, and as much as they could remember of the 23rd Psalm. But most of all, they had clung to Elmo's promise that he would return.

They reached the cabin after dark. Randy went ahead to start a fire, and as the beam of his torch swept the darkness, it illuminated a strange mound in the middle of the floor: fresh groceries! The owner of the cabin had returned after a shopping expedition, found Elmo's note, and gone to get help.

Randy had been at the oars for thirteen hours, with only a one-hour respite at Keg Point. Now, with bare bone protruding from his feet, he took Jena on his back and carried her up to the cabin. Elmo felt great admiration for him.

By the time Elmo had bathed the girls and put them to bed, it was 2 a.m. But, exhausted as he was, he did not sleep. He stayed up all night, watching over his children who had come back from the dead.

Next morning, they heard the sound they had been listening for, for such a long time: a helicopter. It was all over. They had been found.

Elmo Wortman lost half his right foot, and all the toes on his left. Cindy lost some toes, but Jena Lynn, who had spent her first night on the beach with her feet tucked under

Cindy's jacket, and who thereafter kept her feet moving, lost none. Randy recovered the quickest. He stayed in hospital for just four days.

Looking back, Wortman at first felt that his decision to separate from the girls was a bad one. But then he came to see that, although it was based on a faulty calculation of their location which resulted in much hardship for all of them, it might actually have been the key factor in their survival. Within three days of being left behind, the girls' physical condition had deteriorated to the point where they would have been too weak to travel. Had he and Randy stayed with them at Keg Point, and similarly deteriorated, they would probably all have died.

10 Snowbound

If you find yourself trapped in cold conditions in a broken-down vehicle, the first rule is to keep calm, and consider each action carefully before you do anything. You should stay awake, and stay with your vehicle. If a telephone or habitation is visible, you may decide to try to reach it – but remember that deep snow and intense cold are extremely fatiguing.

Quickly get everything out of the boot that will help to keep you warm and fed, or help to dig through the snow.

If you are in a car, tie a marker to the top of your aerial, and put the spare wheel on the roof. Only run the car engine if the exhaust can be kept clear of snow. If the car is likely to be engulfed in snow, ensure that an air channel is kept open. Open windows on the lee side of the car (the side which is out of the wind) regularly to keep air fresh.

Use anything to keep your body warm – car seat covers, newspapers, even seat stuffing pulled out and stuffed inside your clothes. Keep your feet off the floor. Preserve energy by not making vigorous movements.

Where many cars are stuck together, groups of motorists should get together in the vehicle best able to keep warm – or the one which is in the most prominent position for rescuers to see. If you can dig one, a snow cave (described in chapter 4) will make a much warmer shelter than the inside of a car.

Precautions: See the 'Survival Kits' section below. Carry wellingtons, warm coats, hats and gloves inside the vehicle in case you have to leave it. Carry blankets, thermos flasks of hot drinks, chocolates, sweets and other food to keep energy up. Carry a shovel in the boot of your car.

The Kriegers

'This experience taught us a lot about death . . . and a
lot . . . about each other.'

On 12 December 1979, Barry Krieger's wife died after a
long illness. Eleven days later the forty-one-year-old
air-traffic controller took off in his twin-engined Piper
Apache from Longmont, Colorado, bound for Los Angeles,
where he and the rest of his family were intending to spend
Christmas with his cousin. Also aboard the plane were
Barry's sixty-two-year-old mother, Virginia, and his three
daughters: Kathy, who was sixteen; Connie, who was
fifteen; and Claire, aged ten.

At 1 p.m., and already flying at 12,500 feet, Krieger tried
to gain more height to clear the cloud-covered peaks in the
distance. But the air was too thin, and the experienced pilot
was faced with no alternative but to turn back and try a
different route. As he banked the aircraft to the left, disaster
struck. A sudden down-draught of air, roaring along at
nearly 100 m.p.h., crashed over the mountains and pushed
the plane towards the ground.

Krieger responded by trying to steer the Apache through
a gap between two peaks, but the ground was rushing up too
fast. Crashing on its belly, the plane bounced once and then
ploughed across the snow and came to a sudden halt. They
were 12,000 feet up on Chippler Mountain, in Rocky
Mountain National Park.

Krieger sat stunned for a few moments, then reached
down to cut off the fuel supply and prevent an explosion.
Only one of the two valves would shut. The cockpit window
next to him was shattered. He must have cracked his head
against it during the landing. Apart from that, the plane
appeared intact. He asked the others if they were all right.

Virginia Krieger was leaning forwards in her seat. As the
girls pushed her upright, Connie in vain searched her neck
and wrist for a pulse. The crash had broken the old woman's
back, and in turn ruptured her thoracic artery. Her death

123

had been instantaneous. In tears, Connie and Kathy covered their grandmother with a blanket.

Krieger fought to stay calm, for the girls' sake. He again asked if anyone was injured. Kathy, the oldest, reported a sprained wrist (in fact, it was fractured). Connie's back ached, but she told her father she just had a bruise. She, too, had no idea of the true extent of her injuries: two compressed vertebrae. Little Claire was unhurt.

Kathy now asked her father how he felt, and for the first time Barry Krieger was aware of the terrible pains in his back. He could not move his legs, could not even feel them. As it turned out, his back was badly broken. Again, Krieger urged himself not to panic. He switched on his radio and tuned to the emergency channel. The sound of a siren filled the cabin – the emergency transmitter, which had triggered automatically on impact. Krieger explained to his daughters that as soon as someone picked up its signal, the search parties would set out. Just for luck, he would broadcast an SOS on the radio as well.

'Will they find us, Daddy?' his youngest girl asked.

'Of course they will,' Krieger replied with all the confidence he could muster. But as an employee of the Federal Aviation Administration, he knew that the weather had stacked the odds against them. He was concerned about how long they could survive in the bitter cold. The temperature outside was – 40 °C, with 80 m.p.h. winds. Because of the open fuel valve, a fire would be too hazardous. Momentarily overcome by pain and the peril they faced, Krieger slumped forwards against the controls.

Connie and Kathy took over. While Connie bundled Claire up to keep her warm on the back seat, Kathy worked the radio. As she transmitted her Mayday call, she adjusted a jacket around her father's shoulders to keep out some of the cold.

The temperature dropped further as the afternoon wore on. They needed to fetch some clothes from the luggage compartment, Barry said, but that would mean leaving the sanctuary of the cabin. Kathy volunteered to go. Clad only in jeans, boots and a sweater, she opened the passenger door and pulled herself out on to the wing. At once the wind slammed her backwards against the rear passenger window, with such force that the glass shattered. Numb with pain and cold, Kathy waded through snow that was up to her hips, grabbed some clothes from their holiday suitcases, and clambered back into the cabin.

The girls stuffed the broken window with some of the clothes, but the cold crept through and the temperature was soon the same in the cabin as outside.

At 3 p.m. Kathy found some aspirins in her bag and gave them to her father, but the drug did little to relieve his pain. Krieger had the idea of swinging his legs round to the passenger seat, to take some of the pressure off his back. But the moment he tried to lift himself he cried out, collapsing in unbearable pain.

As darkness fell, so did heavy snow. It seemed to come at the plane in thick sheets, and the temperature plummeted. The blackness of the night only served to enlarge each individual's pains and fears. Young Claire began to hallucinate, claiming she could hear dogs and a man's voice asking if anyone was there. Connie wrapped her arms round her young sister, praying that this did not signify the onset of hypothermia. 'Mother is watching,' the young child murmured. 'I just know it.' Connie felt the tears well in her eyes.

Through the long, tormented hours of darkness, Barry Krieger and his daughters took it in turns to ask each other if they were all right: they knew that to fall asleep in such extreme sub-zero temperatures would be fatal. Somehow they made it through the night. At dawn, hunger became another preoccupation. Connie found a pie, a bag of apples and oranges, and a box of chocolates. They were all frozen. Kathy was so thirsty that she could barely force down a sliver of pie. Then she remembered the thermos of coffee that was under the seat. But even the hot coffee had frozen solid.

'What about eating snow?' asked Connie.

Barry vetoed the suggestion. Far from quenching their thirst, the snow would lower their body temperatures and make their condition worse.

As an air-traffic controller, Barry Krieger knew that rescue in the prevailing weather conditions was impossible. How much longer, he wondered, could he and his family hold out?

The day before, Krieger's cousin in Los Angeles had alerted the Federal Aviation Administration that the Piper Apache was overdue. By that time, the crashed plane's emergency signals were already being heard over north Colorado. At 2 p.m. on 24 December – twenty-five hours after the crash – permission came from the US Air Force Rescue Co-ordination Centre for a search to begin. At once Earl Berger, the Civil Air Patrol's emergency services officer for Colorado, telephoned Henry 'Sonny' Elgin, a volunteer pilot who was on stand-by at Denver airport. Within minutes Elgin was airborne. He picked up the Kriegers' signal, but could not get a fix on it. Two hours later, poor visiblity and strong winds forced him to abandon his search.

Connie had received an early Christmas present from her father – a Bible. Now she spent some time marking her mother's favourite passages, and reading aloud: 'Trust in the Lord with all your heart . . .' Barry found the words a comfort, and turned his thoughts once again to his daughters' safety. He reached the conclusion that because the weather conditions would be ruling out a rescue operation, they would stand a better chance of survival if they tried walking. He estimated that they had crashed some fifteen miles west of Granby, Colorado, but he needed the confirmation of landmarks before he would let them set off.

Connie volunteered to climb a high ridge that rose about 300 yards ahead of the wrecked plane. Wearing socks for gloves and a dressing-gown as a hood, and in dreadful pain from her compressed vertebrae, she trudged off through the waist-high snow-drifts. Within minutes the windward side of her face iced up completely. And with each heavy step she took, the pain in her back intensified.

From the top of the ridge, Connie saw only more mountains. Overcome at last by exhaustion, she let herself sink to her knees in the snow, and lay down. Just on the verge of succumbing to the powerful desire to sleep, she was brought to her senses by Kathy's frantic cries from the plane. It was half-past-three in the afternoon before she staggered back into the cabin. Without proper clothing of any sort, she had been exposed to the fierce cold for more than two hours.

In the late afternoon, Krieger seemed unhinged by his pain. He told Connie to pull the cigarette lighter from his back pocket and set fire to the navigation charts for warmth. When Connie protested that one of the fuel valves was still open, he merely repeated his order and told her to do as he said. Connie pretended to fumble under the seats for the charts, and claimed not to be able to find them. A short time later, Krieger sank back in his seat.

'Don't leave us, Daddy,' Connie implored. 'We all need you.' Then she reached for her Bible and read aloud: 'Fear not, for I am with you . . . I will strengthen you, I will help you.'

The odds of surviving a crash in the mountains are one in a hundred. Earl Berger knew that even if any of the Krieger family had survived the initial impact, their chances of staying alive in the brutal cold were next to zero. After spending all night co-ordinating the search, he was forced by heavy winds and blizzard conditions to order fifty ground searchers back to base. It was 3 a.m. on Christmas Day.

At first light, Barry Krieger chipped away at the inch-thick layer of ice inside the windscreen and saw what he had been praying for – blue sky. 'We're going to be saved!' he shouted. 'It's going to be all right!'

'Sonny' Elgin took off again from Denver at 7 a.m. After half an hour in the air he picked up the signals from the

Apache's emergency transmitter, and got a reasonable fix. At 8.20 he made a low pass over an area called Hell's Hole, and spotted the Krieger's plane. From one of the passengers windows he saw a piece of cloth being waved at him, and dipped his wings to say that help was on its way. Just over an hour later, a Civil Air Patrol volunteer and trained emergency medical worker, Steve Osborne, arrived in Hell's Hole by helicopter.

He was expecting to find at least one survivor, but the moment he saw the clothes flapping from the broken windows his hopes were dashed – obviously all that Elgin had seen was this waving cloth: there wouldn't be any survivors after all.

Bracing himself for what was sure to be an unpleasant sight, he suddenly saw a hand waving from the cockpit. Osborne rushed forwards through the snow. It was almost impossible to believe his eyes: there were four people, all alive.

The Kriegers were airlifted at once to Longmont United Hospital. They were all suffering from exhaustion and frostbite, besides their other injuries. Barry underwent surgery on his broken back, and later had to have both legs amputated below the knee because of frostbite and gangrene. But as he said later: 'This experience taught us a lot about death, but it taught us a lot about life, too – and most important, about each other.'

Larry Shannon

'Even in death, my mother saved my father's life . . .'

Larry Shannon, his wife Emma and their pet poodle Andy had been on the road in their twenty-two-foot motor-home for almost four months. They had visited one of their six children in Florida, and were bound for the home of their daughter in Modesto, southern California. They would stay with her for a few months, then return home to Grand Rapids in Michigan.

Nothing unusual in that – except that Larry had celebrated his eighty-second birthday just the day before. Emma was two years younger. A devoted couple, they had been married for fifty-two happy years. When Larry retired as a master welder, they had spent much time travelling around the USA. When Emma became a semi-invalid, Larry dedicated himself to nursing her. Then, in 1974, they suddenly decided to start travelling again, and invested in the motor-home.

It was Tuesday 7 February 1978. They had left Twentynine Palms in southern California two days before, and were now in Sequoia National Park. Checking his map, Larry chose to follow a minor road that starts alongside the fast-flowing Kern River, snakes steeply westwards over a 6,400-foot pass through the High Sierras, and then goes down into the San Joaquin Valley. By midday the weather had clouded over. Soon it was snowing, and Larry began to worry about the lack of turning places on the narrow road, should the route prove impassable. He decided that they would ride out the storm at the next town, just a little further down the road, and drove on into the heavy snow. But Larry was not on the right road. Unwittingly he had driven off on to a Forestry Service track, which stopped at a dead end at a deserted boys' camp.

The Shannons' green and white motor-home did not reach the boys' camp. As he slowed to negotiate a sharp bend, Larry felt the back wheels break through an underlayer of old snow, and the wheels began to spin. Wrapped in two overcoats, Larry got out to investigate. The road was on the side of a cliff, with a 1,000-foot drop below into a canyon. After months of travel in the warmer southern states they had neither shovel, snow chains nor even boots in the motor-home. Larry had to use a saucepan to try to scoop the snow from beneath the rear wheels. After two hours he gave up. Cold, wet and weary, he climbed back into the vehicle alongside his wife and the poodle.

In the early hours of the next morning, the motor-home shook and they heard a loud rumbling. At first light, they saw how close they had come to death – a rockslide had careered down the mountain, completely blocking the road ahead with tons of boulders. The snow had stopped, but if another rockslide struck further down the road, they'd either be crushed or swept 1,000 feet to their deaths.

Larry switched on his CB radio and urgently tried to make contact with the outside world. But, surrounded as they were by high mountains, his transmissions could not be heard. In the afternoon, Larry showed Emma how to work the radio and returned to the task outside.

He used a jack to free the wheels of ice, then switched on the ignition. The motor-home moved forwards, then suddenly lurched and there was a loud cracking sound. The universal joint had broken. 'Now we'll just have to sit it out until somebody picks us up,' Larry said with false cheerfulness.

It snowed all the next day, but by now Larry was confident that their daughter would have reported them missing. They had plenty of tinned food, and Larry toasted their supply of bread on the gas stove to stop it from going mouldy. They passed the day playing cards and reminiscing.

At about four p.m. on Friday, Emma's body went limp. As Larry leaned over to help her, he too was overcome by dizziness and nausea. In the grip of altitude sickness, he fell on to his bunk and passed out. It was dark when he came to. Emma was on the floor, her breathing laboured. But Larry did not have the strength to move her. Instead he made her as comfortable as he could with a pillow and blanket; then he collapsed again.

At 3 a.m., Larry was woken by the sound of Andy barking. He knelt down next to Emma and spoke a few words of encouragement. But his wife was not breathing. When he lifted her hand in his, it was terribly cold. He could find no trace of a pulse. Larry Shannon's wife of fifty-two years was dead.

Hardly able to believe the tragedy, Larry closed her eyes, and prayed. 'We came through life together,' he muttered, 'and we'll end it together. When they find us in the thaw, they'll find me beside her.'

The next few hours passed in a daze. But in the morning light Larry determined to look after his wife for as long as he was physically able. He covered her with blankets and an overcoat, and left her on the floor where it was coolest. Then he turned off the gas heater. 'Emma,' he vowed, 'I won't leave you.'

Bad weather had brought a whole series of mudslides and rockslides to southern California. When her parents had not arrived by the weekend, the Shannons' daughter Patti contacted the police. But they assured her that the scene of every incident had been investigated: no motor-homes with Michigan plates had been involved. When she contacted the Civil Air Patrol, she was told that a statewide aerial survey had revealed no stranded vehicles answering that description. Patti was not satisfied. In case her parents had simply been delayed without contacting her, she had a television station flash a message requesting them to call.

The snow had fallen to a depth of six feet. Larry opened the door several times each day to prevent it from being blocked. Crossing the days off on a calendar, he kept a neat log of both inside and outside temperatures, and wrote a diary. At night, the temperature inside dropped below freezing. Larry wrapped himself up in two sets of everything – thermal underwear, sweaters and socks.

The snow did not let up until 14 February, seven days after they were stranded. The sun was shining and, in Larry's words, 'glittered like diamonds'. He felt motivated enough to venture outside and shovel a clearing round the motor-home with the saucepan. For good measure he cleared the roof, to make it more visible from the air.

Soon afterwards, he heard the sound of a jet and ran inside for some flares. When he returned, the aircraft had gone. Once again he tried using the radio, but to no avail.

Day after day Larry cleared enough space for himself and the dog to exercise in. A few days before the ordeal began, they had stocked up on citrus fruit. Larry ate half a grapefruit every morning, and a piece of toast. He melted snow on the gas stove for drinking water. At night he ate tinned soups and preserves.

Five days of heavy rain followed. Then on 7 March, the twenty-ninth day of the ordeal, the weather lifted and a USAF jet roared low through the canyon. It made three passes in all, rattling the windows of the motor-home. Larry saw what he thought was a signal light flash from the cockpit.

Larry Shannon was so excited he didn't sleep that night. Turning on the cabin lights in case rescuers were already on their way, he treated himself to a shave, and packed ready to leave. But the following day nothing happened. The signal had been no more than a glint of sun on the fuselage. 'It's hard to have your hopes raised and then be let down,' he wrote. 'But that's life, I guess.'

On the morning of the thirty-second day, there was a sudden clattering noise outside. Larry ran out, just in time to see the tail rotor of a helicopter disappear around the side of the mountain.

Pilot Bob Wasik and crewmen John Bethell and Bob McAdams couldn't believe what they saw. They were not on a specific rescue mission – they had been flying to check out the deserted boys' camp when they spotted the white-haired man waving frantically at them. Wasik skilfully set down the helicopter with scarcely six feet between the rotor blades and the solid granite of the cliff-face. All three men raced from the aircraft, pushing through the wet snow towards Larry Shannon.

John Bethell was the first man to reach him. He embraced the old man in a bear hug.

'You're an angel from Heaven,' Larry said in a coarse whisper. And then he wept.

'It was like a dream,' Larry said from his hospital bed in Visalia. 'I couldn't believe it was happening . . . I did everything I could to survive. I just figured I'd have to stay alive long enough to make sure Emma was buried properly.'

The funeral service for Emma Shannon was held a few days after Larry's rescue. On Easter Sunday, the old man returned to the motor-home with his grandson-in-law and a friend. Between them, they managed to replace the broken universal joint. Then Larry manoeuvred the large vehicle round the rockslide and down out of the mountains.

The eighty-two-year-old had lost sixteen pounds in weight, but was otherwise in good health, and soon announced plans to drive back home to Michigan.

'If my mother hadn't died,' said his daughter, Mrs George Spur, 'he would have tried to walk out of there. Even in death, my mother saved my father's life . . .'

11 The tropics

Tropical terrain varies from forest jungle and mangrove or other swamps to open grassy plains or semi-arid plainland. The real dangers of the tropics are not the animals and snakes, but the insects. Many of them carry infection and disease. Most of them are capable of driving you mad.

If you find yourself in thick jungle, it is unlikely that rescuers will find you. Start travelling until you find a stream. Follow that until you find a river. Follow that until you find human habitation. But try to mark your trail as you go. Night in the jungle comes very quickly, so prepare early for bed. You'll need more rest anyway, to keep up your energy and strength in order to maintain resistance to disease. Here are some golden rules for pleasant dreams in the tropics:

- Try to locate your shelter away from swamps, on a knoll or high spot in a clearing.

- Don't sleep on the ground – make a frame of poles, and cover it with palm fronds or other broad leaves. If possible, make a hammock.

- Do not camp too near a stream or pond, especially during the rainy season.

- Do not build a shelter under dead trees or under a tree with dead limbs, or under a coconut tree.

- Keep trouser bottoms tucked into your socks, and either tie them securely or improvise puttees to keep out ticks and leeches. Keep your sleeves rolled down and buttoned.

- Try to keep your clothes clean and dry, to stop rotting and skin disease.

Food and water

Food and water are normally plentiful in the tropics. Water is obtainable from the stream you are following – but purify it first. Animal trails often lead to water. Coconuts (especially green, unripe ones, about the size of a grapefruit) contain drinkable liquid. So do other plants, but remember not to drink any fluid that looks milky (except in a coconut). Water that is almost clear can be obtained from muddy streams or lakes by digging a hole on the land between one and six feet from the bank. Allow the water to seep in and the mud to settle.

Water may be obtained from vines. Not all vines yield potable water, but try any you find. This is how to get the water out:

1 Cut a deep notch in the vine as high up as you can reach.

2 Cut the vine off close to the ground and let the water drip into your mouth or a container.

3 When the water stops dripping, cut another deep notch, below the first. Repeat until the supply of water is exhausted.

Bamboo stems often have water in the hollow joints. Shake the stems of old, yellowish bamboo. If you hear a gurgling sound, cut a notch at the base of each joint and catch the water in a container.

Food is usually easy to procure in the jungle, with sago palms and palm cabbage, bananas and bamboo shoots, coconuts and papaya in abundance. But remember your plant edibility test! Remember there are no poisonous freshwater fish. If you catch a fish, you can eat it (but not the offal). Don't let it spoil, though – fish flesh goes off very quickly in the tropics.

Watch the monkeys. Anything they eat, so can you!

When you're travelling, wearing your sleeves down will help avoid cuts and scratches – which start to fester almost at once in the tropics. You should also avoid scratches, bruises and loss of direction and confidence by developing 'jungle eye'. Disregard the pattern of trees and bushes directly in front of you. Focus the eyes behind what's immediately in front, and rather than looking *at* the jungle, look *through* it. Stoop occasionally and look along the jungle floor. As Juliane Koepcke remembered, a stick or staff should be used to part the vegetation to reduce the possibility of dislodging fire ants. Do not grab at brush or vines when climbing slopes – they may have irritating spines or sharp thorns.

Travel can be conducted safely in the jungle if you don't panic. If you're alone in the jungle, depending on the circumstances, the first move should be to relax and think the problems through. Move in one direction, but not in a straight line. Avoid obstacles: do not fight them. There is a technique for moving through jungle. Blundering only leads to bruises and scratches. Turn the shoulders, shift the hips, bend the body, and shorten or lengthen, slow or quicken your pace as required. Do not hurry. Never try to beat the jungle by speed – it isn't possible.

Avoid climbing high terrain, except in order to take your bearings. A long detour over flat ground is preferable. Prevent heat exhaustion, heat cramps or heat stroke by replacing the water lost through perspiration. Drink plenty of water (but purify it first). Take good care of your feet by changing and washing your socks often. Protect your footwear from cracking and rotting by using grease.

Should you contract a fever, make no attempt to travel. Wait until the fever abates. Keep drinking water. Protect any wounds by covering them with a clean dressing. You should lick even the tiniest of scratches to give some protection against bacteria.

You should put on a mosquito headnet or tie a vest or T-shirt round your head. Wear especially at dawn and dusk.

Move carefully through high grass: some sharp-edged grasses can cut your clothes to shreds.

When you take your clothes off, hang them up. If laid on the ground they may collect ants, scorpions or snakes. Always check footwear and clothing for such guests before putting it on.

Rain forest

Whether you find yourself in a tropical rain forest in South America, Africa, Asia or the Pacific Islands, the principles of jungle survival will hold true. Surviving in a tropical rain forest is comparable in challenge to surviving at sea or in the polar regions: it requires physical stamina, survival know-how, high morale and some equipment.

Tropical rain forests present certain health dangers, which stem from the prolific insect life and from the primitive sanitary and health facilities of jungle villages – vegetables are often fertilized with human faeces, for example, and should at the very least be peeled before eating. The slightest scratch can lead to infection if not promptly treated. Water may be obtainable, but it may be unhealthy. Shelter has to protect you from the insects below and the rain above. Plants play a greater role in diet than they would in polar or temperate regions, because vegetative growth is so prolific. Travel will be more difficult at the periphery of the tropical rain forest than in the interior, because the margins are dense thickets of trees and vines while the interior forest floor is often relatively open. The forest canopy may be 200 feet above the ground, and so dense that little direct sunlight strikes the earth; hence the growth of underbrush is limited.

You can survive in the rain forest if you keep your wits about you! Watch for trees with octopus-like roots, and avoid the swamp which they indicate.

The real dangers of the tropics are the insects, many of which pass on diseases and parasites. Smear mud on your face and exposed skin as a protection, especially when sleeping – it might even improve your complexion. Even if you do get bitten by infected mosquitoes, don't give up. You won't contract malaria for a month, so press on! Check your body every day for ticks. If you're with other people, check each other. Burn ticks off with a cigarette end or ember, or pull them. The mandibles may be left behind, and will have to be treated as if they were splinters – they are an open invitation to infection.

Most stories about the animals, snakes, spiders and nameless terrors of the jungle are pure rubbish. You are probably safer from sudden death in the jungle than you are in most big cities. You probably will never see a poisonous snake or a large animal. If you do, consider yourself lucky. What may scare you most, however, are the howls, screams and crashing sounds made by noisy monkeys, birds, night insects and falling trees.

Juliane Koepcke

'God help me, I thought, they'll amputate my arm if I ever survive . . .'

Just before midday on Christmas Eve 1971, a Lockheed Electra turbo-prop took off on a regular scheduled LANSA Airlines flight from Lima, the capital of Peru, heading for a town called Pucallpa, some 475 miles north-east across the Andes, and deep in the Peruvian jungle. The pilot kept routine radio contact with the ground, but with less than half an hour of the flight remaining that contact was broken. The aircraft, with ninety-two people on board, had encountered a violent storm and disintegrated in mid-air.

Only one passenger came out of the jungle alive: a young German girl called Juliane Koepcke – just seventeen years old at the time – who had been travelling with her mother. Her story is one of remarkable courage and resolution: it was eleven days before she emerged from the jungle, barefoot, dressed in a mini-dress, her collarbone broken, and bleeding from deep wounds which were infested with maggots. But what makes the account of her survival even more amazing is that when the plane shook apart in the storm, Juliane fell 10,000 feet, still strapped into her seat.

Juliane's parents, both ornithologists, held professorships at San Marcos University in Lima. The family spent a lot of time at the jungle hut where they carried out research. They were planning to spend this Christmas together, too. Juliane was sitting in the third row of seats from the rear, next to the window, with her mother next to her. It is said that the flight from Lima to Pucullpa can be one of the most beautiful plane journeys in the world – in clear weather. But when the Electra was over the dense rain forest, visibility closed in, and it started to rain. Severe turbulence followed, then lightning – very near. One of the passengers screamed. It was then that Juliane spotted the yellow flames licking the starboard wing. Mrs Koepcke muttered, 'This is the end of everything,' and as if in compliance with her prophecy there was a violent vibration and Juliane found herself outside the aircraft, in mid-air.

'I felt a sensation of emptiness,' Juliane told a reporter soon after her eventual rescue. 'I was alone, falling, with the noise of the air passing and the tightness of the seat belt on my stomach. The last thing I can remember is thinking that the jungle trees below looked like cauliflowers. Then I passed out.'

It was raining but still light when she recovered consciousness. She realized that she was lying in a row of seats that was upside down. Her shoes and glasses were missing. She did not yet feel the pain from the broken collarbone, from the eye that was so swollen that she could not see out of it, or from the deep gashes on her arms and legs. She was certainly in no condition to summon the energy to move.

The night passed with Juliane swimming in and out of consciousness. In the morning, she called for her mother, but received no answer save the croaking of frogs. She unstrapped herself from the seat and, moving painfully slowly, started to explore the place where she had fallen to earth. She found a small plastic bag of sweets and a Christmas cake, but that was all. The cake was wet, and she discarded it. The sweets were to be her only sustenance for the next ten days of her ordeal. There was no point in looking for other food: despite the time she had spent in the jungle, she didn't know what to look for.

One thing, however, that she did remember from her family's experience of living in the isolated regions of Peru, was to arm herself with a long stick – not as protection against big animals, which are relatively harmless, but as a probe for snakes, spiders and ants. This was even more critical now that she had lost her glasses and was virtually half-blind. Juliane started to look for her mother, but was so dizzy that she had to rest after every few steps. In the mean time, planes and helicopters were searching overhead, above the dense jungle along the Sheobonya River, near the headwaters of the Pochitea.

'I felt very helpless,' Juliane said. 'It wasn't possible to climb up the trees because they were too tall – over a hundred feet high – and I was too weak.'

She came across a row of three seats that had crashed heavily into the ground. Two of the bodies were womens', the other was unidentifiable. She could not bring herself to get close to the bodies, but she moved their feet with her stick. Both women had painted their toenails – something Juliane's mother had never done. She left the place quickly, the jungle by now full of the noise of vultures and flies.

On the second day, Juliane discovered a tiny stream. Her parents had taught her that when lost in the jungle one should look for streams, then follow them to rivers. In the jungle, these are the roads. People live along them. Juliane remembered a young American who had found his way to her parents' hut by just this method. 'I told myself: if he could do it, so could I.'

By now she was covered in insect bites. The zip of her mini-dress was broken all down the back, and the jungle mosquitoes and blowflies had homed in on the exposed flesh. One blowfly bite, on her arm, developed into a deep and painful hole, full of maggots. She had nothing with which to remove them. 'The hole was on the other side of my arm and hard to get at. I tried getting at it with a small stick, but it was difficult. Eventually I got some of them out. They were about a centimetre long. And there were about fifty of them in there.'

It was now two days since the crash. Progress was slow and painful. Like other rivers in the tropical forests of Peru, this one twisted and meandered and doubled back on itself. Walking a mile actually resulted in only a few tens of yards of progress. The banks were a tangled mass of vines and vast, rotting tree trunks. But swimming and wading brought their own dangers: the risk of attack by fish attracted by the blood from her wounds.

'The largest animals I saw were crocodiles, but I knew they were harmless unless you came across a female with young babies.

'At one time I heard the buzzing of flies and followed the sound. There was a row of seats from the plane, with three girls strapped in them. They were covered in flies. I moved on.'

On the third day, she followed the sound of vultures and found a piece of fuselage but no signs of life. Later in the afternoon, the sound of aircraft engines got nearer and nearer. 'I knew it was useless, but I yelled "Hello! Help!" over and over. I never saw them, but they must have been quite near, and of course they didn't spot me.' The drone of engines faded. Juliane was alone again, but her resolve was undiminished: 'I could walk . . . I wasn't hungry . . . and I could drink from the clear water of the stream.'

The jungle is an alien place, never more so than at night. There were noises of rustling. There were things that crawled over her. Even the air seemed oppressive. Juliane slept very little. By the fourth day, the supply of sweets was exhausted. Her whole body was swollen from the bites of mosquitoes and blowflies. But at last the stream she had been following ran into a bigger river, and she knew her chances of coming across civilization had increased.

For five days more she alternately swam and walked downstream. But without food and in the humid 113 °F heat she was getting weaker all the time. 'Huge toads jumped and fell back hard on to the ground. I considered eating parts of these toads, but didn't. And I resisted delicious-looking fruit because I knew that in the jungle many things look beautiful and tempting but are poisonous. Amazingly, I wasn't hungry.'

The maggots in her open wounds were contributing to her debilitation. 'Helplessly I would watch them emerge, their heads like the tips of tinned asparagus. God help me, I thought, they'll amputate my arm if I ever survive.'

The river was widening, the current now so swift that she was not strong enough to swim in it. Nevertheless, she was determined to go on. Although she knew that her mother must now be given up for lost, she clung to the hope of seeing her father, whom they had been flying to meet in Pucallpa.

At last, late in the afternoon of the ninth day after the crash, as she was looking for a suitable place to lie down for the night, Juliane came across a canoe moored on the river bank. Near by was a hut. 'On the floor I found a small outboard motor carefully wrapped in plastic, a can of gasoline, and a big bag of salt. I poured gasoline into the wound where the maggots were. It hurt a lot when they tried to bite their way out . . .'

The next morning, she reasoned that it might be weeks before the boat owners returned. But at the same time – and to someone hearing her story, quite incredibly – she did not want to take a boat that belonged to someone else. In the end, the weather made her decision for her: it was raining so hard that she stayed in the hut.

Later that afternoon, Juliane heard voices. The door suddenly opened and in came two rain-soaked woodcutters, Amado Pereyra and Marcio Ribera. After nine days in the jungle, Juliane Koepcke had at last been found.

Early next morning, after washing her wounds and extracting more maggots, and offering her food which she found herself unable to eat, the hunters prepared their boat for the trip downriver. From the boat she could see that the jungle along the river banks became more and more impenetrable. Further progress on foot would have been incredibly slow, if not impossible.

Juliane received medical treatment at the agricultural colony of Tournavista. Her eyes were so bloodshot that they were almost entirely red. Her arms and legs were ravaged by maggot holes. Her face was swollen and disfigured by insect bites. A small twin-engined plane was summoned to fly her to a mission base run by the Summer Linguistic Institute near Pucallpa, where she was tended by an American doctor.

'All the time I was in the jungle I could walk very well,' Juliane recalls, 'but immediately after arriving at the doctor's house, one leg set rigid like a piece of wood . . . I could not move it . . . it was many weeks before it was better.'

Following her directions, search planes located the wreckage of the stricken Lockheed Electra, scattered over ten square miles of jungle.

It is now believed that at least twelve people survived the crash, including the pilot. Their bodies had decomposed very little, if at all, when found: the bodies of those who had died immediately in the crash had been stripped to the bone by vultures and flies. The body of one woman was found still strapped in her seat in part of the fuselage, her head in her arms, while sixteen other passengers around her were in an advanced state of decomposition. But unlike Juliane, and whether through injury, fear or a belief that they should stay with the wreckage, none of the other survivors seem to have tried to get themselves out of the jungle.

Neither the cause of the crash, nor the nature of the phenomenon that saved the lives of Juliane and the other apparent survivors who fell 10,000 feet, was ever established – although one theory is that a tremendous updraught of air could have broken their fall.

Juliane's survival was miraculous in many other respects, too. The woodcutters who had found her only called at that hut once every three weeks. Had the heavy rain not kept her in the hut, and had she set off downstream again on foot, she might never have left the jungle alive. Not only was the undergrowth almost impassable, but there were no settlements that she could have reached for many days. Besides all the other appalling injuries that she suffered, it turned out that Juliane had badly torn a ligament in her knee, which under normal circumstances would have made it practically impossible for her to walk at all.

But Juliane had walked. For nine days.

12 The desert

If you are to survive travelling in the desert, you should follow the desert nomad pattern of walking in the evening until about 2300 hours, sleep until 0400 hours, walking again until 1000, then dig a shallow well in the sand and lie in it under a space blanket (if you have one – reflective side out) or other covering until the sun has lost its heat. If there is a full moon, you can walk all night. But not faster, just longer.

In the day, there are various ways to protect your eyes from glare:

- Wear sunglasses or goggles.

- Peer from under a pulled-down cap peak.

- Rub soot, boot polish or burnt cork on your upper cheeks and around your eyes.

- Make goggles from paper, camera film, leather or plastic by cutting minute slits – no more than one-sixteenth of an inch – to peer through. Tie them round your head with string, laces, tape or lengths of elastic from underwear.

- Hair, leaves, grass, reeds or moss can be held over the eyes by clamping them to your brow with broad tape tied round your head.

- Wear a face mask of thin material – say a handkerchief or T-shirt.

If you're near a seashore and your skin is exposed to intense sunlight, an effective barrier cream can be made by burning shells or coral, crushing them, and mixing with water or oil.

When you travel in sand dune areas, follow the hard floor valleys between dunes, or travel on dune ridges. Avoid following streams to reach the sea except in coastal desert areas or those areas with large rivers flowing across them. In most deserts, valleys lead to an enclosed basin.

Water

It is important to prevent water loss by breathing through the nose. Avoid talking. The three tables show how much water you need for desert survival.

To maintain your full physical and mental efficiency, you must maintain your water balance.

Cool stones or any exposed metal surface will serve as a dew condenser. Wipe off the dew with a piece of cloth and wring it out. Dew evaporates soon after sunrise and should be collected before then.

Along sandy beaches or desert lakes, you can dig a hole in the first depression behind the first sand dune: rainwater from local showers will collect there. Stop digging when you find damp sand, and allow the water to seep in – deeper digging may produce salt water.

Desert water table: days of expected survival and expected distance travelled if walking only at night and resting in the shade by day

Total available water per person: litres

		0		1		2		4		10	
		days	km	days	km	days	km	days	km	days	km
	50	1	40	2	40	2	48	2·5	56	3·5	64
Maximum	45	2	40	2·5	40	2·5	48	3	56	3·5	64
daily	40	3	40	3·5	40	3·5	48	4	56	5	72
temperature	35	4·5	48	5	48	5	56	6·5	72	7·5	88
in the	30	7	65	7·5	70	8	78	9	100	11	112
shade: °C	25	8·5	83	9	91	10	105	11·5	125	14	160
	20	9	90	9·5	98	10·5	130	12·5	175	15·5	225

Desert water table: days of expected survival if resting in the shade at all times

Total available water per person: litres

		0	1	2	4	10	20
		days	days	days	days	days	days
	50	2·5	2·5	2·5	3	3·5	4·5
Maximum	45	3	3	3·5	4	4·5	7
daily	40	4·5	5	5·5	6·5	8·5	12
temperature	35	7	8	8·5	10	14	20
in the	30	9·5	10·5	11·5	13	19	30
shade: °C	25	11	12	13·5	15·5	22·5	34·5
	20	12	13	14	16·5	23·5	36·5

Daily water requirements to maintain water balance – resting in the shade at all times

Mean temperature (8°C below daily maximum in desert conditions)	Litres required per twenty-four hours
20°C and below	1
25	1·2
30	2·4
35	5·3

Source: UK Ministry of Defence (RAF) pamphlet PAM (Air 225), 1975.

Watch the flight of birds, particularly at sunset and dawn. Birds circle water holes in true desert areas. In the Sahara watch for flocks of doves. Because they are seed-eaters, doves must be close to a source of water. So must pigeons. Their presence can lead you to a shaft, for they nest in cool underground tunnels. Many desert bats visit water regularly at the beginning of their evening flight.

Circular mounds of camel dung often surround wells in Old World deserts – particularly the Persian, Sahara and Gobi deserts. Places where animals have scratched or where flies hover may show where water lay recently on the surface. By digging you may find some. Dig, too, at the foot of cliffs.

Water that smells bad is not necessarily unsafe. Nor is stagnant water: simply strain off the algae and bugs (and consider eating them), and purify as usual.

Desert palms usually indicate surface water. So do salt grass, rushes, sedges, cat-tails, greasewood, willows and elderberry. The large barrel cactus of the American desert also contains a lot of moisture which can be squeezed out of the pulp.

Old camp fires may indicate a nearby water hole. And if you see camel tracks going in roughly your direction, follow them – they will be heading for water.

Quicksand is simply fine sand mixed with water, and usually has a very flat, dry surface. Immediately your legs are caught, throw your rucksack as far as you can towards the solid ground and lie down – you will be able to float and swim out using a slow breast stroke.

Save your urine for your solar still (if you have been able to build one), or mix it with the sand and spread it on your body. It will act as an excellent cooling agent. Insect repellent, too, is good for keeping the body cool.

At night a fire will bring nomads from miles around. You can also flash your torch periodically, like a lighthouse. Try shouting if you see anyone in the distance. A whistle carries further – or a suspended tin can, hit with a knife.

Sandstorms can last from a few hours to several days. Try to anticipate the storm: often a huge black cloud will blot out the sun and then the sky and air will become yellow and dusty. Find shelter, cover your face, and wrap yourself up as best you can. Gather all your gear together, and if it is substantial enough, use it as a shield for your head.

George Owens

'Just a mile from the nearest town, I learnt the hard way that no pilot is immune to misfortune.'*

Early one week in September 1979, a fifty-year-old man called George Owens flew his Mooney aircraft over the barren semi-desert of north-eastern California to the small airport at Hayden Hill. He had mining interests in the area, and was to spend the week there on business. On Sunday afternoon, his work completed, he took off and headed west towards his home in Yreka City. It was perfect weather for flying, over high desert country with which Owens was very familiar. He had flown this route so often, and his home airfield was so close – less than an hour away – that he did not bother to file a flight plan. Owens had no emergency locator transmitter (ELT) aboard, no water supplies and no survival equipment.

The plane took off at 5 p.m., a routine departure. Climbing to his planned cruising altitude of 10,500 feet, Owens moved the controls to thin out the mixture. The engine note roughened. When he tried to enrich the mixture again, the engine stopped altogether. The fuel selector had been directed to the left main tank when Owens took off, and the gauge indicated full. He switched to the right main tank, but was still unable to restart the engine. He was losing altitude all the time. He frantically tried various throttle and mixture settings, but without success. The ground was now coming up fast to meet him.

Owens just had time to send out a quick Mayday before setting up the plane for an emergency landing. His flight path had followed the course of a country road, through a dried-up river valley, over rugged terrain strewn with large boulders and deep gullies. His first instinct was to land on a straight stretch of the road; but there were enough Sunday

*At the survivor's request, information in this account has been altered to protect his identity.

drivers out enjoying the desert to make a collision a real possibility. Then Owens spotted a fairly level patch of barren ground within gliding range, and headed for it.

Tall, spindly pine trees surrounded the clearing, and Owens was unable to avoid them. The left wing of the Mooney struck a pair of trees about six feet from their tops, and sheered off. The plane ploughed into one more pine, then crashed to the ground. A section of the tree was embedded in the engine and cockpit; George Owens was knocked unconscious at once. It was growing dark when the pilot came to. The pain in his right leg was so intense that he knew it was badly broken. A head wound had been bleeding over his face. He was unable to open one eye.

Owens tried to move, and found that he was pinned to his seat – the impact of the crash had jammed part of the control panel and the right control yoke across the right seat, between the injured pilot and the only door. He was trapped. In terrible pain, he decided that there was nothing he could do until daylight. He called periodically for help over the radio, with no way of knowing that the radio was not, in fact, working. As darkness fell, the temperature on the desert plateau dropped down towards zero. Unprepared for such a contingency, Owens had only his lightweight flying jacket for protection. All night he stayed huddled in his seat, shivering with cold, in terrible pain, drifting in and out of consciousness.

When light and warmth finally came next morning, he took stock of his situation. He could not move his damaged right leg: it felt strangely numb, and Owens was alarmed. He needed medical attention as soon as possible. He wasn't certain of his exact location, but he had the impression that a small town was near by. Obviously no one had seen him go down – his only chance of attracting attention was to get himself out of the wrecked aircraft. Since he could not move the buckled structures between himself and the door, he would have to dismantle some of them – the right-hand control yoke, at least. But that would be impossible without tools.

While he was thinking about his predicament, Owens heard the sounds of cars passing along a road. He shouted and beat on the side of the aircraft as loudly as he could in his weakened condition, but there was no response. He hardly expected any. Soon after, he began to hear sounds of human activity, as though some community near by was starting its daily business. The thought of being within earshot of help was frustrating beyond belief.

Owens suddenly remembered that he had a small tool kit on board, behind the front seat. With considerable effort, he managed to get his hands on it, and proceeded to dismantle the control yoke assembly. It was slow, infuriating work. In his weakened condition he tired quickly and rested often. After two hours, only one nut remained on the control wheel. Nothing he could do would budge it: it was practically welded to the spot with rust. Owens strained at it repeatedly, until he was exhausted and his fingers were raw and bloody. Between efforts to free the nut, he beat on the side of the cockpit with his tools, shouted, and called on the radio. But he never got a response.

By now he was getting hoarse and thirsty. Again he remembered something: there was a can of fizzy drink under one of the seats. With much effort he twisted his body, his fingers scrabbling beneath him and behind. At last they touched the can, but no matter how he tried he couldn't get sufficient grip on it to pull it out. Every move was painful, but he kept trying. Finally, he manoeuvred the can into a position where he could close his sore hand around it, and lifted it triumphantly up on to his lap. It was a can of silicone spray lubricant.

Owens was overtaken by a sickening wave of disappointment. Then he realized the value of his find. He sprayed the lubricant onto the solid nut, and waited. When he tried to force it with a wrench, he felt it loosen at once. Soon the wheel was off, and he was able to bend the right-hand seat forwards far enough to allow him to crawl behind it, squeeze out of the door, and move on to the wing.

Concerned about further injury to his broken leg, he tried to support it with his belt as he moved.

It was now quite late in the afternoon. It had taken him nearly twenty-four hours just to free himself from the wreckage. He was certain that by this time he would have been missed, and that a search would have been launched. Several times that day he heard planes fly over his location, but the engine noise was always faint, and soon faded away. As he himself had been the day before, they were probably just ordinary fliers, following the course of the country road.

Or were they perhaps rescue planes that had failed to spot him? He was in a partially wooded area, with no signs of life or human habitation in the immediate vicinity. He was certain that he was not far from a road or town – but in which direction?

Exhausted as he was, George Owens was determined to do something to help himself be found. With his leg injured, the two-foot drop from the wing to the ground posed a serious problem. When he found that it was going to be impossible to slide off gently, Owens simply let himself fall. The impact was so painful that he passed out.

Darkness was falling when he regained consciousness. Realizing that his chances of being found in the dark were minimal, yet unable to stand on his feet, the pilot slowly crawled along the ground, propelling himself on his forearms. He aimed to crawl far enough away from the wreckage to start a fire without fear of an explosion. He gathered dry twigs into a pile and, using dry pulp from a rotten log as his tinder, he struck one of the two matches he had found in his pocket. The fire caught first time – so well, that within seconds the flames were threatening to spread to the aircraft. He had to beat them out with his jacket. There was now no hope of attracting rescue that night, but tiredness had taken Owens past the point of caring. Deciding to make his way in the morning towards what appeared to be the peaked roof of a cabin, he fell asleep under the pine trees in a skimpy shelter improvised from leaves, tree limbs and grass.

At daybreak he began the slow, painful crawl up a hill towards the cabin, hampered by the fact that the terrain prevented him from moving in a straight line. Without water since the crash, Owens's body was rapidly dehydrating in the fierce heat. Even a few minutes' exposure to direct sunlight would actually knock him out; the only solution was to skirt any clearing and stay in the shade of the more difficult, wooded areas.

At the top of the hill, where he hoped to reach the end of his ordeal, Owens discovered to his horror that the roof of the 'cabin' was no more than two tall, dead trees, which had fallen against each other. There was no sign of human life anywhere. He realized that he could never crawl to the town – wherever it was – in his injured state. His best chance of survival was back with the wreckage. On his return journey downhill he found a few prickly pears, which he peeled and chewed. They relieved his thirst a little, for a short time.

By nightfall he was back at the plane. With great effort he managed to haul his overnight case from the luggage space of the Mooney. He chewed aspirin to ease his pain, and moistened his lips with toothpaste. He found, too, a can of liquid wax. So desperate was he for fluid, that he took an experimental swig, but had to spit it out. Improvising a shelter under the aircraft wing, he fell asleep, weaker and more dehydrated than ever.

When George Owens failed to come home on Sunday night, his wife telephoned his business associates in Hayden Hill. Owens had mentioned to them that he had some matters to settle in Alturas, 30 miles north. They speculated that he must have gone there, and stayed the night. So it was only after the second night had passed without word from him that Mrs Owens alerted the Federal Aviation Administration's Air Traffic Service, and a search was officially initiated.

Dozens of rescue sorties were flown over the next three days, by volunteer pilots and sheriffs' helicopters. But since the Mooney had reportedly flown north towards Alturas, that was where the search was concentrated – in an area of wilderness north-east of Hayden Hill, covering thousands of acres of desolate country. The searchers knew that if this indeed was the area where Owens had crashed, and he had no means of signalling his position, then it could be months before he was found.

For three days George Owens huddled in the shadow of his wrecked plane, scarcely moving so as to conserve his energy. He chewed on prickly pears that he could find close at hand, his eyes and ears straining for sight or sound of approaching rescuers.

By Thursday night he was so weak and dehydrated that he was certain he would not live through another day. He simply had to make one last attempt to save himself – or die. In the morning he would drag whatever clothes and rags and portable pieces of wreckage he could lay his hands on into a clearing, and lay out a big X which he hoped might be seen from the air. He was already prone to intermittent blackouts in the powerful sunshine, and he knew that this last-ditch effort might well bring on a state of unconsciousness from which he would never pull out.

At first light he dragged himself around on the ground, gathering together material for his signal. He was in great pain, and only barely conscious.

The sound of an engine, and the sight of a pick-up truck moving through the trees, were at first just illusions. Then, coming to his senses, Owens banged as hard as he could on the aircraft wing. The sight of two high-school boys, approaching with startled looks on their faces, was the finest thing he had ever seen in his life.

The boys, who had played truant that morning to practise their rifle-shooting in the woods, drove back into town at once and alerted the sheriff. The town was only about 1,500 yards away.

George Owens was discharged from hospital a month later. He could not use his right leg: he would need several more operations on the shattered knee before that would be possible. He knew he was fortunate to have survived at all, and that he contributed to his own near-fatal plight by not notifying anyone of his real intentions, and by failing to have either water or a survival kit stowed on board. He says he learned the hard way that no pilot is immune to misfortune, and in the wilderness only those who are prepared are likely to survive.

The irony, in his case, was that he was never more than a mile from a road or a town, but was just as helpless as if he had been stranded in the middle of the Sahara desert.

13 The sea

More than for almost any other survival situation, preparedness for abandoning ship and taking to the life-raft is paramount. So if you are invited for a cruise, take your own panic bag (see the 'survival kits' section below). Sadly, the chances of the boat having one aboard are rather slim. You could take along a copy of this book, too – then you can give the skipper this chapter to read!

Any captain worthy of the name will be proud of the boat's safety arrangements, and delighted to tell you about them and show you how they work. Here is a checklist of what the skipper should tell the *entire crew* before they even leave the harbour:

1 The 'man overboard' procedure.

2 Where the fire extinguishers, fire blanket and buckets on lanyards are stored, and how to use them.

3 When to use flares, where they are stored, and how to use them.

4 How to send a distress signal on the radio.

5 The 'abandon ship' procedure, and where it is on display inside the vessel for you to read at your leisure – especially: where to find your flotation device (and how to use it) and oilskins; allocation of particular responsibilities, for, say, saving provisions.

6 How to use the safety harness.

7 How to use the life-raft, and the equipment aboard it.

Message format for boat or aircraft distress calls

1 **Mayday, Mayday, Mayday . . .**

2 **This is yacht Leo, Leo, Leo/aircraft Cessna** (give call-sign)

3 **Mayday, Leo/Mayday, Cessna** (give call-sign)

4 **At . . .** (give position or estimated position, and state which)

5 If in an aircraft, give heading (true or magnetic), true or estimated air speed (state which), altitude, and estimated fuel on board or flying endurance (in hours and minutes).

6 State the nature of the emergency (e.g. **We've lost our mast.**)

7 State assistance required (e.g. **We're ditching** or **Abandoning ship, will fire distress rockets at intervals**)

8 State other details (e.g. **We are four crew**)

9 **Over.**

Repeat the Mayday message, and continue to transmit for as long as possible – even if you receive no answer.

To explain all this will take an hour or so, but it should be impressed on the crew that it could be the most important hour of their lives. If the skipper is unwilling to discuss it, laughs it off, or says, 'Not to worry, I know all about it' – DO NOT SAIL. It sounds drastic and rather rude, but manners will be the least of your worries when the skipper has been lost overboard in a force nine gale, and the yacht is sinking.

Abandoning ship

You should make every effort within your power to keep your vessel or ditched aircraft afloat – try repairs, or try to ride out the storm. Do everything you can to avoid leaving a larger craft for a smaller one. While you're doing this, someone else should be radioing a Mayday.

If all else fails, this is the recommended 'abandon ship' procedure:

- put on oilskins, warm clothing and flotation devices;
- collect spare clothing;
- prepare survival craft, and unlash the panic bag (see chapter 20) and water containers;
- gather provisions and navigation equipment;
- turn off the engine;
- drink as much water as you can;
- check that the distress beacon and flares are in the panic bag; and
- assemble for disembarkation.

Don't inflate the life-raft until just before you intend to use it. Then launch it from the lee side of the parent craft, to give you some protection from the weather, and to position you well to retrieve other survivors and floating debris.

Don't swim, unless for a very short distance to the life-raft, or to something you can hold on to. Swimming will only cause further loss of heat.

Checklist for abandoning ship

Even when there is no panic, it is easy to forget the major items that you should be taking with you.

Water containers. Store several plastic jerricans, with capacity about twenty litres, near the life-raft. They should be tied together with a strong line, and not quite filled, so that they float. The free end of the line should be easy to locate so that it can be secured to the raft, and the jerricans can be towed if necessary.

Food containers. It is as easy to store tins of food in a strong, see-through bag on a shelf or in a cupboard, as it is to store them loose. And this way, you can grab the bag in an emergency.

Navigation equipment. Experience shows clearly that a minimum of instruments and documents will help you make the best of your time aboard the raft. The bare minimum is a compass and general chart; luxury is a sextant, charts of the area, almanac and reference books, chronometer and writing materials. Keep a bag next to the chart table, into which everything can be tipped in a hurry.

Clothing. Most survivors seem to end up in rafts in their underwear. Make sure everyone grabs at least one warm set of clothing, and oilskins.

Panic bag. Described in chapter 20.

Battery-powered radio transmitter/receiver or distress beacon.

Aboard the life-raft

Someone must immediately assume command, setting priorities and assigning tasks. This will be the single most important factor in staving off the panic that could otherwise now set in.

Here are your priorities (many of which can be carried out together):

● Move away from a sinking or burning parent craft.
● Stream the sea anchor, to keep you in the vicinity.

- Check buoyancy, bail out any water and sponge the floor dry.
- Collect swimming survivors.
- Tie one person to the craft with line, to prevent it from drifting away if it overturns.
- Administer first aid if necessary.
- Check that the ballast pockets have filled with water.
- Set up the radio and prepare all signalling devices for use.
- Collect any debris.
- Get everyone to take a seasick pill.
- Rig shelter, if necessary.
- Post a look-out.
- Make an inventory of equipment.
- Start a log.
- Activate solar stills, if appropriate.
- Rig sail and set course, if desired.
- Read the survival manual.

Swimmers should board the life-raft from the upwind side, to prevent the bottom of the raft being caught by the wind and tipped. If anyone is injured, get them to turn their backs to the raft, push them down slightly to get the benefit of buoyancy when they pop up, and then haul them aboard.

If there are several rafts, connect them at the lifeline, which encircles the outside of the raft. Watch for chafing. The line should be long enough to allow for the motion of the sea – say, twenty-five feet. A group of rafts or boats is more likely to be spotted than a single craft – and resources can also be pooled, and tasks shared.

As soon as possible, a system of watches should be instituted, preferably with two people 'on' at once. The people on watch should be tied to the craft, and given extra clothing if the weather is cold. The watches should be no longer than two hours – especially if a lot of bailing or inflating is called for. The look-outs' responsibilities are to:

- check the craft's buoyancy and general seaworthiness;
- check that lines are not chafing the craft;
- check for leaks, and repair them at once;

- ward off sharks and other predators with an oar or paddle;
- attend to any fishing lines;
- check that others are sleeping safely – not trailing their arms or legs over the side, or lying in pools of water;
- note the craft's direction, speed and the weather conditions; and
- look out for lights or signs of land.

Keeping a log is useful for recording navigational data, the number of days afloat, the number of survivors, first-aid treatment, supplies and issue of rations and water, conditions of the craft, rainfall, numbers and types of fish caught and so on. What is more, it will help to keep your minds off the crisis, and perhaps provide much valuable data for survivors in the future if you all perish but the raft is later found.

In most cases you will want to use a sea anchor to stay in the vicinity of the accident if a radio message has been sent, or if it is worth waiting for debris. If, however, rescue is unlikely and you know your position, you may consider sailing. Be realistic about your progress, and overestimate rather than underestimate your travel time.

Remember that no matter how savage the sea, your greatest enemy lurks not outside the craft but within yourself. The tendency to panic will be strongest in the first twenty-four hours after abandoning ship. Control yourself for that period and you will inevitably come to exercise some measure of control over your environment. Just sit back and enjoy it!

Protection

After administering first aid to anyone who needs it, you will turn your attention to your first survival priority, protection. A number of factors which are unique to a sea survival situation can affect your health and well-being – mainly those caused by shortage of fresh water and exposure to the weather and salt water.

Exposure. Do not expose yourself needlessly to the sun and wind. In hot weather, it's better to wear a light layer of clothing than nothing at all. If it's very hot, try dipping your clothes in the sea, wringing them out, then draping them over yourself. The effect of evaporation is quite cooling. Use sunscreen cream from your panic bag on any area of skin that must remain exposed. Wear a hat, preferably one with a brim. Wear sunglasses – the reflection off the water will cause sore eyes very quickly. Again, improvise if necessary. If your eyes do become sore, don't rub them. Apply an antiseptic cream to the eyelids and use a light bandage.

Seasickness. No bravado about this: if you have seasickness pills, take them. The motion of a raft is very different from what you are used to, and sickness often results. With limited water supplies, vomiting vital body fluids can be fatal. Keeping your mind occupied with various tasks will help to prevent the misery of seasickness. Try to stay relaxed (you should be rationing your sweat anyway, remember?), and if you feel it coming on, try keeping your eyes fixed on the horizon. If the weather is cold, make doubly sure that you keep warm.

Immersion foot. You can recognize this condition, caused by prolonged exposure of feet and legs to cold water, by a red colouring and pain. In extreme cases, the affected area will swell and blisters will appear, interspersed with dark blotches on the skin. Try to prevent it by removing tight-fitting shoes, and keeping your feet as warm and dry as possible – keeping the raft floor dry is a good start. Treatment consists of moving the feet and toes to assist blood circulation: do not massage them. Wrap them in dry clothing, and keep the body warm.

Salt-water sores. These are caused by prolonged exposure to salt water. Prevention lies in keeping clothing as dry as possible. The only real cure is thorough rinsing with fresh water – if you can spare it.

Parched lips/cracked skin. Prevention and treatment are the same: apply sunscreen cream or vaseline (or fish or bird oil) and don't lick your lips. Cover lips or skin to prevent further drying out by sun and wind.

Constipation or difficulty in urinating. Nothing to worry about in the short term: both are natural reactions to food shortage, inactivity and lack of fresh water.

Location

You should check and prepare all signalling devices as soon as possible.

Pyrotechnic signals should be kept dry and ready for immediate use. Do not use them, however, until you actually see an aircraft or ship. Keep them clear of your body, and make sure none of the burning residue falls on or into the raft.

Use your heliograph mirror any time the sun is shining. Sweep the horizon with it, even if no ships or aircraft can be seen or heard.

Water

Don't drink sea water, urine or human blood. They are so salty that they will take much more water *from* your system in order to be processed than they actually put in. All you'll do is hasten dehydration. If you have enough time before abandoning the parent craft, drink as much water as you can.

Sources of water

Your panic bag contains solar stills. Get them going immediately. Use every means available to catch and store rainwater – plastic shoes, hats, even the intestines of turtles. If salt is dried on the canopy of the raft, rinse it off with sea water just before it rains.

Dew might form on the inside of the raft canopy during the night – not much, but every little helps.

Icebergs (in the northern hemisphere) are a source of fresh water. Approach them with caution because of the danger of them overturning, and harvest the old (bluish-looking) sea-ice. It splinters easily.

Fish eyes contain a lot of water. Fresh turtle blood is drinkable.

Going without water

- If no water is available, don't eat – particularly not proteins, such as fish. The process of digestion requires a lot of water.

- Ration your sweat: be inactive. Stay in the shade. Sleep. Rest.

- Try to prevent seasickness.

- Remember that alcohol dehydrates the body, as does smoking.

- To decrease the desire to drink, suck on a button or piece of cloth.

Food

The amount of food that you may eat in sea survival is in direct proportion to the amount of drinking water available. The body needs water for the digestion process, as well as for the elimination of the waste products of eating. But if you have ample water, eat whatever protein foods are available first, and save your emergency carbohydrate rations for a less rainy day.

Fish juice is not a substitute for water, because it contains so much protein – but wet fish is better than dry! All sea birds are protein food. So is seaweed – check it for tiny crabs and shrimps.

Remember the rules about edibility (chapter 8). Avoid all fish that are brightly coloured, covered with bristles or spines, have no scales, retain the indentations after you have squeezed them, puff up or have parrot-like mouths or humanoid teeth. And don't eat fish offal or eggs.

When you're fishing remember these rules:

- Never fasten the line to something solid – it may snap if a large fish strikes;

- fish are more apt to see and strike a moving bait than a still one;

- don't encourage sharks by trailing your hands or feet in the water. Throw waste overboard during the day, when you can watch for them.

Turtle fishing

Turtles can be caught with your bare hands. There are two problems though: how to approach the turtle, and how to get hold of it. If you spot what you think is a turtle, paddle up quietly – or wait for the turtle's natural curiosity to lead it towards your raft.

Now get your turtle into the raft. Catch a fin at its thick front edge, as close as possible to the point where it emerges from under the shell. With the other hand grasp the shell halfway along its far side. Now tip the turtle so that its shell is resting first on the outer side of the inflated ring and then on top of it. Let the turtle slide on to the bottom of the raft, keeping clear of blows from its claws and nips from the beak.

Cut its throat, and be ready to collect the blood in a container. Drink this as soon as possible, as it will start to coagulate in less than a minute. Dismemberment is the next process, and will depend on the tools you have available. The intestine can be turned inside out and used as a long cylindrical container. The blubber which lines the shell, when melted in the sun, makes an oil which has many uses: the Robertsons used it as a seasoning for dry fish fillets, for rectal enemas to cure constipation, for lubricating rusty instruments, for massaging stiffened joints, for dressing skin lesions and protecting them against salt spray and even for pouring on the sea to calm the waves.

The eggs are very nourishing, as is the bone marrow. Eat as much of the meat as you can (and your water supply allows) while it is still fresh. Dry the rest.

The Robertsons

'I knew we would have to make it on our own . . . I became a savage.'

In January 1971, Dougal and Lyn Robertson and their family set sail from Falmouth in their forty-three foot schooner *Lucette*, with the intention of circling the globe. Seventeen months later, at 9.45 a.m. on 15 June 1972, a pack of killer whales attacked the nineteen-ton boat and shattered the hull. Just four minutes after that, *Lucette* sank. The Robertsons were 200 miles off Cape Espinosa in the Galapagos Islands, in the largest stretch of open ocean in the world.

Dougal Robertson had spent twelve years at sea, obtaining a Foreign-Going Master Mariner's certificate. Lyn was a State Registered Nurse and midwife. Douglas, their eldest son, was eighteen, while Sandy and Neil, their twin boys, were only twelve years old. Having given up the hard life of farming in order to undertake their voyage, they were all in good, almost tough, physical condition. Also on board was Robin Williams, a twenty-two-year-old Welsh student who had joined the boat at Panama.

They all reached the comparative safety of the nine-foot-six inflatable raft, with nothing but the bags of onions, oranges and lemons, water and few bits of equipment that they had been able to grab as they abandoned the sinking yacht. The rigid dinghy was swamped. As the terrible reality of their circumstances slowly dawned on them, Lyn recited the Lord's Prayer and sang 'For those in peril on the sea' to comfort herself.

Douglas and Robin kept watch at the doors of the canopy, ready to retrieve any wreckage or debris that might float by. They watched in dumb longing at the sight of a five-gallon water container, blown further and further away by the steady wind.

Dougal Robertson was overwhelmed by feelings of guilt. Both because it was his unorthodox views on bringing up his children that had led them to sail round the world in the first place, and because he had failed to anticipate such an instant disaster.

The situation looked bleak. They were 200 miles downwind and down current from the Galapagos Islands, with no way back. The Marquesas were 2,800 miles to the west – even if they survived the journey, the chances of hitting one of them were remote. The coast of Central America lay more than 1,000 miles to the north-east, on the other side of the Doldrums, the dreaded area of calms and squalls.

What if they stayed put? They wouldn't be missed, and the alarm raised, for at least five weeks. Dougal's decision was to sail with the trade winds to the Doldrums, 400 miles north. The only feasible shipping route lay 300 miles in that direction, as well as their only chance of rainwater – and their only chance, however small, of making a landfall.

'We'll stay here for twenty-four hours to see if any other wreckage appears,' he announced, 'then we must head north.'

They had no choice but to stay inside the life-raft, six people packed into an inflatable raft of just nine-foot six. Movement was severely restricted. They opened the survival kit and took stock. They had eighteen pints of water, glucose and vitamin-fortified bread for twenty man-days, eight distress flares, a bailer, four fish-hooks and a twenty-five-pound fishing line, a knife, a flashlight, signal mirror, first-aid kit, two sea anchors, inflating bellows, a Genoa sail from the schooner and three paddles. They also had the bag of twelve onions, ten oranges, six lemons, and a tin of biscuits. Enough, Dougal estimated, to last the six of them ten days.

As darkness fell, so did the temperature. Draped in sheets they had improvised from the salvaged sail, the six survivors from *Lucette* tossed and turned all night in a vain attempt to ease their cramped limbs. They experienced the first of the many strange bumps and nudges from beneath the inflated floor of the raft that were to nag at their tired bodies until the raft, too, sank. Douglas discovered that the bumps came from large fish that had taken shelter under the raft. 'We'll have to do something about them,' he said, '. . . .like catching them.' It was a discomfort that they never managed to get used to. The pressure in the raft's inflatable compartments dropped during the night. Their first task at dawn was to top them up. The bellows performed badly, so Douglas cut the tube from the rest of the air pump and blew into it hard. Pressure was soon back to normal.

Breakfast was a meagre quarter-ounce of biscuit each, a piece of onion, and a mouthful of water.

Douglas and Dougal hauled on the steel wire and brought the fibreglass dinghy, *Ednamair*, alongside. They bailed it dry, and found Douglas's watch – still working – together with a stainless steel knife that Dougal had thrown aboard as the schooner sank. The knife was to prove a most valuable possession. Using part of the salvaged sail and the dinghy's oars, they rigged a makeshift sail. At 2 p.m. that day, the sail was set and a force 5 wind soon had the dinghy 'tugboat' pulling the raft on its 1,000-mile journey north, adding 25 miles a day to the drift of the Humboldt current which was taking them in the same direction.

Meanwhile Robin and the boys wrote letters to their family and friends on scraps of salvaged sail. Lyn wrote a moving letter of farewell to her nineteen-year-old daughter, Anne, who had left *Lucette* in the Bahamas. They all felt depressed as the letters were packed in waterproof wrapping and stowed in one of the pockets of the raft. Neil lay in his mother's arms, staring sadly into space.

The next morning, Dougal Robertson found an eight-inch flying fish lying in the dinghy. He gutted and scaled it, and Lyn marinaded the flesh in lemon juice. They ate slowly, each savouring their tiny portion of fresh fish, onion and water. But this first fish held a significance over and above the few ounces of protein that it yielded. It told them that providence was not entirely against them, and that fish could be caught if they only knew how.

The water supply in the meantime was critical. Their total stocks on 15 June consisted of the two gallons of water in the raft's survival pack, plus the liquid content of the oranges, lemons and onions. Dougal Robertson knew that rain was unlikely in that area for six months, and the survivors as a group decided immediately to ration water consumption to a pint and a half a day between the six of them. They would need the ten days' grace that this would give them to head north towards areas where rain might be expected. However, they had a rain shower later that day. From the centre of the rain-catching area on the yellow rubber roof, a pipe led down inside the raft. But as the first drops of rain splashed down, the only liquid to appear in the raft was strongly salty and bright yellow. After the salt had been washed off the roof, they managed to collect half a pint of undrinkable, rubber-tainted liquid. They could not use a single drop of it. Dougal knew they would have to do a lot better if they were to survive.

By dawn of the fourth day the sea was calmer, and Dougal climbed into *Ednamair* to adjust the sail. He found two flying fish lying on the bottom of the dinghy. He decided to try his hand at catching one of the large brightly coloured dorados that were swimming around the raft. But even trolling at different speeds from *Ednamair*, with variations of red and white bunting on the spinner from the survival kit, and using fish heads on a hook, he met with no success. The dorados would follow the lure, but refused to strike. Exhausted, his mouth dry with thirst in the midday sun, he gave up.

Lyn, Robin and the boys were not idle. 'There was a lot to do,' she remembers. 'We played games, like noughts and crosses, until Dougal took the pencil from us because he wanted it for his log. Robin worked out crossword puzzles for us. We tried Desert Islands Discs. All sorts of things . . .'

The raft now required topping up with air at almost hourly intervals, and they were reaching the point where the person on watch spent all the time either blowing up the raft or bailing it out. It had been given to the Robertsons by friends in Iceland, and was an old model.

Lyn was the first to spot bubbles rising from under the towing straps, during her watch on the fourth evening. They spread out the repair kit and discovered that the adhesive solution had dried out, and that the patches lacked a crucial coating of sealing compound. Next day, with rubber plugs, patches of ordinary rubberized fabric, a nylon fishing line and a piece of emery paper, they set about effecting some sort of repair to the four holes they had discovered, three inches below the waterline. By deflating the raft at the towing end, they could double the floor back and bring it inside the raft for repairs.

A short, heavy rain shower just after dark produced a pint and a half of water tainted yellow by the roof, then they settled as best they could for the evening. 'I rarely slept at all now,' Dougal Robertson says. 'I was listening all the time to the sounds of the raft, the sea, the dinghy, and thinking of ways to catch fish, of the possibility of straining plankton from the sea, of what we could do when the raft began sinking, as it must do in time . . .' Later that night, a large whale surfaced many times around the raft, often cruising quite close to it. The tension was broken only when Sandy fell asleep and snored in unison with the whale's blowing. Everybody managed a nervous laugh.

The morning of the sixth day brought a rare treat. In the early hours, Dougal had heard a noise in *Ednamair*. Quickly pulling the dinghy alongside, he found a large dorado thrashing around in the bottom. He sawed the head completely from the body of the thirty-five-pound fish to stop it from jumping out again. With a full stomach and renewed vigour, Dougal Robertson tried his hand once again at fishing, but lost the spinner, hook and line. As the day wore on, hot and unrelenting, he lay back in the raft and went over and over in his mind various methods of cashing in on the plentiful, but so far unexploited, fish supply around them.

The survivors lay gasping in the oppressive heat, sucking

on pieces of rubber to create saliva and ease the burden of their thirst. Items of tattered clothing had been discarded to ease the pain from areas of raw flesh on buttocks and thighs, developed through continuous contact with salt water.

As he opened another tin of water that evening, Robertson wondered with a sinking heart whether they had come to an end. The raft was becalmed. They still had 150 miles to go before there was any chance of rain. Yet they had just six pints of water left, including the yellow liquid collected in the last shower.

If Lyn was praying, as she often did, then her prayers were about to be answered: gathering clouds obscured the stars and at dawn it started to rain. The water from the collecting-area pipe was soon running clear and untainted, and they could fill every available empty tin and plastic bag – as well as their shrunken stomachs – until they could use no more. As they lay with their faces turned to the sky, the clear fresh water washed all the salt from their skin and hair. That single shower of rain lifted the survivors from the depths of despair back to the optimism and resolve with which they had rigged the makeshift sail on *Ednamair* and pointed the boat northwards. Chewing on strips of dorado that had been drying in the sun, they began to chatter about food and plentiful water supplies. It was then that Douglas spotted the ship on the horizon.

It was a large cargo vessel, on a bearing that would bring it within three miles of the raft. Dougal shouted for the flares. Hands trembling, he fired a red magnesium parachute rocket that roared off high above the raft. Pausing only a moment or two for the vessel to alter course towards them, he then triggered a red hand flare, grasping it high above his head. And as the smoke rose in a giant plume into the air, he lit another. 'This chance might not come again,' Dougal said. 'I'm going to use our last rocket flare and one more hand flare.' Now only three hand flares remained.

The ship sailed on, and over the horizon, as they stared bitterly at its diminishing shape.

In a strange way, however, something positive came out of this sad and frustrating incident. Something happened to Dougal Robertson that changed his whole perspective of their predicament. In his words: 'If these poor bloody seamen couldn't rescue us, then we would have to make it on our own and to hell with them. We would survive without them, yes, and that was the word from now on, "survival", not "rescue" or "help" or dependence of any kind, just survival . . . From that instant on, I became a savage.'

As if in reward for his new surge of strength, a turtle arrived the same day with a hard thump on the bottom of the raft, quite different from the blows to which they were used from dorados.

'The turtle's flippers had become entangled in the sea anchor line, so first passing a rope from the dinghy under the raft, we made it fast to one of the back flippers, then, carefully avoiding the searching beak, freed the turtle from the sea anchor rope and towed it around the raft to the *Ednamair*.' Robertson scrambled on to the dinghy and pulled the now struggling turtle alongside, reaching down to grasp the back flippers. He twisted the turtle round until its back was next to the dinghy, and heaved. It was surprisingly heavy and as it came aboard, the dinghy tilted its gunwales alarmingly close to the water. Robertson thrust his knife into the leathery skin of the turtle's neck, deep into the spinal column, severing the arteries.

By now the laws of survival, as the Robertsons saw them, certainly applied. In the words of Dougal: 'We would struggle and endure, and if our reflexes were not as swift as the animals and fish around us, we had cunning, and we would improve with practice.' The turtle was butchered and turned out to be a female, full of eggs. Soon the family were feasting on raw flesh and egg yolks; then they began the work of drying the surplus fillets.

They waited as long as they could in the area where they had sighted the ship, in accordance with common sense and the ordinary practices of seamen. Then, on the tenth day after *Lucette* sank, they again set sail northwards. The raft, however, now needed bailing every ten minutes, and everyone's physical condition was deteriorating rapidly from the exertions of keeping it afloat. Their mouths were raw from the rough surface of the inflating tube; their lungs and cheeks ached from the effort of inflation.

Transfer to the fibreglass dinghy *Ednamair* seemed inevitable – and horrifying: the slightest imbalance with six people plus supplies and equipment aboard the tiny nine-foot-two tender would spell disaster.

At dawn on their fifteenth day adrift it rained. They drank as much water as their bodies could take, and saved about thirty pints besides. There was a lot of rainwater in the bottom of the dinghy, mixed with turtle blood and a little seawater. As it was unpalatable, they felt it was safe to introduce it into their bodies through the bowel by means of a retention enema. 'It was an old nursing practice for dehydrated patients,' said Lyn. 'Douglas got a hollow piece of rubber from the raft ladder and we tied a piece of plastic on the end of it like a funnel. Everyone had a rectal enema except Robin – he didn't want to lose his dignity, although he was very dehydrated at that time.'

They had arrived inside the Doldrums: 400 miles down, 700 to go. But by day seventeen, it was clear that they would have to abandon the steadily deteriorating raft. Douglas cut the door pieces of the raft into capes to shield them from the rain, and fitted a small canopy to the bow of *Ednamair* to shed spray. Then, while he and his father finished stripping the raft, the others made the transfer to the dinghy.

They dropped the sail, caught and dressed a turtle, and lay at sea anchor in calm weather the first night in the dinghy.

The twins tucked themselves under the canopy in the bow, while the others found places in the cramped space that was left. Since only Dougal and Douglas could steer the dinghy it was necessary for one of them to be in the steering position at all times.

The twentieth day, 4 July, was Lyn's birthday. After a

birthday meal of fresh turtle meat and water, the family sang Happy Birthday to her. 'It sounded a bit odd on a small boat in the middle of the Pacific, but it did our morale good,' says Dougal.

Two days later, fresh water became a curse as squall after squall beat down on them. The seas got higher, and they prepared grimly for a rough night. Soon waves were breaking over the boat, and they had to bail continuously. Later, at about 8 p.m., it started to rain with increasing intensity, until they were being lashed by a torrential downpour. In the early hours of the morning the wind dropped, but the rain suddenly fell twice as hard. After long hours of exposure to the full force of the storm, Dougal Robertson became aware of a loud moaning noise. 'I did not realize that it came from myself.' The onset of hypothermia was averted only by chewing turtle fat and huddling together.

Lightning and thunder now filled the dark sky, and still the rain fell harder and harder. Above the din of the storm Sandy was sobbing. Lyn prayed, her hands a blur as she bailed frantically. The twins held the canopy up to stop any extra water from pouring down into the boat. Dougal clutched the sail, ready to trim it if another squall struck, Robin rubbing his numbed body for him to keep the circulation going.

There was no change in the weather at dawn. Throughout the day and into the next night, the family were exposed to the vicious wind and cold, torrential rain. Douglas took the helm. Kneeling side by side, Dougal and Robin bailed mechanically, sometimes succumbing to exhaustion and falling asleep, only to jerk awake moments later.

'We could no longer feel pain,' Dougal was to write. 'Our hands and limbs were soaked to the bone, our skin was a crumpled mess of nerveless wrinkles. We shivered and bailed and sang songs . . . and when we were too tired to sing, Lyn pummelled and rubbed our insensitive bodies to life again.'

By dawn, all six castaways had fallen into a deep, exhausted sleep. Robin's kneeling body sagged sideways against the dinghy, his bailing cup still in his hand. Lyn knelt asleep against the stern seat, her body close to Dougal's for warmth. Dougal Robertson's arm still moved in the motion of bailing, until he realized that the rain had stopped. 'Death could have come to us at this moment, without our knowledge or any resistance to its coming.'

On day twenty-nine Dougal caught a small shark. Two days later, his first dorado, with an improvised gaff. The day after that, another three. Lyn gave the eyes to the twins. 'The rest of us sucked the bones for liquid.'

They had a good quantity of fish and turtle meat hanging up to dry. Now all they needed was water, but by noon on the thirty-first day they were roasting under the hot sun. Dougal ladled sea water over Robin and Douglas in order to cool them. Lyn did the same with the twins.

Douglas remembers the attempts they had made to put Robin at his ease. 'He was the stranger in the house. We tried to make him feel he wasn't the odd one out, but petty things happened. Like, there was a box that had to be exactly in the middle of the boat – if it was one centimetre closer to me then I'd push it back with all my strength, and he'd push it back to me. There were always short tempers.'

As far as Robertson was concerned, Robin's strong strain of human sympathy made up in many ways for his practical inability, and his unshakeable belief in their eventual rescue, and their ability to survive until then, was a spur to Robertson's determination to ensure that such a satisfactory conclusion to their ordeal should be reached. The following dawn brought an hour of heavy rain – enough to replenish their stocks and fill their stomachs.

They were now in better physical shape than when they had transferred from the raft. Sores were healing and, after the enemas of water and turtle oil, their bodies were functioning properly. They had food. They had water. Dougal's announcement that they were now nearing the direct shipping route between Panama and Hawaii was greeted with indifference: all hopes were now pinned on making their planned landfall on the coast of Central America, sailing by day and rowing by night. Then, towards evening on their thirty-eighth day adrift, they saw a Japanese tunny boat in the distance, on a course that would bring it within a mile of their position. 'Hand me a flare,' Dougal demanded, 'but remember what happened with the last ship we saw.'

The grey and white paint of the fishing vessel stood out clearly against the darkness of the ocean as they steadied *Ednamair*. The first flare failed to ignite, but the second burst into brilliant red light. It burned Dougal Robertson's hand in the calm air, forcing him to wave it to and fro and, finally, hurl it high into the air.

It was this curving arc of light that the Japanese spotted. They did not at first acknowledge the distress signal, and the Robertsons could not be sure that the alteration in the boat's course was not merely due to it rolling in the swell. In fact the Japanese *had* seen the dinghy but had not intended to investigate such a small craft, believing it could not support life so far from land – but they turned to the rescue the moment they saw the flare.

'Our ordeal is over,' said Dougal Robertson as he sank back down on to the seat.

Unable to contain his emotion, Douglas burst into tears and hugged his mother. Robin laughed and cried at the same time, slapping Dougal on the back and shouting 'Wonderful!' over and over.

Dougal felt that death could have taken him quite easily then: he could never experience another such pinnacle of contentment.

The Japanese fishermen took Neil aboard first, then Sandy and the rest of the survivors. None of them was able to walk, but Dougal tottered up to the bridge to give details of their identity, and more interestingly for him, to check their position.

So good had Dougal's navigation been, that his estimated latitude was only five miles wrong, and they were actually

100 miles nearer to land than he had estimated. Four days later, they arrived in Balboa in Panama, where it seemed that every press man on earth was waiting to greet them.

14 Avalanche

The advice on surviving an avalanche is easy to give but may be quite impossible to follow. It is, however, the distillation of the experience of many victims over a period of years, so do your best to follow it.

Whether you have triggered the avalanche or it has started above you, try to ski to one side of it if you are on a steep traverse. Unless you are near the bottom of a slope, don't try to beat the avalanche by skiing in front of it – you won't succeed.

If you *can't* ski away from it, jettison skis, poles, day-sacks. Then either swim in the torrent – a sort of double-action backstroke seems to be the most effective, with the back to the force of the avalanche and the head up – or use a vigorous sideways roll: anything to give you the momentum to stay near the surface and to keep moving.

Keep your mouth shut: the snow dust will melt in your lungs and could either panic you or drown you. Keep fighting, all the way.

Just before the avalanche stops there may be periods of intense compression. When this happens still try to keep moving, make a tremendous effort to keep your nose and mouth in the crook of one elbow, ready to clear a breathing space, and thrust the other arm upwards as a marker. These last actions are crucial, because:

- the majority of fatalities are due to suffocation – a particular hazard in wet snow, which consolidates on stopping; and

- the average depth of snow covering avalanche victims is about one and a half metres – hence the importance of the out-thrust arm.

When the avalanche stops, make one great effort to get yourself out. If you don't know which way is up, spit: go the way your saliva doesn't fall. If you're trapped, don't panic – that will use up your oxygen and energy supplies very quickly.

If you're skiing off-piste, carry either a day-sack or a bum-bag, holding your survival blanket, candle, matches and high-energy food, all in a small tin which you can also use for melting snow. If you can afford them, you can have your party kitted out with electronic transceivers.

If you are the survivor on the surface, speed is of the essence. You are the victims' best chance of survival. Do not go for help unless help is a very short distance away (in a ski resort, the avalanche will be investigated, so stay where you are). Remember, you must consider not only the time required for you to get help, but also the time required for help to return. After thirty minutes, the buried victim has no more than a 50 per cent chance of survival – and their chances diminish by a further 50 per cent every subsequent thirty minutes.

Mark the spot where you last saw the victims, and search for them directly downhill. If they are not on the surface, probe with a pole or stick. But do it quickly, and the moment you make contact, start digging like mad. Every second will count. The time to stop digging is when you drop with exhaustion.

Anna Conrad

'I'm OK, I'm alive! . . . gimme a beer!'

Anna Conrad woke up to find herself trapped in a chamber of snow and wood that was not much bigger than her own body. She had no idea where she was. No idea how she had got there. All she knew was that it was cold, and that in the utter darkness and silence she was more alone than she had ever been. It was, she says, 'just total isolation'.

On the previous day – 30 March 1982 – heavy snow and 120 m.p.h. winds had forced the Californian ski resort of Alpine Meadows to close. For days, blizzards had been piling as much as three feet of snow a day on to an already deep and unstable mass. The danger of avalanche was enormous. By the afternoon of 31 March resort manager Bernie Kingery had sent most of his employees home. He stayed on in the ski patrol office in the summit terminal building, supervising the skeleton crew of maintenance men, lift operators and avalanche dynamiters.

At about 3.30 p.m., he watched angrily from the window as one of the lift operators, twenty-two-year-old Anna Conrad, ski'd over to the resort from her house half a mile away. With her was a friend, a visitor to the resort, Frank Yeatman.

Kingery called her into his office and gave her a dressing-down. When she left a few minutes later, she headed for the locker room on the second floor of the three-storey building.

It was now 3.45 p.m. Also in the ski patrol office, awaiting further instructions, were maintenance man Randy Buck, night security officer Jeff Skover, and lift operators Beth Morrow and Tad DeFelice. Pisteur Jake Smith was out on the approach road to the resort, checking the snow conditions. When the message came, sudden, and mostly garbled, from his patrol radio, nobody in the office could make out what he was saying, apart from one word: 'Avalanche!'

Seconds later they heard a low whistle, which at once became a deafening thunder. Gliding on a cushion of new layers, huge slabs of snow – each weighing thousands of tons – had slammed down the mountain and over the road, killing Jake Smith and three skiers. Then they engulfed the large A-framed terminal building, and everyone inside it. The shock waves came first, strong enough to bend and twist the mammoth steel beams of which the terminal building was constructed. Then, as the snow-laden wind screamed down, the building simply blew apart. It was as if a huge bomb had exploded outside. Finally the snow came, burying everything left standing.

As the building erupted, Jeff Skover grabbed a desk-top. DeFelice and Buck fell to the floor. In Skover's words, 'Time stood still.' Kingery was lifted bodily by the first blast of wind and seemed to float across the room. The noise of the wind changed to a thundering roar, and Skover threw himself under the heavy desk and fought to keep his grip. But so strong was the force of the wind that the wall behind him seemed simply to evaporate. Skover, too, was lifted and hurled out into the whiteness.

In the locker room, a row of heavy wooden lockers crashed on to Anna Conrad's head, knocking her unconscious. When she came to, the deafening roar of the wind had gone. So, too, had daylight. She was trapped in a dark cocoon of snow and wood. When the row of lockers had toppled, it had fallen across one of the benches and taken the brunt of tons of snow. But in the tiny space beneath, just five feet long and two feet high, Anna had no inkling that there had been an avalanche, and could make no sense of her surroundings. Worse than that, she had no idea how she was going to get out again. 'It was a cramped space. I could move a little, but not much. It was total isolation.'

Outside, Randy Buck and Tad DeFelice owed their lives to a twenty-ton concrete ski-lift counterweight that saved them from being buried alive inside the demolished terminal building. Quickly digging himself free, Buck helped pull DeFelice to safety. Together, they excavated Jeff Skover, who had been thrown some 100 feet away by the wind: apart from one hand, he was totally buried.

The scene that greeted them as they emerged was staggering. Only the shells of buildings remained. Piles of splintered wood and twisted steel lay everywhere. In all, the wreckage was scattered over an area of five acres. Snow was rammed into hills twenty feet high, trees uprooted or broken like sticks. But where even a cry of pain would have been welcome because it pinpointed their buried colleagues, there was nothing. Only silence, frightening and conclusive.

It took 150 rescuers less than a day to find the bodies of Jake Smith, Beth Morrow, Anna's friend Frank Yeatman and three skiers. For Anna Conrad and Bernie Kingery, the search continued. It was America's worst avalanche disaster for almost twenty years.

During the first twenty-four hours of the search, Anna was either unconscious, or awake and in pain, and unbelievably cold. In the dark, she had no means of telling the time. She started to explore her surroundings, running her hands over every square inch of her freezing tomb. She was rewarded with a miraculous find: a book of matches. She struck one, and the first thing she saw was a name on one of the lockers. Anna realized at last where she was. She was immediately able to pull more clothes out of the lockers to combat the numbing cold.

Up on the ground, they brought in dogs to help the rescuers. One of the animals, a nine-year-old German Shepherd called Bridget, an avalanche veteran, picked up Anna's scent on the morning of 2 April. 'That dog was doing everything but talking to tell me she had found something . . .' said Bridget's handler, Roberta Huber.

Anna heard voices shouting her name. She yelled back, but nobody heard her. Then she heard another sound. It was the muffled crunch of retreating footsteps, fading into the distance: because of the imminent danger of new avalanches, all rescuers had been ordered to leave the site.

Anna was powerless to do anything about it, and the loneliness and cold and pain flooded back around her. It would be another two days before the noises returned – but Anna had lost touch with that part of reality: 'I was conscious most of the time,' she said after her rescue, 'but I had no sense of time passing. I didn't think it was quite as many days as it was . . .'

Even though she was now wearing three pairs of ski trousers, Anna was beginning to suffer from the intense cold. Her feet were numb; the ordeal was ultimately to cost her most of her left foot, and all of her right. Worst of all, she was by now desperately thirsty – and dehydrating rapidly. She was sustained only by handfuls of snow. 'I was grabbing snow and eating it as fast as I could. I prayed a lot that day.'

But the rescue teams returned, and Roberta Huber's dog again caught Anna's scent. Ten feet above her, fifteen rescuers began hauling aside the wreckage. It was 1.10 p.m. on 4 April – ninety-four hours after the avalanche.

Anna heard the sounds and strained her face upwards. Suddenly there was a beam of light streaming in through a small area of the ceiling of wood above her, and some snow flurried down. Anna made a grab for it.

'Anna, is that you?' one of the rescuers shouted. His name was Lanny Johnson, a friend of Anna's.

'I'm OK, I'm alive!' came the reply.

Within a few minutes, Johnson was able to reach into the hole and hold Anna's hand. 'It's good to see you. We love you, and we're going to get you out,' he said, his throat feeling suddenly so tight that he was scarcely able to speak.

'It's good to see you, too!' Anna smiled.

'They were all friends of mine,' Anna recalls, 'every single one of them. It was like a reunion. Seeing people you love is great. I knew they'd come . . .'

Johnson called over another rescuer, Bernard Coudrier. 'We both kind of had a feeling of disbelief,' he said. Minutes later, he was giving her oxygen – although her first request was for a beer.

'She was smiling and talking to us the whole time,' said ski patrolman Gordon Girton.

When they finally brought her out, Bridget the German Shepherd bounced over and licked her face. It was the first time in North America that a dog had found an avalanche victim alive. Anna was carried to a helicopter which was waiting to air-lift her to hospital. As it left the ground, she heard a spontaneous cheer from the rescuers louder than the roar of the aircraft's engines.

'It was like God was right there with her,' Johnson said, '. . . and held that space open.'

'It's absolutely unbelievable,' said Gene Conrad at his daughter's bedside at Tahoe Forest Hospital in Truckee. 'Miracles really do happen.'

But Marshall Lewis, assistant marketing manager of Alpine Meadows, felt Anna had survived without divine intervention. 'Just her will to live saw her through five days of cold.' Mountain experts attribute her survival to an extraordinary combination of lucky factors. Her cocoon was big enough to provide her with oxygen to breathe and a little room to move, and it was snowy enough to allow her something to drink, but small and dry enough to keep her from freezing to death. Inside the tiny space, the temperature would have been about 32 °F, while the temperature outside plunged well below freezing, and was pushed down further still by the wind chill factor. Outside, Anna Conrad would probably not have survived two days.

Under twenty feet of snow, she patiently waited longer than that for the rescue that she was confident would come. Panic would have accelerated her loss of body heat and could have been fatal. And all the while, she also made a conscious effort to try to keep her circulation moving. Without a doubt, the predominant factor in Anna Conrad's survival was the presence of mind and sheer determination of the woman herself.

Dr Roger Mason, one of the physicians who treated her, said he thought she 'might have gone another five to seven days . . . her body heat was amazingly close to normal . . .

Someone without the tremendous inner strength she obviously has might have given up and succumbed after two or three days.'

But the final word must go to Anna herself. Asked by reporters to what she attributed her survival, Anna Conrad said simply, as if it were the most natural thing in the world: 'I never gave up.'

15 Held hostage

In terms of what you can physically do to help yourself, being held hostage is the worst kind of survival situation. It's not a battle against the elements, but a battle of minds: against your captor's, and inside your own. Do not, however, underestimate the role you can play in your own rescue. You *can* make a difference.

It may appear to you when you have been kidnapped or taken hostage that your survival is completely dependent upon everyone else but you. Your captors, the police, the people being asked to pay ransom – they all appear to have a much larger say than you in what happens to you. In many instances, this is simply not the case. Quite possibly *you* will play the most significant part in determining how the incident is resolved. You, your personality, your attitudes, your actions and your behaviour will often make the difference between an unpleasant outcome and one which you will live to tell your grandchildren about.

The police and experts can isolate several different types of hostage-taker – political extremist, fugitive, institutionalized, estranged, wronged, religious fanatic, mentally disturbed. But as far as you're concerned, there is only one kind of captor: a human being, with a weapon.

As human beings, captors, too, have personalities, feelings, emotions and – who knows – a sense of morality. The more contact you can establish with them, the higher the chances that they will have second thoughts about pulling the trigger if the time comes. Whatever the age, intelligence, background or personality of your captors, make sure that all your efforts are aimed both at avoiding their ire and at gaining their compassion.

While each kidnapping or hostage situation will be unique, there are some universal, basic measures you can take to maximize your prospects for survival. All of these measures are practicable and at the least, they won't in any way make your position worse.

Initial response. Right after the attack, don't resist. If you're hurt at all during the time of your captivity, it is likely to be in these first few seconds. Obey all commands quickly, and to the letter. Try to remain calm and quiet. It might, in turn, have a calming effect on your captors.

Self-control. In the next few minutes after a hijack, or when you arrive at your place of detention after a kidnap, try to regain your self-control. Irrational or erratic behaviour on your part may result in similar behaviour by your captors. Tell them of any injuries, medical problems or medicinal needs you have. The sooner these problems are taken care of the better. Remain passive, do not provoke. Do not ask questions: any extra pressure on your captors may spark off a violent reaction.

Evaluation. When you're settled in, collect your thoughts and evaluate your situation. It is important that you start thinking clearly, calmly and rationally as soon as possible. Plan your movements carefully and avoid instinctive actions – try to trade punches and you've had it.

Passing time. Start to look for ways of escape – covertly, of course. Escape may be difficult or impossible but you should not miss a good opportunity if it presents itself. Keep busy with mental activity, and avoid depression. Try to make yourself a daily schedule, and keep to it – it's good for morale. Practise your religious faith if you have one (secretly, if necessary). Do some physical exercise. Maintain your hygiene. Always remember that the captors can control your body, but they cannot control your mind. You are free to think, perhaps to review your life – as far back as you like.

Dealing with your captors. When it comes to handling your captors, feel your way carefully. Find out what they are like, and try to act in a manner that will meet with their approval. Presenting an image of hostility will only result in harsher treatment, and lessen your chances of gaining sympathy. Try to gain your captors' respect as a person. Try to be as real a person to them as possible – share your thoughts on your family, your hopes, your plans, your problems. Choose the most stable person to make contact with. Logic is not valid in this sort of situation: relate on an emotional level. Try to work out what sort of person they will be well disposed towards – a poet? a doctor? a scientist? Talk on the level of: 'I love a country where there is desert . . .' or: 'You know, in the West our lives are so restricted. We can learn so much from you . . .'

Be prepared for strange things to happen to your mind. You might find yourself becoming sympathetic to the captor's cause – the so-called 'Stockholm Syndrome'. You might hallucinate, become intensely fatigued, lose your intellectual ability and concentration.

Avoid all political discussions. If you must take part, try to tailor your comments so as not to offend or incite. Beware all female perpetrators and anyone who appears mentally deficient or unstable. These are the people who are most prone to violence and to erratic or sadistic behaviour. On the other hand, you want to establish bonds with any of your captors who appear receptive. It is hard for anyone to pull a trigger when the person on the other end of the gun is a friend.

Eat any food offered to you, and take cigarettes – even if you don't smoke. Stay face to face with armed perpetrators if at all possible, and if the situation is starting to look desperate, try not to be noticed – even at the expense of other hostages, by sitting next to someone who is failing, and who is likely to be singled out as one of the first to go. It's callous, but it's your life!

Interrogation. If you are grilled, avoid discussing secrets or any other information which might be useful to your captors. Such information will only reinforce their opinion of your value. By the same token, never tell a captor that ransom or other demands are unrealistic, or that they can or cannot be met. It will only interfere with the job the negotiators are trying to do. Don't discuss anything to do with the negotiations. If in doubt, play dumb.

Don't become a pawn in anyone's propaganda, either: if you look useful, it could actually prolong your captivity. Just try to keep your captors optimistic about the negotiations: treat lengthy negotiations as normal, and don't appear to be surprised by the delay.

Release. Be ready for rescue. Have a plan of action worked out, and be prepared to put it into effect at a moment's notice. This plan should include avoiding obvious lines of fire, and possible assault routes. Hide behind furniture if possible, or stay on the floor. Help your rescuers in any way possible. Identify the perpetrators, and yourself.

Be prepared to run for it – escape as soon as possible.

After-effects. After your release, rest and recuperate until you are physically recovered. It might take longer than you think. Seek psychiatric help if you have problems re-adjusting. Help your family to recover, too. They will have suffered as much as you.

Throughout, try to remember that regardless of how things may appear to be going, you should keep a good attitude and make the best of the situation. If you survive the first three days, the chances are excellent that you will eventually be released.

Just keep calm and alert. Don't fight. Follow instructions. Try to build a positive relationship with them. And control your anxiety and fear by the methods already discussed in chapter 5.

The Cossanos

'Please – let Lester live to see the baby.'

Richard Gantz, a twenty-eight-year-old ex-Marine, was serving a twenty-year gaol term for robbery and rape when he escaped from Fishkill Prison in New York State during the afternoon of Saturday 11 August 1979.

At 2.30 on Sunday morning he flagged down a car in the rain, carrying a couple from Wallkill, New York. He made them drive him to their home, and after forcing them to drink a quantity of alcohol, the six-foot-five, fifteen-stone convict tied the man to a bed and raped the woman.

Armed with a .410 bore shotgun, Gantz fled in the couple's car, crashing it less than a mile away. He then stole another vehicle, which the New York State police found abandoned at about 8 a.m. near some woods in the town of Gardiner. More than 150 prison officers and police were immediately drafted into the area to join the search.

Jack Soto was entertaining his daughter to morning coffee when he heard the news on the radio. He asked her to stay to lunch, but Mary Ann politely declined the invitation. She had promised her son Justin a visit to the cinema that afternoon, and wanted some time at home before they set out. Mary Ann was thirty-nine, and lived in Gardiner with her husband Lester Cossano and her six-year-old son, Justin. She was eight months pregnant. Lester, a technician with IBM, was away on a business trip in California, and would not be back until later that evening.

On their way home, Mary Ann and Justin drove into a road-block. The policeman said he thought it was safe for her to go home, but warned her to be careful with strangers. Mary Ann carried on through the driving rain.

The Cossanos' house on Phillies Bridge Road was an isolated, white-shingled, split-level house surrounded by woods and approached by a long drive. Mary Ann parked and they went into the kitchen through the back door.

Picking up the telephone, she called a girlfriend who worked as a switchboard operator at the nearby Wallkill Prison, and asked more about the search. According to her friend, the escaped rapist was last seen near the railway tracks behind the Cossanos' house. Then her friend asked her to hold on: she had to handle another call. As Mary Ann cradled the receiver in her hand, sixth sense made her turn round. Watching her from the stairs was a huge man with blond hair. He was carrying a shotgun.

Gantz was wearing a pair of Lester's jeans and one of Mary Ann's coats. Both garments were much too small for him.

'When she comes back on, tell her you've got to go,' he ordered, coming into the kitchen.

Mary Ann realized that he must have been listening on the upstairs extension. She did as she was told. Everything her friend had said about the convict flashed through her mind. Particularly about the woman in Wallkill. My God, she thought, if he rapes me I'll lose the baby.

'If you don't do anything foolish I won't hurt you,' Gantz said. 'All I need is some rest and a place to hide.' He sat down at the table and asked about the road-blocks. Mary Ann told him everything she could remember about the one she had passed through, and described to him the local roads. She felt that if she could only convince him that there was an escape route, then he might take it.

A little later that afternoon, Captain Stanley Kowalik, commanding the search operation from a post on Creek Bridge Road, was joined by detective George Rebhan. A policeman with thirteen years' experience in the New York State Police Department – the last five of them with the US Bureau of Criminal Investigation – Rebhan was also a trained hostage negotiator.

Police tracker dogs were proving useless in the driving rain. The helicopter wasn't much good either. Kowalik had experience of the dense woods and wet lowlands that surrounded the area. He knew that the only way to find

Gantz would be to tread on him. What he feared most was that Gantz would eventually need a place to dry out, and might take a hostage. This had happened before, when Gantz had forced a young woman to go along with him on a robbery. After the robbery, he had raped her.

After church that morning, Genevieve Soto decided to call in on her daughter on her way home. As her car came up the drive, Gantz jumped up from the table.

'Who's that?' he demanded.

'It's my mother,' Mary Ann replied. 'What do you want me to do?'

'Let her in.'

Sensing immediately that something was wrong, Genevieve Soto asked her daughter what the matter was. Mary Ann shrugged and said, 'Nothing.'

When Gantz stepped into view behind Mary Ann and motioned her into the house with his shotgun, Genevieve realized at once who he was. She felt relieved to have arrived when she did: she had a background of twelve years of work with juvenile delinquents, enough to tell her that Gantz was unlikely to rape a pregnant woman if her mother was in the house.

She walked into the kitchen as if Gantz were just a workman enjoying a break. She offered to make him a sandwich, and asked his name.

'Eric,' Richard Gantz said defensively.

'Well sit down, Eric,' Genevieve said cheerily, 'and we'll organize a bite to eat.'

Gantz put down his shotgun and came to the table.

After lunch, Gantz worked out a plan for Genevieve to tour the area and take note of all road-blocks. He was just at the point of telling her not to inform anyone of his presence in the house when Mary Ann's stepson, Lester Jr, and his fiancée, Betty Jane Kuhnan, pulled in to the driveway. Gantz snatched up his gun and went to welcome his next two hostages.

It was still raining when Lester Cossano's plane landed in

New York City. As he and his colleague drove home in their rented car, they listened to a news bulletin on the radio about the search for an escaped convict called Richard Gantz. Lester was dropped off at home at 8.15 p.m., and went round to the back door. Mary Ann greeted him; he was dumbfounded by the scene awaiting him in the living room.

'What the hell do you want?' the fifty-year-old, five-foot-seven executive demanded of the giant man who was wearing his jeans and carrying a shotgun.

Gantz told him to sit down. Nobody was going to get hurt, he said.

Lester Cossano complied with the order. As he sat down, he noticed that Gantz was not pointing the shotgun at anyone. He quickly worked out his chances of grabbing it and killing the escaped convict. But Gantz had strapped Lester's hunting knife to his belt: if Lester's attempt was unsuccessful, Gantz might use it to stab him – or worse, one of the family. He decided not to try anything.

Gantz now had six hostages under his control, and the strain was starting to show. His remedy, however, could not have been predicted – shortly before Lester arrived home, Genevieve had returned from her enforced reconnaissance of the neighbourhood. She reported that only one road was not covered by a road-block. Now Gantz looked at her and said simply: 'You and Betty can leave. But you'd better not warn anyone about me being here.'

As soon as she was released, Betty went straight to the police. Within minutes an all-cars message was broadcast that Richard Gantz was in the Cossanos' house. He was armed, and holding hostages.

After eight hours of fruitless searching, George Rebhan had been heading for home and a dry change of clothes when he heard the transmission. He drove at once to the house on Phillies Bridge Road. He arrived to find Captain Kowalik positioning rifle teams around the house and, beyond them, a second cordon of police and road-blocks. He set up his command post behind the Cossanos' garage.

Rebhan had studied prison reports on Gantz. The convict had, as a US Marine, been trained in jungle reconnaissance. Now the time had come for Rebhan, and his three fellow negotiators, to use their own experience and training in an encounter with the convicted rapist.

Two hours earlier, Gantz had sent Lester Jr out to do a further check on road-blocks. Lester was now in the command post, helping the police piece together the scene inside the house. 'Your son's been gone a long time,' Gantz remarked to Lester.

'He's probably going the long way round,' was Lester's reply.

From where she was sitting on the couch, exhausted and scared, Mary Ann could sense Lester's tension. She knew that if Gantz made a move to harm her or Justin, Lester would attack him – and probably be killed.

Just then the telephone rang. Gantz motioned for Mary Ann to answer it. 'It's for you,' she said.

Gantz listened. 'Mr Gantz, this is George Rebhan speaking . . .'

The fugitive swore loudly into the mouthpiece and hung up. Within seconds, the phone rang again. Once more, Mary Ann passed it over to Gantz.

'We are concerned about your welfare,' said Rebhan, 'and the welfare of the other people in the house.'

Gantz let loose more obscenities and hung up. The phone rang a third time, and Gantz picked it up. 'I want a bottle of Scotch,' he said.

'OK, Mr Gantz. I'll see what I can do.'

George Rebhan was pleased. Gantz had made a demand – the first step on the way to a successful negotiation. Even better, Lester Jr was able to tell him that there was already a bottle of Scotch in the house. By not offering it to Gantz, Cossano was therefore maintaining some measure of control inside the house. At this stage, as an Ulster County deputy sheriff explained, there were 'no plans to forcibly remove him. It's sit and wait.'

'Mr Gantz, we're working on the whisky,' Rebhan said when he dialled again.

'I don't want any publicity – you understand?' Gantz replied.

'I'll do my best,' Rebhan said, but he wasn't hopeful. Television and press reporters were milling around outside the house in increasing numbers. Several policemen were detailed to telephone every news agency in the area with a request not to broadcast the story.

Inside the house on Phillies Bridge Road, Richard Gantz suggested turning on the radio to get some music. When Mary Ann switched on, they found themselves listening to a news bulletin about the siege. Gantz telephoned Rebhan at once and swore loud and long at him.

'We're doing our best,' was all Rebhan said in reply. Then he added: 'Why don't you let the lady and the boy go now? All you need is one hostage.' Rebhan was planting the germ of an idea to which he would return often as the night wore on.

When he replaced the receiver, Gantz apologized to Mary Ann for his bad language. Lester detected that a subtle shift was occurring in Gantz's attitude towards his hostages.

Rebhan now began to telephone every five minutes. His excuse was that he needed to report on his progress in stifling the press. Every time he called, he brought the subject of Mary Ann and little Justin into the conversation.

Mary Ann felt angry and helpless, and frightened by the growing tension. At two o'clock in the morning, she broke down in tears.

'Take Justin and go to your mother's,' Gantz said.

'Not without Les,' Mary Ann replied.

'Go.'

Gantz dialled Rebhan, and announced that the woman and the boy were coming out. Moments later, they got into the car and drove off. Rebhan could not believe it: by letting Mary Ann take the car, Gantz was depriving himself of his only means of escape, apart from on foot.

The siege continued all day Monday. Power to the house was shut off at 4.30 p.m., but restored at 7.20 p.m. at Gantz's insistence. When the telephone rang later that evening, Lester picked it up. It was Genevieve, asking to speak to Gantz.

'Eric, I'll help you in any way I can when this is over,' she said, 'but please – let Lester live to see the baby.'

'You know I wouldn't do anything to hurt him,' Gantz replied. Unless, he added, police action forced it. To Genevieve he sounded 'very, very relaxed and a perfect gentleman', but she remembered only too well how she had said she felt only a few hours earlier: 'It was like a powder keg. He wanted his freedom and he told us he had nothing to lose.'

In the early hours of Tuesday morning Lester's head began to swim with tiredness. Gantz placed the shotgun on the mantelpiece and sat down opposite him. Lester tried to reckon his chances of reaching the gun before Gantz did. Then a strange thing happened. Lester realized that he no longer had a desire to kill Gantz. Gantz had let his loved ones go free. It would be impossible now to shoot him.

The next time Rebhan called, Cossano told him that he desperately needed some sleep – even only an hour. Rebhan could not agree to the request. The police were ready to storm the house the moment they thought Cossano might have been harmed. If he fell asleep, they had no way of knowing what was going on, or whether Gantz had in fact harmed him. When Cossano repeated his request, this time more forcefully, Rebhan persuaded Gantz to wake him in exactly one hour. Then Lester lay down on the sofa and fell into a deep, exhausted sleep.

At 5.30 a.m. the police heard a shot from the direction of the house. They moved in at once. They found Lester Cossano stretched out on the sofa, sound asleep. There was no trace of Gantz. Scrambling out of a ground-floor window, he had fled through a patch of grapevines into the woods and vanished. When he came across two policemen patrolling a road, he pretended to surrender. He advanced with his hands above his head, but dived into thick undergrowth at the last minute. One of the officers raised the alarm by letting off a shot.

Gantz emerged at the northern edge of the wood. He was intercepted by Sergeant Brian O'Connor, but the sudden clatter overhead of a police helicopter gave Gantz the split second's diversion he needed to flee once more into the undergrowth. George Rebhan joined O'Connor, and the two men started a search.

Minutes later, O'Connor spotted Gantz lying flat on his stomach, almost completely camouflaged in a pool of mud. O'Connor jumped on top of the giant man, followed by George Rebhan.

After more than two days, the longest siege in the history of the New York State Police was at an end.

By mid-morning, Lester Cossano was reunited with his wife and family. 'Les was tired, but everything was OK, physically and mentally,' said Charles Eidel, a member of the rescue squad who examined Cossano.

Two police sharpshooters armed with Winchester rifles with telescopic sights had edged close to the house during the night. One of them said he had Richard Gantz in his sights at least twenty times as he passed in front of windows, but did not fire. 'Life is precious,' the firearms officer commented. 'We don't want to take it unless it's absolutely necessary.'

Inside the house, Lester Cossano apparently managed to get along as well as could be expected with his captor. 'They had a bond together, no arguments, no fights, no nothing,' said Eidel. 'They cooked together and they even managed to sleep.'

The strain, however, was tremendous. All the while, Gantz had the .410 bore shotgun he had stolen from the Wallkill couple. He also had access to four rifles owned by Cossano himself.

At hourly intervals during the final night, the four policemen serving on specially trained hostage negotiating teams made telephone calls to Gantz from the nearby house

16 Fire

Hotel fire

Know where the exit is. The moment you've put your luggage down in your room, go back out into the corridor and find the emergency exit. Open it. Are there stairs beyond, or another door? Open that, too. Now, as you return to your room, count how many doors there are between it and the exit. Is there anything in the corridor that would be in your way, like a vending machine or a large pot plant? Now back to your room.

Check your room. Does your bathroom have an extractor fan? In an emergency you can turn it on to help remove smoke. Do the windows open? If so, look outside: are there any ledges? How big? How high up are you?

Now relax, and enjoy your stay!

Leave the hotel at the first sign of smoke. If something wakes you up in the night, trust your in-built alarms. Investigate thoroughly before you go back to sleep.

Always take your key. Don't rush out and lock yourself out of your room: you may be forced back by smoke or flames. Get into the habit of always leaving your hotel keys in the same place – on a bedside table, say.

Stay on your hands and knees. If you do wake up and find smoke in your room, grab your key, roll off the bed and crawl towards the door. Even if you can tolerate the smoke when standing, don't. Save your eyes and lungs for as long as possible: at head height, the air may be full of carbon monoxide. Feel the door handle. If it isn't hot, open it slowly and check the corridor.

If you decide to leave, close the door behind you. Most doors take about half an hour to burn down. They are good fire shields, so close each one behind you. Crawl to the fire exit, staying against the wall closest to the exit, counting doors as you go.

Don't use the lift. Smoke, heat and fire can render lift controls useless, and the lift shaft can fill with smoke. Always use the stairs.

If you can't go down, go up. Hold on to the handrail as you go down the stairs: other people may be panicking around you, running and stumbling. If you encounter smoke 'stacked up' at lower levels, turn round and go back up again. Go right up to the roof. Settle yourself on the windward side of the building (the side the wind is coming from) and await rescue.

Look before you leap. From the first floor you might just about get away with a sprained ankle. If you're any higher than the second floor, forget it. You're better off where you are, fighting the fire.

If you can't leave your room, fight the fire. If your door is too hot to open, or the corridor is completely filled with smoke, don't panic. Open your window to help vent any smoke in the room (don't break it, in case there is smoke outside and you need to close it again.) If your telephone is working, call the fire brigade: some hotels have a nasty policy of trying to fight fires themselves! Switch on the bathroom extractor fan.

Now fill the bath with water. Wet some towels or sheets, and stuff them into the cracks around the door to keep out smoke. If the door is hot, douse it with water to keep it cool. If possible, put your mattress against the door, and jam it in place with a wardrobe or chest of drawers. Wet them, too, if necessary.

Keep everything wet. A wet towel or pillow case around your nose and mouth can be an effective filter of smoke particles. Swing a wet towel around the room: it will help to clear the smoke.

If there is a fire outside the window, remove the curtains, move away as much combustible material as you can, and throw water around the window.

Then just keep hanging on in there until help arrives.

Ron Flory

'Tom and I were down there together. We'll go out together.'

Six miles east of Kellogg, Idaho, and nearly a mile beneath the earth's surface, came a shout that terrified every miner who heard it: 'Fire! . . . Fire on the upper levels!'

It was noon on Tuesday 2nd May 1972. The fire had started mysteriously in an abandoned section of the Sunshine Silver Mine, feeding itself on piles of discarded timber. Now it erupted with a sudden, fierce intensity, filling the mine shafts with smoke and deadly fumes which cut men off from their escape routes. Eighty miners were lifted to safety before the fumes overcame the hoist operators. Ninety-three men were still trapped, along 100 miles of shaft. In the words of a mine official, Sunshine Silver Mine was 'like a big apartment house with many, many rooms'. Locating survivors, let alone rescuing them, was going to be very difficult indeed.

When twenty-eight-year-old Ron Flory heard the shout, he and his partner Tom Wilkenson, a year his senior, jumped into a battery-powered locomotive and drove west along the mile-long tunnel in which they had been working – known as Syndicate Drift – in order to alert two other men. The four of them then returned to a small shed they called 'the station', at the vertical No. 10 shaft, to await a cage to take them to safety. There was a telephone at the station, but it wasn't working.

Donning emergency respirators, the four men activated the chemicals that would neutralize any carbon monoxide in the air. They were soon joined by five other miners. No cage appeared, but smoke did – swirling in to engulf the station, and forcing the men 100 yards back down the tunnel to the locomotive garage.

Every five minutes, two men walked back to the station to check for the cage and to try the telephone. But without success. Then the garage, too, was engulfed. Perhaps because he wore spectacles, Wilkenson's respirator slipped off, and within seconds he was unconscious.

Ron Flory sprinted to the station and pulled the emergency cord. Then he and driver Dick Allison lay their stricken friend on top of the locomotive and drove westwards again. As soon as they were clear of the smoke they propped him against the side of the passageway, and went back to get the others. The others wanted to check the station one more time, and drove off. But Flory, by now dizzy and weak, walked back towards Wilkenson. He stopped on the way to scribble a message in chalk on the wall: 'Ron Flory was here. May 2 to –?'

By an ironic twist of fate, the AGM of the Sunshine Silver Mine was in progress in Coeur d'Alene, forty-five miles away. Martin Chase, the mine's general manager, had informed shareholders that in 1971 Sunshine had produced seven million ounces of the precious metal – one-sixth of the entire US output. After his speech he telephoned the mine, and was told about the fire. Chase left the AGM at once and headed for Kellogg.

By the time he arrived, 1.25 p.m., smoke was issuing from the mine's main ventilation shaft. Chase knew at once that the fire was serious, and he was faced with a difficult decision. The mine's enormous fans pushed thousands of cubic feet of air into the 100 miles of passageways every second, and sucked foul air out. In a fire, the fans circulated deadly smoke and carbon monoxide — yet none of them could be switched off until the miners' whereabouts were known.

of one of the state troopers. George Rebhan said that the tactics were mainly to keep Gantz talking and even-tempered. 'It was mostly maintaining the good rapport we did develop on the phone during the day,' he said. 'We got quite redundant and he did at times, too. The big thing is time and keeping the proper atmosphere for him and keeping him in a proper frame of mind. At no time did he ever even suggest he would harm the hostage. And at no time did he hallucinate or lose his train of thought.'

As the negotiation wore on, Gantz talked more and more about his personal safety. 'We tried to assure him he would be all right,' said Rebhan. 'Many of the conversations dealt with small things – he ran out of cigarettes and sugar for coffee, and asked for fresh supplies.' The police never provided them. Gantz also asked for sleeping pills, and a bottle of them was placed on the rear step of the home. 'We were told he is an active insomniac: he can go for six or seven days without sleeping and still function in a normal manner,' Rebhan added.

'He led us to believe he wanted to fall asleep and let himself be captured,' said Captain Kowalik. 'He wanted to let us take him while he was asleep.'

Then, in a negotiation call shortly after five o'clock, Gantz demanded that the police cordon be pulled back. It was. Half an hour later, Gantz made his bid to escape.

Back at the Cossano home, Charles Eidel was still talking about a written note Richard Gantz had left clipped to the kitchen refrigerator. It said: 'Thank you for your hospitality.'

Even as Chase was arriving at the mine, so were the rescue services and miners' wives. Myrna Flory was told by one of the rescued miners that her husband, too, could have escaped, but had gone instead to help his friend Tom Wilkenson. Frances Wilkenson was already there, after hearing the news on the radio. They joined the other relatives in their silent vigil under the grimy towers that worked the hoists. Behind them was a sign which read: 'This is the first day of the rest of your life. Live it safely.'

A mile beneath them, Ron Flory made out a light about 100 yards away. The other miners had been gone for an hour and a half. The light must be on the returning locomotive. Flory shouted, but got no response. He walked towards the light. What he saw nearly made him retch. Dick Allison was slumped motionless in the driver's seat; three others were lying on the ground. They were dead, victims of carbon monoxide poisoning when they drove back from the station with their respirators off. Flory backed off and ran back to get Tom Wilkenson.

The two miners double-checked that there was nothing they could do to revive the others, then took stock of their situation. They did not know where the fire was. They had no means of communication with the ground, or with the other trapped miners – if there were any. They had no food. The only form of lighting came from their cap lamps and the locomotive's headlight; when the batteries went, they would be in darkness. On the plus side, the waterline to their level was intact, and fresh air was definitely flowing from the four-foot shaft which had recently been bored down from the higher levels.

Later that evening they drove further westwards along Syndicate Drift. At the point where the new air shaft entered the tunnel, they found a green bag containing a field telephone. Flory unfastened the bag, and turned the crank. But there was no reply to his call; a sharp rock in the shaft had severed one of the lines, making the telephone useless.

They settled down for their first night underground. The fear that they might be trapped for a long period was slowly creeping up on them – the fear that they might starve to death, or suffocate if their respirators began to fail. Flory wondered who would teach his two-year-old son to fish, and how the child would manage without a dad. Wilkenson was tense, constantly asking Flory to talk to him, wondering why the rescuers were taking so long. He speculated about returning to the station, or climbing the wooden escape ladders to the higher levels. Flory was adamant that with no guarantee of an air supply up above, such an attempt would be suicidal. At least down at the lower level they had fresh air. Wilkenson protested that they had to tell the rescuers – somehow – that they were still alive.

Flory walked off down the drift towards the station. He felt dizzy again, a sure sign that his respirator was not working properly. When he reached the bodies of the four miners he hesitated, then helped himself to their cigarettes, and returned to Wilkenson near the four-foot shaft. During the night he thought he heard voices. One of them belonged to Dick Allison, the dead driver.

As time wore on that night, the two men talked about many things. The main topic was fishing, but the conversation always came round to food. They had not eaten since their break on Tuesday morning, and hunger was starting to gnaw at their stomachs. Wilkenson argued again that they should make their way back to the station, and this time Flory reluctantly agreed. With their respirators no longer working reliably, they would need protection from the smoke as soon as they were away from the shaft. They decided to remove their T-shirts and soak them in water, then hold them over their mouths and noses.

They made it past the four bodies, but then the smoke thickened and they couldn't breathe. They had no choice but to turn back.

Sitting back against the wall near the shaft, Flory remembered that his wife had been complaining for a long time that she didn't have any photographs of him, or of the family together. The first thing he'd do when he got back home would be to organize a family photograph.

Meanwhile, Martin Chase had centred the rescue operation on No. 10 shaft, above the station. Using giant exhaust fans, the eighty-strong rescue team had started to clear the smoke away from the head of the shaft, which was 3,100 feet below the surface, at midday on Thursday. The plan was to send a hoist down as soon as they could reach the shaft, to gauge the level of smoke at the lower levels.

At about midnight a temporary bulkhead keeping the smoke away from the rescuers began to leak. It was six hours before they could resume their task.

The US Bureau of Mines rescue team had arrived at Sunshine, and Chase decided to deploy them on a back-up rescue effort, via the four-foot shaft. They lowered a television camera 3,700 feet underground into the mouth of the shaft, to see if it would accommodate a two-man rescue torpedo.

Frances Wilkenson was beginning to lose hope that she would ever see her husband again alive. At one stage she had refused the name badge handed to her by the Red Cross, saying that she didn't need one: her husband was going to walk out alive. Even when they found the bodies of four miners on Wednesday evening, she had not been discouraged. Now she wasn't so sure. Her twelve-year-old daughter and three-year-old son, Eileen and Tommy, kept asking when Daddy was coming home. She could not share with them her fear that in the darkness, when their cap-lamp batteries had failed, the survivors might go mad.

At 5 p.m. on Friday, Flory's hopes plunged when he found that water was only coming out of the waterline in a tiny trickle. With the water supply finished, they would be done for. Now they had no option but to reach the station. Wilkenson led, because his lamp was brighter. They found that the smoke had thinned considerably, and they got to the station without many stops to catch their breath. They found the lunch boxes of their dead colleagues; after a second or two of hesitation they opened them and began feasting on sausages, chocolate and coffee.

On Saturday morning it seemed to Wilkenson that Flory had indeed become unhinged. He started to sing, banging a wrench in time against the water pipe.

'That won't do any good,' Wilkenson said.

'I know,' Flory countered, 'but it sure makes me feel better.'

The weekend passed, and still there was no sign of rescue. On Sunday evening, Flory and Wilkenson found two more bodies in the vicinity of the station. The area now seemed clear of smoke, and they debated trying the escape ladders. As if in answer to their question, they suddenly sensed a strange stillness in the air. For some incomprehensible reason, the fans must have been switched off. Without air, climbing the ladders was now unthinkable. As soon as the fans stopped, a swirl of hot steamy air closed in on the two miners. Flory and Wilkenson thought it was smoke, and started to run along the drift. Then the humid cloud caught up with them. With much relief, they found that they could breathe in it.

Nearly a week of rescue attempts had now come to nothing, and the headline in the *Kellogg Evening News* for Monday 8 May read: 'Rescue Hopes Dimmer.' At 9 p.m. Donald J. Morris and Wayne Kanack, two inspectors with the Bureau of Mines rescue team, climbed into one of the two-man torpedoes and were lowered down the shaft. But it was so clogged with loose rocks, all needing to be removed by hand, that after six hours they had made only 450 feet of progress.

Flory and Wilkenson were near the end of their reserves of hope. The batteries in their cap lamps were running very low now, and without good light it would be impossible to climb the escape ladders. They were down to their last tin of sausages. In a final desperate attempt to attract attention, they went once again to the station, and tried pulling the emergency cord.

At midday on Tuesday, exactly seven days after the fire had begun, a fresh team was sent down the four-foot shaft.

They reached the 4,800-foot level without problems. With great excitement they discovered footprints near the shaft, and the green telephone bag – unfastened. The team explored the drift for 1,000 feet towards the No. 10 shaft, but they found nothing. They called off the search and another descent was organized for later that afternoon.

Flory was peering hard at the dim light of his calendar watch – it was 5.30 p.m. on Tuesday 9 May – when he suddenly spotted a flash of light down by the four-foot shaft. Wilkenson could not believe him. Flory picked up the wrench and banged it against the water pipe. He saw the light again. Wilkenson flashed the locomotive light on and off and shouted, 'Over here!'

'Stay right there,' came the reply through the gloom.

Tom Wilkenson tried to smile as the rescuers approached, but broke into tears. 'Thank God you've come,' he cried. 'Thank God . . .'

Ron Flory was the first to go up in the torpedo to the 3,700-foot level. He was examined by a doctor, and offered the chance to go up to the surface immediately. 'No,' he said firmly. 'Tom and I were down there together. We'll go out together.'

At 8.20 p.m. on Tuesday, millions of television viewers watched as Ron Flory and Tom Wilkenson stepped out of the Sunshine Silver Mine. Bearded and bedraggled, they were the only two men out of ninety-three to have survived the disaster. As they walked out under the harsh glare of the television lights, Myrna and Frances were waiting for them.

Tom Wilkenson stayed on at the Sunshine Silver Mine. But not Ron Flory. 'I've had enough,' he said. 'I'm taking the State Governor's offer to relocate and be retrained for another job.'

17 Other dangers

Falling overboard

Your predicted survival time in cold water will be greatly increased if: you are wearing a flotation device; and you assume the HELP and HUDDLE positions (detailed below), rather than try to swim to safety.

Keep your clothing *on* – including shoes and hat. This helps flotation and every layer slows heat loss. Cling to whatever floats. Get as much of your body out of the water as possible, especially your head, through which you can lose 50 per cent of your body heat.

Assume the HELP and HUDDLE positions if possible – which is to say, if you are wearing or can improvise a flotation device.

HELP (Heat Escape Lessening Posture). If the head is not immersed, the greatest heat loss is at the sides of the chest and from the large blood vessels around the groin area. In the HELP position, the arms are held tightly into the sides of the body and the hands are held against the chest. The knees are drawn up to minimize groin area exposure to the cold water, and the legs are kept in contact with each other by crossing them at the ankles.

HUDDLE. Two people should huddle together chest to chest, with children (whose heat loss is faster) sandwiched between adults. Three people or more should press themselves together, making firm body contact against their sides. It's worth remembering that both HELP and HUDDLE positions can also be used in a lifeboat or life-raft, or even on a hillside, to minimize heat loss.

If you are clothed, but have no flotation device, you can improvise one (or more) with trousers, a shirt, a raincoat, a dress, a blouse, stockings – anything is worth a try. The principle is that you create a balloon by, say, taking off your trousers, tying the legs together, and flipping them overhead to trap air. (It does work: try it the next time you go for a swim.) If you have no flotation device and nothing to cling on to, try either floating on your face (it's easier than on your back) and snatching the occasional breath when you need it, or treading water very gently.

If you have absolutely no hope of rescue, start swimming for shore. But that's really the last resort, because the cold dramatically impairs even a strong swimmer's ability and judgement (the average person is unlikely to swim more than one kilometre in water at 10 °C) and activity increases heat loss by reducing the insulative effect of clothing and by stimulating blood circulation to arms and legs instead of keeping it close to the vital body core.

If you are injured and unable to adopt the HELP position, you can still survive in all but the coldest and roughest seas, using a technique called *survival floating*. The technique is based on two premises: that almost everyone will float while their lungs are full of air, and that it is much easier to float vertically than horizontally.

1 While floating vertically with both hands limply held at the sides, take a deep breath and hang relaxed in the water with your face below the surface.

2 As the need to breathe occurs, exhale through your nose slowly while raising your arms and crossing them in front of your face.

3 Then, as if parting a curtain, extend both arms and push downwards with your palms towards your sides, and at the same time tilt your head back.

4 As your mouth comes out of the water, take a breath, lower your head and relax again.

5 If you are relaxed with this technique, alternately switch between slow, horizontal movement towards shore and survival floating.

6 Even with cramp, it is possible to stay afloat this way. Relax the cramped muscle by slowly massaging it between breaths of air.

If other people need resuscitation, start at once, even in the water. And don't give up too soon, especially with children – a doctor in the USA, Martin Nemiroff, has pioneered research which has led to the reviving of young drowning victims after as long as forty minutes in the water. As with every other survival procedure, just hang on in there!

Earthquake

Remember the essentials: stay calm and think through the consequences of any action you plan to take. If necessary, tell others what to do, speaking in a firm and controlled voice – you are in charge.

If you're inside a building, stay inside until the shaking stops. Crouch under a desk or table, with your face away from windows and glass. If there is no desk to shelter under, stand in a strong doorway, against an interior wall, or in a corner away from an outside wall. Watch out for falling plaster, bricks, light fittings and other objects – and for high bookcases, shelves and other furniture that might slide or topple.

Don't go outside until after the shaking stops.

Don't use candles, matches or other open flames during the tremor. Douse all fires.

Don't use lifts, even if the power is still on – warping in the shaft could make the lift jam.

Don't use stairways unless you are certain that there is an exit and that there is light in the stairwells – there could be a blockage below.

If you're outside, avoid high buildings, walls, power lines and any other object that could fall on you. Do not run through the streets. If you are surrounded by high buildings, take shelter in the nearest strong-looking one. But if possible, move to an open area away from hazards.

If you're in a car, stop in the safest place available – preferably an open area. Stop as quickly as you can, but stay in the vehicle – it could be the best shelter you've got.

Lightning

When an electrical storm threatens, get inside a house or large building, or inside an all-metal vehicle.

Inside a house, do not use the telephone, except for emergencies – lightning may strike the outside lines. Close any open windows. Do not touch radiators, stoves, metal pipes, fireplaces, sinks or wiring. Do not touch or use plug-in electrical equipment or appliances such as radios, television sets, electric razors or toothbrushes, lamps or fridges. Do not shower or bathe during an electrical storm.

If you're caught out of doors, avoid the highest objects and structures around you – such as trees, hill-tops, antennae, telephone poles, electricity pylons and exposed sheds. Avoid being higher than the surrounding landscape in an open field, on a golf course, on the beach, or if you're fishing from a small boat. If necessary, take shelter in a ditch or ravine – but watch out for flash floods.

Don't stand underneath a natural lightning rod such as a tall, isolated tree in an open area. In a forest, seek shelter in a low area under a thick growth of small trees.

Don't stand in small, isolated sheds or other small structures in open areas.

Get out of, and away from, open water.

Don't use metal equipment such as a fishing rod or golf clubs. Remove your shoes if they have metal spikes. Don't work on or touch fences, power lines, pipelines, clothes lines, rails or other metal structures which could carry lightning to you from some distance away. Get away from tractors and other metal farm equipment, motorcycles, scooters, golf carts and bicycles. Stay away from overhead wires and railroad tracks.

Avoid sitting on moist or wet ground. Use a dry groundsheet, jacket or any other dry, non-conductive material or object.

If you're inside a vehicle, don't touch any metal part. If you're on a large boat, stay inside. If possible, get off a small boat and go ashore.

If you're isolated in a level field or area and you feel your hair stand on end or your skin tingle – indicating that lightning is about to strike – drop to your knees and bend forward, putting your hands on your knees. Do not lie flat on the ground: you must ensure that as small an area as possible is touching the ground, whilst not acting as a conductor.

The natural inclination in a really violent storm is to seek shelter, especially if the rain is driving down hard. But don't go into a cave unless it gives you at least ten feet headroom and three feet on either side. Small caves and hollows in the rock are often simply expansions of natural fissures: as such, they will conduct earth currents. For the same reason, don't shelter at the base of a cliff or peak, or under large boulders.

The best position is out in the open, on a broken scree slope. Sit on top of something dry with your knees up and your hands in your lap. Don't support yourself on your hands or by leaning back. The object is to keep your points of contact with the ground as close together as possible, so that any current flowing along the ground would tend to pass through a non-vital part of your body, such as your bottom!

Crowds

At the first sign of a surging crowd, try to edge away from anything solid, such as a wall, barrier or pillar. If the crowd is small – too many people trying to get out of an emergency exit, for instance – try to calm them by shouting some of your finest humorous understatements, or by issuing controlled, authoritative orders.

In a crowd stampede, aim to ride it out like a cork on the sea. Take a deep breath, and tense your whole body against pressure. Bunch your arms in front of your stomach (small children should be picked up even if they can walk – shield them inside your bunched arms). Now lift both feet off the ground so that they are not trampled on, and let yourself be carried with the flow. Try to keep moving all the time, and work yourself away from solid obstructions but towards the edge of the crowd. If your feet touch the ground, spring up again.

Trapped in a lift

Follow any emergency procedures detailed near the lift buttons, and extinguish any cigarettes.

If you're alone, sit down and wait. Go through your wallet, or any reading matter you may have with you. If you have a pen, write a shopping list or list of odd jobs to be done at home. Anything to keep your mind off the situation.

If the lift is crowded, announce *immediately* – before the first surge of panic hits anyone – that you know what you are doing. Get everyone to turn so that they are facing the rear of the lift; it may not achieve much, but it sounds good. If there is room, all sit down. If you know the people, and their talents, get the joker to tell a few jokes, and so on. If you feel that panic is mounting, now is the moment to announce that you are a member of the police force or SAS or a doctor or whatever you can think of, or that you will personally cause considerable bodily damage to anyone who dares to panic and jeopardize your own safety.

Car under water

If the car windows are open when it plunges into the water, if the car floats the right way up, and if the water does not come up to window level (yet), simply get out of the window as fast as you can.

It's very hard to escape from a car once water is pouring in through the windows. The doors won't open, either, because of outside pressure, until the car is nearly full of water. So if water *is* coming in, do as much of the following as time and your memory allow:

1 Close all windows.

2 Shut any open ventilators.

3 Release the seat belts.

4 Switch on all the lights as a signal, even in daytime.

5 Don't try to open the doors.

6 Wait for the car to tilt, motor end down. Take advantage of the air pockets.

7 Grasp the door handle, ready for your getaway. When the water level stops rising, the pressures outside and inside have been equalized. Take a deep breath, and . . .

8 . . . open the door and escape. If it doesn't open, unwind the window and go out that way.

9 Swim up, breathing out as you go.

If there are more than one of you in the car, either leave all at the same time, or form a human chain, to make sure no one is left behind.

Surviving a nuclear war

I don't want anyone, anywhere to believe a nuclear war is survivable: if you think that, you might go ahead and have one.

Survival kits

The previous pages have outlined the rules of survival, and the various techniques which will help you carry them out – techniques that will enable you to secure fire, shelter, water, signals and food, under most conditions. Often the methods involve improvisation, using natural materials. The methods work. But I can assure you that it is a damned sight easier to light a fire with a match than with a bow drill, and to slip into a survival tube tent than to build a lean-to shelter!

So now is the time to plan your own personal survival kit, tailored to your activity, your needs and the weather, and convenient enough to be carried with you at all times: even the most minimal kit can save the day.

A home-made kit has some real advantages over even the best-designed commercially available kits. Not only can you tailor it to your needs, but you will know each item and why you included it. By and large, that's better than breaking open a bought kit in an emergency and wondering what various items are for – or why they aren't there!

First, start with a suitable container, since your activity will usually dictate the maximum size of the kit. For casual walks from the car, or day-long rambles, something that fits in a small day backpack is ideal. A small pack can carry much survival equipment, and can also double as a carrier of your camera, lunch, extra clothes and water bottles. Make sure it's brightly coloured. If you do a lot of backpacking over periods longer than a day, make sure that your survival-kit container can fit in a side-pocket of your main rucksack. You may prefer a bum-bag to a back pack, particularly if you're going skiing.

18 Walker's survival equipment

Day pack

Basic

Protection:
survival bag or blanket;
wax-coated matches or special lifeboat matches;
candle stub.

Location:
signal mirror;
whistle;
small torch.

Water:
puritabs or similar.

Food:
concentrated glucose – tablets or mint cake.

The survival blanket is a compact and lightweight sheet of aluminized non-stretch polyester, which will provide instant protection from the elements, and reflect body heat back to the body. It is both windproof and waterproof, and will stay flexible even under freezing conditions. With its shiny reflective surface, it can also be used as a signal device.

Puritabs are a quick and convenient way to sterilize water. The tablets (or similar ones) will kill bacteria, but will not of course remove dirt and suspended matter.

Comprehensive

A comprehensive day pack contains everything in the 'basic' pack, plus these extra items.

Whole candle. Preferably a tallow one, which will light in any temperature. A four-inch candle will weigh less than one ounce and burn for almost four hours, if protected from the wind. Practically indestructible, even if you drop it or soak it in water, it will provide light for reading, and heat for a snow cave or bivi bag. A candle burning inside a tin can makes a heater for a small, snug shelter. A candle will ignite fuel so damp that matches alone would never ignite it. You can rub the candle on the heels and toes of your socks if your shoes or boots begin to chafe, or use it to lubricate zippers. You can use a candle flame for cooking on, or heating up water. It can lubricate the hand-held socket used in the fire drill and bow (see chapter 4). Melted wax will seal the seams of pre-heated leather boots. And best of all, you can even use a tallow candle as emergency food!

Three condoms. The condom is one of the most useful survival-kit items. It can be used as a water carrier if you support it by placing it in a sock or shirt sleeve; as a covering for small items to prevent rust or exposure; as a protective covering for wounds, or to keep them closed; or to keep fire tinder dry. Two stretched together can be used as a catapult, and they can be blown up and used for fishing (see chapter 8) or as an emergency flotation device. Use only the cheap, non-lubricated, heavy-duty ones.

Small compass. A button compass is very useful and easily packed away. But if you have room, a Silva-type compass is far better.

Fishing equipment. About thirty yards of monofilament line will suffice, together with six very small hooks, six swivels, weights and a cork for a float.

Snares. Buy ready-made ones, consisting of brass wire and cord. Remember, the more traps you set, the more chances you have of catching your food. Have about six in your kit.

Small magnifying-glass. Useful for checking wounds and tick sites, and for lighting fires.

Parachute cord.
Plastic bags.
Safety pins.
Heliograph.
Mini-flares.
Razor blade.

Needle and thread. Useful for removing thorns and splinters, as well as repairing clothing.

Rubber tubing. Useful as a spring for a trap, and for obtaining drinking water from difficult or inaccessible places, such as small depressions in fallen logs, or among rocks. You can also use it in a solar still. An appropriate size would be outside diameter 5 mm, length 600 mm.

Plastic film container of sugar. Used as a fire-lighter, with potassium permanganate.

Plastic film container of potassium permanganate. A very versatile item. For first aid: dissolve a few grains in clean water to make an excellent antiseptic solution. For water purification: add a few grains to a litre of water, leave it to stand for thirty minutes, and drink. (Ignore the red colour.) As a snow marker: sprinkled on snow, it makes an excellent signal. For fire-lighting: put half a teaspoon of the chemical and a teaspoon of sugar in a shallow 'bowl' depression in a piece of dry wood. Rotate a stick, with a blunt rounded end, in this depression, between the palms of your hands. Even more dramatic, if you have anti-freeze, is to put a teaspoon-sized heap of the chemical on a sheet of paper or on dry leaves, add a few drops of anti-freeze, and scrunch the bundle into a ball. In a few seconds it will burst into flames.

Writing materials. A sheet of waterproof paper (take a whole notebook if you've got room), plus a pencil stub.

Insect repellent and sunscreen cream.

Plastic film container of curry powder. If you don't include this in your kit, you've obviously never eaten a rat or newt in your life!

Small pack of disposable cleansing wipes. Useful for general cleansing. And as anyone who has ever suffered from 'walker's bottom' will tell you, these are indispensable.

And finally, take a copy of this book.

First aid kit

Basic

Sticking plasters;
roller bandage;
triangular bandage;
small roll of plain sticking plaster;
plain gauze pad, 150 mm × 900 mm;
solmin – or other aspirin not requiring water.

Comprehensive

Extra quantities of 'basic' items;
sterile cleansing wipes;
scissors;
tweezers;
field dressings;
safety pins;
inflatable splints.

Sample journey plan for hikes and outings

You should leave this with a friend, relation, pub landlord, boarding-house owner or even at a police station – but don't forget to notify them of your safe arrival, or of cancellation of the outing.

Date . . .
Name of leader . . .
Address . . .
Telephone number . . .
In the event of emergency, please notify . . .
Telephone . . .

Major route – with planned stops, and estimated time and date of arrival and departure for each location

Alternative route – if conditions change, or the planned route is impassable

Description of vehicles – any which might be involved, for example, the car you have left in a car park

If we have not returned by . . . please notify . . . (name and telephone number of appropriate search and rescue team, or police station)

Now list the *name, address, age* and *telephone number* of each member of the outing. List also the name of a contact for each person on the outing – 'In the event of an emergency, please notify . . .'

Include any special information about any member of the party which would aid in rescue or survival – if there is a health problem, rescuers can deliver vital medical supplies.

Larry Ritchey

'If at first you don't succeed . . .'

Larry Ritchey was thirty-five, a keen outdoors man, and proud. When he found himself unemployed in 1982, he decided that a solo hiking expedition would be the perfect way to boost his sagging morale.

He loaded his pick-up on Thursday 25 November. Leaving a map of his route with some friends – half-joking as he asked them to tell the police if he was not back by five o'clock the following Tuesday – he headed sixty miles east of his home in Portland, Oregon, to the spectacular slopes of Mount Hood in the Cascade Mountains.

Pulling off the main road, he slept in the back of the pick-up. Then at dawn he hitched a lift for seven miles back down the road, with the intention of snow-shoeing down a ridge below the road, circling a lake, crossing White River Canyon, and climbing back to the road along another ridge. By Monday afternoon he should comfortably have finished the thirty-mile trek, and be back where he had parked the pick-up.

Ritchey was well dressed for the conditions in thermal underwear, woollen trousers and shirt, long mitts, a parka and rubber-soled boots. The alternate snow showers and sunshine which he encountered on the first two days presented no problems to him.

Black snow clouds were massing from the north as he reached White River Canyon at noon on Sunday. He had to negotiate massive boulders and icy streams, and his progress slowed. Two hours later the snow began to fall, so heavily that he had to feel his way ahead with a ski-stick. The ground sloped away, but Ritchey continued a straight traverse of the incline. Before long his snow-shoes were packed with snow. Leaning on his ski-sticks, he knocked one shoe against his leg to clear it, and took a pace forward before clearing the other shoe.

Suddenly the snow-shoe disappeared through the ground

and Ritchey fell forwards, hitting his forehead so hard on the snow that he was then pitched backwards. Then all he can remember is plummeting downwards through the inky blackness of the chasm. His fall was broken with a splash, and freezing water instantly soaked into his clothes and chilled him. Temporarily winded by the fall, Ritchey pulled himself to his feet. His rucksack had cushioned the impact, and he was unhurt. He retrieved some matches from the waterproof container in his pocket, and lit one of the five candles that were in his rucksack. At once, his predicament was clear to him.

The subterranean stream in which he stood was about a foot deep, and was in a large cavern of snow, rock and ice, about ten feet wide and fourteen feet high. A patch of grey light, some six feet by three, signified where he had fallen through the canyon floor. The sheer rock walls back up to it were unscalable.

Downstream, the water disappeared through a wall of rock. Certain that the stream would surface further upstream, Ritchey set off with a candle in his hand to investigate. He waded some two hundred feet into the cave, with stones falling from the roof into the water, and sudden flurries of silt. Then a sixth sense made him stop dead, and he watched the candle flame. It was burning brightly, and steadily – but without a single flicker. That could mean only one thing: there was no wind and, therefore, no exit.

By the time he had retraced his steps, the oblong patch of light in the roof had faded. It was night. With any chance of excape now closed off until daybreak, Ritchey began to worry about the onset of hypothermia. His clothes were soaking wet, the chill aching into his bones. A hot meal or drink was out of the question: his gas stove had been broken in the fall. So he rehydrated some freeze-dried beef and eggs in the stream and ate them cold. He chewed on some jerky – dried strips of beef – and drank some water in which he had swilled a tea-bag. Then, to save the candle, he extinguished it and propped himself against a wall in the cold, pitch darkness.

When Ritchey closed his eyes, he pictured the large boulders that were scattered around in the snow outside, and he suddenly remembered the thirty-foot nylon climbing rope in his rucksack. Here was hope: he reasoned that, by tying a heavy stone to one end, he ought to be able to hurl the rope out of the hole and use it as a grapnel.

He slept little that night. At daybreak, he put his plan into action. Several times the stone anchor seemed to drag over an obstruction, but it always dropped back down into the cave. After thirty or forty throws, he took a rest.

When he resumed, he decided to be more systematic. This time, he would work the anchor through all 360 degrees of a circle.

As daylight failed, Ritchey had moved through much of the circle. Making a mental note of where to resume in the morning, he now turned his attention to the problem of how to keep his feet dry through the following night. A lean man for his height, Ritchey had little reserve of fat for his body to break down into calories. Everything he could do to help retard the process – like stopping his wet feet from being heat sinks – would prolong his chances of rescuing himself. He piled together heap after heap of stones to stand on, but the stones were too smooth and wet to hold together and each pile collapsed under his weight. He had to resign himself to another night of fitful dozing against the wall.

In the morning, he started once more to throw the stone anchor up and out of the roof. On one throw the stone missed the hole and thudded against something inside the cave. Three feet of tree root, as thick as his arm, were projecting out of the rock face near the top of the wall – too far from the hole to be of any help with his escape, but it might provide a means of hoisting himself out of the water should he still find himself in the cave that night.

Even when the stone occasionally broke free from the rope, Ritchey would mechanically tie on another, and continue with his circle. Recalling his days as a salesman, Ritchey now told himself that the problem in hand was similar in many ways to the process of selling: try enough people, and somebody will buy. Throw enough stones, and one of them will bite.

Late on Tuesday afternoon, the stone caught on something and held. Ritchey tested the rope, then tied his rucksack, ski-sticks and single remaining snow-shoe to the free end, and began to climb. Hand over hand in his thick mitts, until his feet were clear of the water. Then, with a cruel suddenness, the rope went slack and he was falling back down into the stream.

Eyes firmly shut and fists clenched, Ritchey shouted and shook with frustration and disappointment. Summoning the will to start all over again, he threw the stone several times in the direction of the obstruction which had, however temporarily, given him some hope of escape.

It was now evening, and Ritchey started throwing towards the tree root. When the rope was over it, he was able to lift himself clear of the water by passing one end of the rope through his belt, over his shoulder and between his legs, and hauling on the other end. By tying the two rope ends together, he created a sling in which he could hang. He was cramped and uncomfortable, but no longer subject to the numbing coldness of the stream, and he sank into an exhausted sleep.

Larry Ritchey slept for twenty-four hours, unaware that his friends had reported him overdue to the police on Tuesday evening, and that on Wednesday volunteer searchers on snow-mobiles had scoured the ridges and canyon terrain without success, following the map he had left behind. Two helicopters also joined the search, but were soon grounded by dense fog and the general bad weather conditions.

Ritchey was roused by the pain of restricted circulation in his legs. He felt very weak as he climbed out of the sling, but knew he must not succumb. His only chance of escape was by the success of the stone anchor, and for that he needed all his strength. He ate strips of raw bacon from his rucksack, together with the rest of his dehydrated food supplies.

Later that morning, as the snow-mobiles were again out

searching unsuccessfully for the missing hiker, Ritchey threw the stone – and it held. But the moment his weight was on it, the stone flew back down into the cave. A few hours later, the same thing happened. This time, Ritchey responded to failure by belting out his favourite country and western song, as loud as he could. As the strains of 'Your Cheatin' Heart' echoed around the cave, Ritchey was aware of how slurred the words sounded. He suspected that he was falling victim to hypothermia – already shivering constantly, he now found it difficult to walk without stumbling. It was imperative that he get himself out of there, especially as the water level had risen after heavy rain to above his knees.

Long into the night he hurled the stone. Quite apart from the prospect of escape, he had to keep moving just to keep warm – to sleep now would be fatal. Exactly when, Ritchey cannot remember, but at last the stone jammed. The rope was taut and took his weight. Ritchey frantically tied on his equipment and started to climb as best he could in his weakened condition. The mittens slipped on the rope, so he tucked them into a pocket. With bare and painfully numb fingers, he inched himself upwards, periodically clenching the rope between his teeth for a rest.

At last he got his reward: the feel of rain and wind on his face. As he neared the surface, Ritchey kicked up with his right leg, jamming his boot and calf into the snow. With a twist of his upper body, he got his head clear and completed the bridge. His body was across the hole. With one last jerk, he rolled over and lay panting with a mixture of fatigue and elation in the dark night.

Tired beyond belief, Ritchey hauled himself to his knees. He saw that the stone anchor had caught around a limb of a dead fir tree, just five feet from the hole. Hauling up the equipment on the other end of the rope, he wearily searched in the snow until he found his lost snow-shoe. His body desperately craved rest, but Ritchey forced himself to keep going. He walked and stumbled for ten miles through the night, through relentless rain, until he heard the sound of a truck engine in the distance. Scrambling over a high bank of snow on his hands and knees, he found himself on the main road, in the glare of approaching headlights. Just seconds later he was sitting in the warmth of the motorist's car.

When he recounted his ordeal to the gathering of journalists, Ritchey said that he was satisfied that he had done everything possible to get himself out of the cave. He recalled how he had repeated to himself, over and over, the old saying: 'If at first you don't succeed, try, try again.'

He did admit to a reporter from the *New York Times*, however, that on occasion, 'I thought there was a good chance I wouldn't make it.'

But Larry Ritchey was a trier, and he made it.

19 Car survival kit

The equipment listed below will make it possible to deal with most emergencies. For a trip along main roads with service stations, phone boxes and police patrols, you won't need to carry all of it. Just think of the greatest number of vehicle and weather problems you might encounter on your journey, and stock accordingly. All of the equipment should be carried *in addition to* a standard basic survival kit, which should be stored in the glove compartment or under the seat. If you are trapped in your seat, it may be critical to have signal devices readily to hand: mini-flares, a pen-torch and a signal mirror should therefore be mounted with Velcro fastening above the sun visor – but beware of petrol vapour when using them.

CB radio;
fire extinguisher;
emergency heater – something along the lines of a metal tray or baking tray, loaded with squat, wide-based candles;
shovel and axe;
torch;
flares;
vehicle spares: fan belt, fuses, bulbs, hoses and clamps;
battery jump-leads;
tow rope;
insulating tape;
a petrol can which will not explode – the kind which is filled with wire wool;
plastic bags, of various sizes;
kitchen roll;

container of water;
first-aid kit;
sunglasses;
old clothes;
blankets or sleeping bags;
high-carbohydrate foods, canned (with a can opener) or in
sealed packets: sweets, biscuits, unsalted nuts, dried fruit,
muesli bars;
sheet of heavy-duty plastic.

John Vihtelic

'If John Vihtelic is still alive out there, he's going to have to
help himself.'

On Tuesday 7 September 1976, John Vihtelic stepped off a
plane in Portland, Oregon with a few days in hand before
starting a ten-day training course in the servicing of kidney
dialysis machines. After the course, he would be setting up
a service territory in Philadelphia for Drake-Willock
Systems, the manufacturers, and marrying his childhood
sweetheart Mary Fahner, a teacher from his home town of
Whitehall, Michigan.

As it turned out, the twenty-seven-year-old former Green
Beret medic was to spend the whole duration of the course
trapped in the wreckage of a borrowed car, 160 feet down a
ravine in the Cascade Mountains.

His ordeal started on the Saturday after his arrival in
Portland. He borrowed a station-wagon from Drake-
Willock, and headed north with the idea of exploring
Mount Rainier National Park in southern Washington
State. He spent most of the day walking on the
snow-covered slopes of Mount Rainier. Then the weather
closed in and forced him back to the car. With a few hours of
daylight left, he headed south – not back to Portland but to
the Mount Hood area, a little more than 150 miles away. He

intended visiting Gifford Pinchot National Forest, which seemed a feasible detour in the time available. But what Vihtelic did not realize was that the route he had chosen was one of the most difficult in the whole region.

The rough, single-lane gravel track was cut out of the mountain-side. With his headlights bumping and lurching in the murky twilight, Vihtelic had to concentrate hard to keep the car on the twisting road. It was early evening – and two hours after he had left Mount Rainier – when the car hit a bump in the gravel and veered out of control towards the edge of the road. The next thing he knew, the car was cartwheeling off the edge and down a steep ravine, and all he could hear was the sickening crunch of compressing metal.

When the crumpled station-wagon finally came to rest at the bottom of the ravine, Vihtelic was lying face down on the inside of the roof. Miraculously, he had escaped with just a few cuts and bruises. But when he tried to move, he discovered that his left foot was trapped.

As he twisted around in the cramped confines of the wreckage, he noticed that his watch said 8 p.m. It was now almost dark, but sufficient light remained for him to see what was gripping his foot. A two-foot length of tree root, some six inches in diameter, had come through the windscreen and pinned the limb against the dashboard.

Vihtelic switched off the ignition, then there was nothing else that he could do. The full enormity of his predicament hit him like a wave, and in panic he tried to wrench his foot free. Long into the night he kept jerking and pulling on it, until the pain became too much for him. Then he pulled his sleeping bag over himself as best he could, and dozed.

At daybreak, he was able to take stock of things. To his horror, he saw for the first time how badly damaged the car was – and how lucky he was to be alive. The roof was crushed in places to below window level; on the driver's side, there was just enough window space for him to wriggle through. But until he could free his foot, it was a space he could only reach by twisting agonizingly on his left leg.

Just a few feet from the wreckage was a swollen mountain stream, whose roar echoed around the ravine. The car lay close up to the base of the steep slope down which it had fallen, its muddy chassis blending in with the earth and grey rock.

From the road 160 feet above, the car was practically invisible. Vihtelic did not realize this when he looked up through the trees early that morning and saw a car go by. He felt sure he had been spotted – rescue would surely follow. But as the day went on, more and more cars went past the point where the station-wagon had left the gravel road, and no one showed any sign of having spotted the wreckage.

Some of the vehicles belonged to the park rangers who were already searching for him – alerted by Vihtelic's boss at Drake-Willock, who knew the grim reputation of the Rainier region, the rangers took only a few hours to check all 110 miles of park road and ravines. Before the day was out, the head ranger reported that Vihtelic's station-wagon was not in Rainier Park.

Food was not an immediate problem for the trapped driver. He could reach the huckleberries on a bush near the wreck, and he managed to reach an apple that remained from his picnic lunch. As a medical technician he knew enough about nutrition and body chemistry to realize that, weighing in at more than thirteen stone, his body could call on its reserves of fat and muscle tissue for quite a while before starvation set in. He was helped further a day or two later, when field mice discovered a lump of cheese and dragged it within his range – they did, however, eat the crackers that went with it!

However, John Vihtelic was desperately thirsty, and water was now an absolute priority. Thousands of gallons of it were flowing tantalizingly close to him, just twelve feet or so beyond the window of the wrecked car. His own technical ingenuity came to the rescue. Out of the heavy-gauge metal strips that pinned the lining to the roof, he improvised a sort of fishing rod. Then, with cord from his sleeping bag, nylon string from a tennis racket, and

233

lengths of electrical wire ripped from the door panels and roof, he made up a fishing line. One end was tied to the rod, the other to a T-shirt. By easing the rod and line through the buckled driver's window, he was able to cast the T-shirt into the swollen stream. It was then simply a matter of hauling the sodden garment back into the car and wringing out the water into his mouth.

By Wednesday following the crash, Vihtelic's elder brother Frank had flown to Portland from his home in Detroit and was trying to piece together the fragments of evidence which might lead him to John. A woman in the town of Ashford, on the perimeter of the park, reported having seen a man who answered John's description and who had asked directions to Portland the previous Saturday morning. Unfortunately this led Frank Vihtelic to concentrate his search in the area west of Rainier, rather than to the south.

Meanwhile John was attacking his next problem, escape from the wreckage. His attempts with a spanner to jab at the tree root, and then twist and split the wood fibres, were getting him nowhere. They were painful, too: often his blows with the heavy tool would hit his ankle instead of the six-inch root.

His next manoeuvre was to try rocking his body backwards and forwards, in the hope of lifting the car off the root. When that didn't work either, he tried to puncture the spare tyre in order to retrieve the jack behind it, hoping to be able to lift the car free. But this, too, was unsuccessful.

It was now Friday, and with a weekend coming up John's morale lifted. The weather had improved, and the more adventurous families of Oregon might come to the wilderness for a drive or a picnic. There had to be a good chance that he would be spotted. Prising the mirror from one of the car's sun-visors, Vihtelic attached it to his tennis racket with masking tape. Although the sun never fell directly on to the wreck, there were two and a half hours in the afternoons when it came close enough for him to reach with this new outstretched signalling device. During that time he could flash distress signals at traffic on the mountain road.

Vihtelic's guesswork was right. Saturday dawned bright and clear – perfect picnic weather. Even though he could only signal during the short period when the sun fell on to his improvised heliograph, he managed that weekend to flash the mirror at dozens of cars travelling along the gravel road 160 feet above. But by Sunday evening, eight days after the crash, his frustration reached an angry climax. Why the hell couldn't anybody see him? Why was it that he could see them, but not the other way round?

Two more of Vihtelic's brothers now flew into Portland: Larry an airline pilot, and his younger brother Joe, an engineer. Three more of John's friends from his home town were with them, including Tom Fahner, his fiancée's brother.

They hired cars and split into three teams of two – one man driving, the other perched on the bumper to get a better view into the ravines. They carried leaflets with John's description, which they handed out at cafés, restaurants, hotels, garages, local police stations – every public place they could think of.

One policeman told them: 'We have over one hundred missing persons on our books. If John Vihtelic is still alive out there, he's going to have to help himself.'

Still trapped in the wreckage, Vihtelic was coming to the same conclusion himself. Trucks followed that route in a steady stream that week. Not one of them responded to the flashing mirror. After counting a hundred vehicles on the Friday, he knew the terrible truth at last: the wreckage was invisible. He was invisible. Nobody was going to help him. He had to get out alone. And just to make matters worse, night temperatures would soon be dropping to below freezing. If he hadn't got himself out by the following weekend, he would surely perish.

The rescue team became more and more despondent. Money and hope were both now in short supply. On

Saturday morning, Joe Vihtelic and Tom Fahner handed out leaflets in the Mount Hood area, then headed back to Rainier for a final sweep of the ravines and gullies. To save themselves a bit of time, they took a short-cut through the mountains. Without realizing it, they were driving the exact route – in reverse – that John had followed. Tom Fahner was driving. Joe was on look-out. Just before seven o'clock that evening, Tom slowed right down to negotiate a hairpin bend, then accelerated on up the hill.

That made them roughly the five-hundredth vehicle not to spot the wreckage 160 feet below.

On Monday, the fifteenth day after the crash, Vihtelic made his decision. The root had to go – even at the expense of losing his foot. With customary ingenuity, he emptied his small suitcase of its contents and threw it towards the stream. Then he fashioned a metal strip from the car into a sort of shepherd's crook, and used it to scoop small rocks towards the open suitcase. Time and again, he would manoeuvre a rock carefully up the side of the suitcase, only to see it fall back when it was just inches from the rim. At last, near evening, he succeeded in getting a rock the size of a small melon into the case. With the shepherd's crook he then pulled his prize back into the car. After all this time, he at last had something with which to hammer the spanner into the root. The steel began to bite into the grain of the wood, but darkness and exhaustion intervened.

At dawn, he started again. His foot had been trapped for sixteen days, and as he cut into the root and the pressure eased, blood surged back excruciatingly into the parts of it which were still alive. The pain was almost unbearable, but just three hours later he was free. Scrambling through the buckled window, he waved his arms manically in the air and shouted: 'I'm free! I'm free!'

Using a branch from a tree as a crutch, he could now begin the treacherous climb back up to the road. It took him an hour. At the top, he lay down by the side of the road, and turned his face towards the sun. It was the first time he had felt its warmth and light in the sixteen days of his ordeal.

Vihtelic was still sunbathing when a truck driver found him and called for an ambulance.

Doctors reported his condition as 'remarkable'. He had lost nearly two stone in weight, but was otherwise in good health. Much tissue had died in his foot, however, and the limb had to be amputated just above the ankle. After just three weeks in Emanuel Hospital in Portland, John Vihtelic was discharged, and allowed home to the hero's welcome he deserved.

In the words of Elaine Webb, a deputy in the Skamania County sheriff's office: 'The ingenuity this guy displayed in keeping himself alive was phenomenal . . .'

20 Boat panic bag

With a bit of shoving, all these items will fit into an ordinary waterproofed sailing holdall. The bag should be stowed as near to the tiller or helm as possible, and you should keep your boat's supplies of flares in it as well. This is a list of the *minimum* extra supplies for four people, over and above what you'll find with your life-raft.

Small portable transmitter/distress beacon;
six 500 g packs of compressed glucose and vitaminized survival biscuits;
100 multi-vitamin tablets;
first-aid kit;
insect repellent and sunscreen cream;
torch, with spare batteries;
heliograph;
four spare red rocket flares;
four spare red hand flares;
four smoke flares;
four white flares;
two fluorescent dyes;
fishing kit – including some large hooks with which to improvise a gaff/spear;
solar stills (as many as you can afford and room allows);
two knives;
compass;
two sponges;
half-filled water containers;
portable bilge pump;
repair kit – the plastic patches and adhesives used for

inflatable swimming pools are best;

two inflatable beds of dimensions matching those of the raft interior (there is nothing like them for comfort, when the bottom is freezing cold and being bumped by a big fish, and as a last resort, they become mini-rafts);

as much cordage as there is room for – parachute cord is best;

tins of carbohydrate foods (which retain water in the organism, and are almost entirely lacking in the basic fish diet);

can of mussels – for bait;

plankton net;

antibiotics;

antiseptics;

inflatable plastic splints – not only an excellent first-aid item, these can also serve as containers or floats;

plenty of plastic bags, in different sizes;

stainless steel scissors – for cutting up fish, turtles, birds;

underwater mask and snorkel – useful for checking damage underneath the raft, and for gathering the shellfish and seaweed that colonize underneath (the mask can also become a sun visor, if the glass is smeared with fish or turtle blood);

heavy gardening gloves – useful when handling fish or flares;

towel;

sewing kit;

packs of cleansing wipes;

toothbrush, toothpaste and sea soap;

waterproof notebooks and pencils;

books;

four survival blankets;

warmpacks – for instant heat.

Steve Callahan

'I love all of you . . . I will fight to survive, to rejoin your company . . .'

The sickening crash against the yacht's hull came just before midnight on 4 February 1982. A few minutes before, Steve Callahan had settled down on his bunk. Now tons of seawater cascaded into the cabin, and the boat seemed on the point of sinking. 'This is it,' he remembers thinking. 'I'm going to die.' Snatching up a knife, he fought his way topside, clad only in a T-shirt and underpants. Suddenly the boat started to list, and he escaped as fast as he could through the hatch. The bow was already completely submerged, and waves were breaking over the deck.

Callahan cut the life-raft adrift, and yanked the inflation cord. As he leapt aboard, the anti-collision strobe light on the yacht's mast short-circuited in the water and began to flash urgently over the sea. Callahan found two cabbages and a tin of coffee floating near the boat and retrieved them from the water. He also managed to cut away part of the mainsail. But he knew that to be sure of survival he would need his emergency 'panic bag', which was lashed inside the cabin. Tying the raft's cord to the stern, he waded back aboard. The cabin was awash, battered by nine-foot waves. To get to the survival kit he would have to dive into the dark water.

'If she sank while I was down there,' he recalls thinking, 'I'd die. But I'd die just as dead, and slowly, if I didn't have more than what was on the raft. I was in there for several minutes trying to get things out. I'd come up and get a breath of air in between waves . . .'

Working mainly by feel in the frightening blackness, Callahan retrieved his sodden sleeping bag, a floating cushion – and his panic bag. He had to come back up for air several times before he finally managed to cut through the cords. Disaster struck when he struggled back up towards the deck. The hatch was shut, held closed by tons of water.

Lungs near to bursting, Callahan scrabbled frantically to open it. He could do nothing to budge it. Suddenly, of its own accord, it blew open. Callahan heaved himself on to the deck, choking and gasping. Exhausted, he managed to re-board the raft and secure it to the stern of the wallowing wreck with a long cord. If the boat was still afloat in the morning he would try to go back on board, to plug the holes or at least get water, food and clothes. The seas grew stronger, making sleep impossible. For Steve Callahan, this was to be the first of seventy-six wretched nights spent adrift.

The twenty-nine-year-old boat-builder from Maine had set sail from the Canary Islands on January 26 in his twenty-two-foot sloop, *Napoleon Solo*. He had built the boat by hand the previous summer, and entered it in the 1982 Mini Transat, a single-handed sailing race from Penzance to La Coruna in Spain, and then on across the Atlantic to Antigua in the West Indies. He had been forced out of the race with bow damage but now, after repairs, he had sailed 800 miles in seven days. With luck and fair winds his self-designed, home-made ocean cruiser seemed likely to reach the Caribbean island of Antigua ahead of his scheduled arrival date of 24 February. But now Steve Callahan found himself adrift in darkness on a hostile ocean, in a seven-foot circular raft.

Just before dawn the thirty-foot cord connecting the raft to *Solo* snapped. Designed to break under load rather than let the raft be dragged down by wreckage, it could not take the strain imposed by the heavy seas. The flashing light on the mast grew smaller and smaller as the two craft drifted apart, then it vanished altogether.

For the next twenty-four hours, gale-force winds whipped up waves as high as twenty feet. They broke over the tiny raft, often submerging it. Callahan had suffered deep cuts on his back and thighs while struggling to escape from the boat's flooded cabin. He also quickly developed salt-water sores on his knees and elbows, which made bailing – with his salvaged coffee tin – a painful operation.

By his own reckoning, Callahan was 450 miles east of the nearest shipping lanes, between New York and South Africa, and was drifting in a westerly current. He knew it would be at least twenty days before his family even began to suspect that he was in trouble and raised the alarm.

In all, his survival kit consisted of eight pints of water, three pounds of food, a distress-signal radio, two waterproof torches, three solar stills (each capable of producing a pint of fresh water daily – as long as there was sufficient sunshine for the condensation process), a speargun, flares, an air pump, a rocket-gun, ropes and cords, a set of utensils and a plastic box containing navigational charts and a manual on sea survival. During lulls in the gales, he listened to the signals being broadcast by his radio, studied the chart and made plans. He read in the survival manual that a man can live for thirty days without food, but only ten without water. The solar stills had no chance of functioning in the present conditions, and so Callahan immediately rationed himself to half a pint of water per day. He ate little.

After nearly two days of transmission, he switched off the radio, accepting that no one was within range of its signals. He found himself thinking about his parents and family back in Maine, and resolved that he was going to survive. Somehow, he swore, he was going to make it home.

He began keeping a log. Every day he would evaluate his situation: 'With what I have now, I can last — more days.'

'At the beginning,' he says, 'my chances of making it even to the shipping lanes were very, very slim. Making it to the Caribbean was probably one in billions.'

After four more days the storm ended. The solar stills were not yet working, and his food supplies were almost exhausted. Drifting westwards, carried by the North Equatorial Current towards the Antilles, life soon began to form around the raft. An eco-system evolved. 'Anything floating at sea becomes an island,' Callahan explains. 'Barnacles start growing on it. These attract fish. Fish attract other fish. I would pick up seaweed and there'd be little crabs or shrimp in it.' First, flat-bodied, pouty-mouthed trigger fish appeared. They tasted awful. Then a flashing, irridescent school of some fifty or so dorados suddenly showed up. Highly prized as a delicacy, these brilliant blue game fish are common in tropical waters, ranging from three to six feet in length. These specimens weighed about twenty pounds each. 'They came closer and closer to the raft until I could spear them. I was their island. They would go off to fish, then come back. During the night they would surround the raft, cruise right along with me, just stay there all night long.'

Callahan took to calling them his 'little doggies' (they have a toothy, canine grin), and felt buoyed up by their companionship. Watching them leap several feet out of the water was a big joy to him. He came to recognize them individually. 'Each one definitely had a personality. Some just loved to come up and bang the bottom of the raft hard. Others would hit it, but softly . . .'

He calculated his approximate speed by timing the passage of heavy seaweed. He estimated his progress at between fifteen and thirty miles a day. He checked his direction at night by sighting the Pole Star and the Southern Cross, and by day through the positions of the rising and setting sun. He tied pencils into a rough sextant, and by sighting it on the Pole Star and the horizon he could guess at his latitude.

One day the raft was attacked by a shark. Tearing at the water-filled ballast pockets hanging below, it only retreated when Callahan thrust hard at it with the spear-gun.

He had never felt so alone in all his twenty-nine years. But as if they had been sent to encourage him, the dorados were there whenever he looked, daring to swim closer and closer to the strange rubber craft. 'By the end, I could reach down and touch them. They would shy away, but then come back again and again.'

As a designer and boat-builder, Callahan had often toyed with life-raft designs. Since 1976 he had sketched preliminary designs for a number of self-sufficient but sailable dinghy-type rafts. Now as he sat or lay on the cold, gyrating floor of the raft, he was able to devote a lot of time to refining his ideas with hard-won experience. He now knew that to the classic list of enemies of the survivor at sea – drowning, exposure, thirst and hunger – should be added a fifth threat to life: panic, distress, the crumbling of morale. To his mind, the ideal lifeboat should somehow provide an adequate counter to every enemy of survival. The designs took shape in his head as the raft drifted westwards.

On the eleventh day he managed to spear-gun his first dorado. The flesh was delicious, and over the following days and nights he sucked every ounce of fluid and meat from the fish. He felt more encouraged now about his chances of survival – as long as his band of dorados stayed with him. Sharks still bumped the raft during the night, but would disappear after a few sharp jabs from the gun. All the same, Callahan's fears for the safety of the raft were increasing.

On day fourteen, the solar stills yielded their first fresh water. Every three or four days now he managed to spear another dorado. Then the rubber-powered mechanism in the spear-gun gave out. Callahan had to improvise a hand-held harpoon by lashing the shaft of the spear to the gun, and then a very strange thing happened. As if to help the shipwrecked man, the dorados moved in close enough to the raft for him to gaff them. Callahan remembers being profoundly moved.

None the less, as days dragged into weeks, Callahan realized that he was slowly starving on his raw fish diet. To make matters worse, it was round about now that he spotted the first of the seven ships which he sighted during his ordeal. He fired a flare, but nobody saw it. He turned on his emergency transmitter, but nobody heard it. He felt a sense of frustration, hopelessness and unfairness stronger than at any other time of his ordeal.

Callahan took scrupulous navigation notes in his log, together with details of his water and food intake and weather conditions. Even if he died, the data might prove valuable if the raft was retrieved. He wondered if this was in fact the reason for his existence: to suffer what he was suffering, to man's very limits, so that others might learn what those limits are.

Back in Maine, Edward Callahan reported his son missing on 9 March, twelve days after his scheduled arrival date in Antigua. The US Coast Guard made a check of possible ports of departure and arrival, and for two weeks the Coast Guard's Search and Rescue Branch, Atlantic Area, broadcast an alert that *Napoleon Solo* was overdue and unlocated, requesting listeners to keep a sharp eye out for it. There was no response.

Steve Callahan's mother had had a terrible dream on the very night that *Napoleon Solo* sank. She had seen her son clawing his way up through dark and murky water, fighting for his life – at the exact time that he was in fact struggling against the closed hatchway. Now she resolved not to rest until she knew her son was safe. But when no trace of the boat was found by 17 March, the Coast Guard abandoned the search. Only ham radio operators kept the alert alive.

'The ham radio operators of this world are marvellous,' says Mrs Callahan. 'We felt we had someone helping us. Without them, it would have been a terrible, vast emptiness.'

On 1 April Steve's elder brother Edgar, a former deep-sea diver, flew home from Hawaii to work full-time on the search. Convinced that his younger brother would never give up, even in the direst of circumstances, he immediately set up a centre of operations in the family kitchen. With the help of sailing friends, Edgar and his father gathered wind, weather and current data, and plotted Steve's probable drift pattern.

Aboard the raft the temperature was now oppressively hot. Steve Callahan was doubting his ability to live through another week, when another strange thing happened to him. As he stood to search the horizon for ships, he saw a large rainbow, with a smaller one inset. Callahan was overcome by its beauty, and at that moment he believed he saw the whole scheme of nature: the beauty and the unpleasantness, both fitting together into the cycle of life. Although he had never been a religious man, Callahan began awkwardly to say a prayer.

On 20 March, day forty-five, as Callahan gaffed a dorado and hauled it aboard, the spear snapped, ripping a hole in the side of the raft. As he tried to repair it, a sudden storm hit.

He struggled to close the hole, first frantically plugging the gash with foam from a cushion and finally tying it off with cord. But still it leaked, and the sharks moved in closer as he worked with his hands underwater. He had alternately to pump air and bail for the next twenty-four hours. When exhaustion set in, he had to allow himself brief spells of sleep between the bouts of hard physical work. At night he worked in the light of a torch tied to his forehead.

'I'd tried everything I could possibly conceive of to make the repair and nothing, nothing worked. I saw no answer. At that point I broke down for a while and yelled and cried – even though I felt I was just being stupid and acting like a five-year-old.

'I couldn't find a solution, but I couldn't live if I didn't. There's nobody there to give you advice. Nobody to calm you down. This was the time when I probably would have died in a couple of days if I hadn't found a solution . . . There was a kind of duality in my mind. I could see myself being childish and I disapproved of it, but I couldn't help it.'

On the fourth day after the accident with the spear, the storm intensified. His log that day reads simply: 'My body is rotting away before my eyes.' Screaming and shouting with frustration, Callahan reached one of the lowest mental points of his experience. He broke down completely, and cried, 'Oh Lord, did I come this far to die?'

The night before, a large shark had passed the raft. At

daybreak it was still there. The shark knew he was weakening, Callahan thought to himself.

As he lay sobbing on the floor of the raft, the lower tube was deflating. But seconds later, mysteriously galvanized back into action, he got to his knees and started pumping once more. In response to his efforts, the foam plug simply blew out of the hole. As he stuffed it back in, Callahan knew that time was running out. The next time the plug blew out, he might be asleep, and the raft would founder. He had to find a permanent solution, and fast. 'I came very close to just giving up, saying, "OK, that's it . . ." Then all of a sudden, boing! I slapped myself and said: "Look! You *are* going to die if you don't find the answer. Keep calm. You're not in immediate danger. Think again! Think again. Think again. Go through all the equipment you have and see if there is any way you can figure out a solution."

'And then the answer came. It just dawned on me that a Boy Scout fork in a utensil kit I had thrown into my duffel bag a long time before was the answer. All I had to do was ram it through the end of the nylon I had gathered up around the hole and fold it inward. It fit so perfectly! It even had holes in the handle right where they should have been, so that made it easy. If that hadn't worked, I wouldn't have had enough strength to do anything else.'

Shooting the North Star at night with his crude sextant, Callahan assured himself that he was no more than eighteen degrees above the equator. With luck, the current would now carry him into the web of the West Indies. 'But there was no joy in this. I was constantly wet, a sunburned prune. Cold by night, hot by day. Where my skin rubbed against the raft, it sloughed off and the salt stung the sores . . . I couldn't stretch out or stand, and my legs cramped. It was like living for ever in a half-filled waterbed, with a couple of kangaroos kicking at the bottom.'

The dorados returned, but Callahan was by now too weak to do any harpooning. His body was in such a bad condition that his fingernails had loosened in their beds. Once again, as if to save him, one of the large fish seemed to sacrifice itself. Rolling over on its back, it revealed its soft underbelly to the debilitated survivor. Callahan was able to kill it easily. The flesh and fluid went a long way to restoring his strength and spirit.

In the family kitchen in Maine, Edgar Callahan studied weather data and drift patterns right round the clock, trying to work out the probable path of any wreckage or life-raft. He established that his younger brother must be somewhere within a 200-mile quadrant north-east of the group of islands at the edge of the Caribbean Sea.

Meanwhile, the wreckage of *Napoleon Solo* was wrongly reported as having been washed ashore in Puerto Rico. The Callahan family wept, but they were determined to carry on. Certain that Steve was still alive, his father was even contemplating selling the house to finance a private rescue operation.

On day seventy-six, 21 April, three black frigate birds flew around the raft. Callahan noticed that the sea had turned a deeper blue. The dorados were joined by other fish. Then, on the horizon, he saw land.

As the raft drifted closer to the steep cliffs, he saw a reef of coral in his path, pounded by heavy surf. The razor-sharp coral would cut the raft – and him – to shreds. After 2,600 miles adrift, he was about to face the final test of his resolve and ingenuity.

He had begun to wonder if he would ever make it ashore. 'You reach a point, adrift like that, when you know it will never end. You're doomed, a Flying Dutchman, to drift on for ever and ever. Same sharks, same seas, same birds and sun and thirst. Always.'

Callahan began feverishly stripping plastic and foam from the cushion and bandaging it around himself with pieces of the mainsail, to protect himself against the coral reef. Then, suddenly, a fishing boat appeared in the distance. Callahan waved like a madman, and the boat changed course. 'I had turned on my emergency beacon,' Callahan says. 'I thought air traffic would probably pick up the signal. Then I heard the motor, looked out, and there they were.' His joy was immense.

The three fishermen, from the tiny island of Marie Galante, eighty miles south of Antigua, looked on in amazement as the dorados continued to leap around the raft and its long-haired, bearded occupant. It seemed that yet again the dorados had saved him: the fishing boat changed course not because it had seen him waving, but because it spotted the birds hovering overhead, attracted by the leaping fish. 'The whole experience with them was mystical,' Callahan says, 'even spiritual.'

He waited while the fishermen slaughtered all of his fish. As he rode to the island of Marie Galante in their boat, the dead 'doggies' lay all around him. 'I had mixed feelings,' he recalls. 'They had come 1,800 miles with me, saved my life, and now they were being rewarded with death and the fish market. That's the sea for you.

'The fish were, in essence, my salvation, because it was they who attracted the birds. Now you may say, well, this doesn't mean anything. But to me the fact that the fishermen had never fished in that area before, that they saw the birds and came right to me because of the fish, this is significant to me.'

At 12.30 p.m. on 21 April, the telephone rang at the Callahans' house in Maine. A ham radio operator in Pompano Beach, Florida, relayed the news that Steve had been picked up off Marie Galante Island by three fishermen.

'If I hadn't gone back aboard *Solo* I probably would have died from exposure that first night,' Callahan now recalls, thinking about the lessons to be learned from his time aboard the 'so-called six-man raft that's suitable for one person . . . The only reason I am alive is because I was able to recover my own safety gear from the boat before it sank.'

Asked how he felt, Callahan said at the time: 'It feels

exactly as you would expect. But it's not just talking to people again: it's seeing reds or yellows or smelling a flower . . .'

In his log, he wrote:

To live in a liferaft is living Hell. Even those lovely scenes – the beautiful swim of the dorado, the swirling fluff of clouds becoming sunset, the explosion of sequinned galaxies at night – all are views of Heaven from a seat in Hell . . .

. . . I long to feel the breeze and ease of the downhill glide after my bicycle has reached the summit. I long to hear the laughter of children. I long to feel the warmth of family, friends and neighbours. I long for a simple glass of water, for putting my feet up on the woodstove and reading a book as snow comes down outside . . . I love all of you and long. I will fight to survive, to rejoin your company . . .

Steve Callahan was taken to hospital suffering from severe malnutrition, dehydration, exposure and multiple wounds. He had lost three stone in weight, and could scarcely whisper, but just three hours after being carried ashore he could stand without assistance, and was able to telephone his home in Maine.

After-effects

When you have been rescued and your ordeal is finally over, you should rest until you have completely recuperated – physically, at least. It will take longer than you might think. If you have been starved, you will be gripped by almost pathological greed; if you have been desperately thirsty, you might drink up to ten gallons of liquid in the first twenty-four hours after rescue. And of course, any physical wounds and injuries will also take time to heal.

Some survivors are strengthened by their experiences, while others are crushed. So, sadly, there might also be mental wounds and injuries. There will be bad dreams, certainly. Guilt, perhaps, that you survived and others didn't. Guilt about the way you behaved, or things you said. And there might be other, more damaging, psychological scars. Don't hesitate to seek psychiatric help if you are having problems readjusting. Help your family to recover as well as yourself. They too will have suffered.

On a more positive note, the chances are high that, with the right mental attitude, you will come home unscathed. The struggle to survive against all odds seems often to bring out the best in human nature. A person may be thrown back on solitary resourcefulness, or may combine forces with others – but you will, with luck, bring back with you a surer knowledge of yourself, your abilities and your powers of endurance and inventiveness.

There can be no more eloquent testimony to the after-effects of a survival ordeal than the words of the survivors themselves. The next chapter recounts what some of them have had to say.

21 Recovery

Elmo Wortman

'In retrospect, I now see that although [my faulty decision that we should separate] was based on a miscalculation in our location and resulted in a very difficult time for all of us, it might possibly have been the key factor in our survival.

'Within three days after Randy and I had left them, the girls were too weak to travel. Jena never stood or left the sail after that time. Cindy's movements were limited to less than a hundred feet, and even then she was afraid of not being able to return to the sail. If Randy and I had stayed with them and we all declined to that physical condition, it is pure speculation as to how long any of us could have lived. No one would have known our location or even been looking for us for some time.

'There is no simple reason why Cindy, Randy, Jena and I are not on the list of dead or missing. Each person who knows anything about such matters can find a reason that parallels and supports his personal convictions. Paul Breed, former Coast Guard commander, bush pilot and present airline owner, who has known us for several years, was quoted as saying, simply, "If any family could survive it, they could."

'The results of our experience have been different for each of us. What do the children now say about it? "A real 'bummer' of a trip, but no big deal" . . . As we returned to a more normal life style, their personalities also returned to normal.

'As for me, when I lay down to die after we were wrecked,

Cindy and Randy picked me up and made me go on living. When, because of my error, the girls were left alone for so long, they hung on, took care of each other and lived. In so doing, they made the balance of my life worthwhile. I had a good crew for the *Home's* last trip, a hell of a good crew.'

Lauren Elder

'For perhaps ten days following the accident and my descent from the mountain, Jean and Jay would appear at the foot of my bed at night, standing side by side in a rather formal pose. They were devoid of emotion, mute; they did not try to speak to me. I looked at them and prayed softly.

'During that time I spent whole days sitting in the sun, trying to sort out all that had happened, trying to understand it. Friends brought me books; strangers shared experiences and, quite often, confidences. Visions are not uncommon, I have learned. It is simply that those who have them are wary about admitting it.

'. . . I have since returned to the High Sierra. I made the trip in August, three months after the accident. My arm was in a cast and my foot had not yet healed, but I had to go back . . . it had some power that I didn't understand. I needed to return, to see for myself what it looked like from another perspective. I had been wrenched away from it too quickly, so that I hadn't been able to absorb what it was.

'. . . As we began to work our way into the mountains, I could feel the anxiety rising within me, but still I went. We hiked into the Center Basin, below the place where the plane had fallen, and I was sick with fear, with anxiety, with the absolute knowledge that I should not be alive, should not have come through that experience alive. I knew then that it was time to get off the mountain, to go home. If, like a cat, I should have nine lives, I had used up eight. I insisted we hike out as fast as we could . . .'

Iranian Embassy siege

After the SAS had stormed the Iranian Embassy in London on 6 May 1980, the hostages were suddenly free, and elated that it was all over.

'I remember lying on the grass outside feeling petrified and overjoyed at the same time,' said Ron Morris, a forty-seven-year-old employee at the Embassy.

The feeling of excitement continued as the exuberant hostages were transported to hospital for medical check-ups before being taken to a police college for debriefing. A leading psychiatrist was denied access to the released hostages by senior police officers, despite his protestations that they should be encouraged to talk about their ordeal at the first opportunity. For the hostages the excitement continued, together with a strong sense of togetherness, a common bond, as they discussed their dramatic rescue.

This sense of belonging among the hostages lasted for many months after the siege. Eight of them held frequent get-togethers, a positive form of therapy which provided not only a platform to air their fears about the episode, but also an essential form of self-help on the long road to recovery. These eight had reacted in different ways to their frightening confinement, but they were all perceptive enough to realize that the experience had changed their lives.

'In my private life I'm a much more reserved person now,' wrote Chris Cramer, a thirty-two-year-old BBC journalist, two years after the event. 'My home and my family mean a lot more to me than they did before.' For a short time after the siege Chris lived on his nerves. He was afraid of being alone and became very security-conscious. 'I felt haunted, almost hunted, by something. When I got into my car in the mornings I was afraid it would blow up. When I came home at night I crept up the stairs in case someone was waiting for me.'

Ahmed Dadgar, the Iranian medical adviser at the Embassy, was transferred to a private hospital ward within a few weeks of his miraculous recovery from his appalling injuries. It was there that the first delayed shock reaction to the six-day siege began to manifest itself. Ahmed would wake up in sheer fright, his body bathed in sweat.

'I imagined that I was back inside the telex room with [one of the gunmen] on guard outside the door . . . I could see [him] there with a gun in his hand, waiting to kill me.' The nightmares continued when he was finally discharged from hospital and returned to his London home. He became obsessively preoccupied, too, with his state of health. 'I was terribly depressed. I knew that I had escaped death by a miracle and yet resented the fact that I couldn't be as active as I was before the siege. Everything became an effort. I found that I couldn't concentrate for any length of time. I couldn't eat properly and I couldn't sleep.'

In common with many of the hostages, Ahmed Dadgar found that the siege had changed him from a normal person into an aggressive one. 'I was blunt with people at the Embassy, not the shy man I had been before. I started to tell them exactly what I thought of them.'

During the third day of the siege, fifty-one-year-old Muhammad Faruqi, editor of the Islamic magazine *Impact International*, was asked by another hostage if he regretted becoming involved in the incident. His answer reflected his entire reaction to the ordeal. 'It's a unique opportunity,' he said. 'And now that it's here I think I'd like to make the most of it.'

Of all of the hostages, Faruqi appeared to have suffered the least after-effects – which was due in great part, perhaps, to his being a devout Muslim with a passionate faith in his fellow human beings. He prayed several times a day, spent many hours in patient conversation with the gunmen and recorded an hour-long interview with the terrorist leader. He saw the siege more as a journalistic exercise than a terrifying experience. 'It was a very valuable time of my life,' he says. 'I saw it as a fascinating insight into a terrorist incident.'

Faruqi returned to work immediately after the incident

and started to write a series of articles on the siege for his magazine. He was lucky, perhaps, that he had access to such a valuable method of catharsis – a form of therapy also adopted by Chris Cramer and Sim Harris, in their book *Hostage*.

Sim Harris, a BBC sound recordist, found his obsession with the event lasted for at least nine months, coming to a head when he gave evidence at the Old Bailey trial of the surviving gunman. It then gave way to a completely new feeling, a delayed shock reaction which left him feeling severely depressed. 'I'm not sure I knew myself after the siege,' he recalled. 'I seemed to be acting out a part like a complete stranger. It was as if I was on roller skates, a different person with a different purpose.'

He threw himself into the writing of the book, discovering that the siege 'had a hold over me which I couldn't resist . . . Yet in a strange way [writing the book], seemed to be providing me with the right therapy. It was all coming out of my system, gradually, bit by bit.'

But Sim Harris knows that, as psychiatric specialists told many of the other hostages, some of the after-effects are likely to stay with him for ever: the memories will not fade; the best that they all can hope for is that in time the pain will diminish. In no survival story is this more apparent than in that of Martin Hartwell.

Martin Hartwell

'Shut up, I'm going to die now.'

In December 1972, the story of a bush pilot who had survived for thirty-two days in temperatures of minus thirty centigrade in the North West Territories of Canada was considered sensational enough to make headline news all over the world.

The name of the German-born pilot, a native of Cologne, was Martin Hartwell. Both his ankles were broken when the plane hit the ground, as well as his nose and one of his knees. But it was not so much the agony of his ordeal or the length of it that attracted attention, as the fact that his survival had depended on eating human flesh. World opinion did not legitimize the act of cannibalism in survival situations until after the rescue of the Uruguayan rugby team in the infamous Andes air crash. Unfortunately for Hartwell, they were still stranded on their mountain at the time of his eventual rescue. If only they had been rescued – and their story publicized – just a few weeks earlier, he could have been spared incalculable remorse, isolation and personal distress.

Against his judgement, Hartwell had been persuaded to undertake a 500-mile, three-and-a-half hour mercy flight in bad weather from Cambridge Bay to Yellowknife in the North West Territories, just inside the northern tree line and not far from the Arctic Circle. Aboard the plane were Judy Hill, a British nurse, and her two patients – Mrs Neemee Nulliayok, an Eskimo woman with pregnancy complications, and David Kootook, a fourteen-year-old with suspected appendicitis.

Misdirected by faulty navigation equipment, Hartwell flew far off course and was forced to lose height in order to fix his position. One of the plane's wings clipped a tree, cartwheeling it into the side of the only hill for 100 miles around. When the pilot came to, he found that the nurse beside him was unconscious, and breathing noisily. His first instinct was to try to lift her up, but he could not manage it on his own. Ordering David to climb over and out through a gap in the aircraft hull, Hartwell then tried lifting again while the boy pulled. They laid the nurse on the level ground, but within minutes the British girl had succumbed to her injuries, and the noisy breathing stopped.

Two hours later, the Eskimo woman also died.

Hartwell's own injuries were severe. It was immediately obvious that his survival was going to depend on the young boy, who, despite the pain of his suspected appendicitis and the shock of the crash, at once organized a fire and retrieved food and sleeping bags from the wreckage. He found meagre supplies of corned beef, sugar cubes, salt and soap.

Under Hartwell's guidance, David switched on the plane's Emergency Location Transmitter. Then, for the next seven days, they both sat back and waited, expecting rescue at any moment. The biggest air search in Canadian history was indeed under way. But Hartwell's faulty instruments had flown him so far off course in the bad weather that the ELT signal could not be detected by aircraft searching along his proposed flight path.

After the seventh night spent in below-freezing conditions, and with their emergency rations dwindling rapidly, Hartwell decided that they would have to take matters into their own hands if they were to have any hope of rescue. They had to move, even if it was no further than to a lake they could see in the distance – seemingly just four miles away – which would supply them with fish.

Hartwell came up with the idea of improvising a sledge from pieces of aircraft wreckage, and David hauling him downhill to the lake. David dutifully salvaged a piece of metal fuselage, and Hartwell dragged himself aboard. But the boy was unable to pull it, and the plan was abandoned.

In his crippled state, Hartwell found David's natural dependence on him more and more disconcerting – and his inability to supply answers to the boy's questions was sapping his own morale. When David asked when the rescue plane would come, Hartwell found himself answering that he didn't know – but that if one did come it would be tomorrow rather than today. When a high-flying aircraft once crossed over their position, David ran to switch on the ELT, and asked if the plane was looking for them. Hartwell replied as he believed: that he doubted the plane was part of an air search, but that it might pick up the ELT signal and send other planes to the area.

The stock of food was running dangerously low. Hartwell put it to David that he should strike out for the lake alone, and try to catch some fish for them both. The boy stalled, reasoning that because rescuers would be along very soon, there was no point in such a journey. Eventually, though, the boy did set off for the lake, carrying with him enough food for the journey. Soon afterwards he returned, reporting that the snow was too deep to be negotiated. Worse than that, he had eaten all the food.

Next day he tried again, but again he came back quickly. Finally, Hartwell talked him into a full-hearted attempt to reach the lake. The boy was away from the crash site for a night and all the following day. During the second night, an aircraft passed directly overhead. Hartwell activated the ELT, then heard another noise. David had returned, within five minutes of the plane flying overhead. Hartwell suspected that instead of making any attempt to reach the lake, the boy had merely been hiding behind a tree all the time.

Any further attempts to reach the lake were out of the question. It was obvious to Hartwell that the boy was now physically very weak, and beyond much effort. They investigated the drugs in Judy Hill's bag, and ended up sharing a one-inch piece of candle for nourishment.

Hartwell remembered having read that the last resort in a survival situation was not infrequently to turn to the dead as a source of nutrition. David, however, had not heard any such stories.

One night, Hartwell asked him if he would eat human flesh if it meant their survival.

'Shut up,' the Eskimo boy said simply. 'I'm going to die now.' Drained of all hope of rescue, and with their supply of food now completely exhausted, fourteen-year-old David Kootook died quietly that night in his sleep.

It was now twenty-four days after the crash – and five days since the Canadian armed forces had called off their search. Hartwell was finding that his hunger pains had subsided, but was not happy with the discovery: it would only mean that from now on he would just slowly die of starvation – unless he did something about it. Cursing the broken legs that were immobilizing him and making it impossible to forage for food, he began to think about the people who would like him to return, the people who might *need* him to return. He realized that if he was to survive to see them again he would have to eat the flesh of those who had died. The corpses lay around the wreckage in the snow, preserved by the bitter cold in the state in which they had died.

It was a ghastly prospect, but the pilot knew he had to be realistic. An early rescue by others now seemed a remote possibility. Yet he was almost literally glued to the spot by his injuries, only a matter of feet from what should be considered as life-giving meat. The facts of the matter seemed incontestable, yet what preoccupied Martin Hartwell now was how others would judge such an action. Would it get on the television? On the radio? In the newspapers? Or would the media be sympathetic and choose to gloss over it?

He felt that an act of cannibalism would go unreported. There had, after all, been many rumours over the years of survivors eating human flesh – but nothing was ever confirmed in the world's press. Even if it was reported, what then? What could they possibly do to him that was worse than his present predicament? If he was executed, he would be dead. If he didn't eat the flesh, he would be dead. A little earlier, but dead all the same.

Hartwell's emotions swung now towards anger. Anger against his own impotence in the situation, and anger against God. Yet if he did not help himself, why should he expect divine help? The only resource he had left was simple courage. He shouted as loud as he could into the wilderness around him: 'Is there nobody around here?'

He shouted in all directions, but no reply came. Only the wind. And there was nothing to be seen, either – nothing but the same unchanged areas of trees and snow and wreckage. A grim determination began to grow inside him to get himself out alive, by whatever means. 'I crawled to a tree 12 yards away and back,' Hartwell wrote later in the twenty-four-page statement he submitted to the Canadian police. 'The pain was unbelievable and it took me two hours. No food for three days. I had to get something to fill the gap until my legs got better and I could get to a lake. From here it's clear to the authorities what I did . . .'

The first bite of flesh was the worst. But once Hartwell had overcome his natural repugnance and had brought himself to swallow it, the taboo was broken and he experienced no further negative reactions.

Meanwhile, a public outcry was going on in the North West Territories, where residents' lives depended on air travel. The biggest air search in Canadian history was resumed, and on the thirty-second day of Hartwell's wait, purely by chance, an aircraft picked up the ELT signal.

Corporals Harvey Copeland and Al Williams, parachutist medical orderlies, jumped from their rescue helicopter at 1,000 feet. They had to wade through heavy snow for an hour before they reached the wreckage of Martin Hartwell's light aircraft. 'You wouldn't have believed anyone could have lived through it,' Harvey Copeland reported to the press on his return.

As the paramedics surveyed the grisly scene around Hartwell, they did their best to reassure him. They told him not to worry: the means of his survival would never be made public. Keep cool, they said. Keep quiet.

Hartwell smoked a cigarette, then another. For the first time, he felt himself getting tense and nervous. Deep inside, he knew that here the horror started.

At the hospital in Yellowknife he had a bath, then two Royal Canadian Mounted Police arrived to question him. They asked Hartwell if he had anything 'special' to say about what had happened.

'Yes,' Hartwell said simply, 'I survived because I ate human flesh.'

Echoing the words of the two paramedics, the Mounties told him to keep quiet about it. Nothing of this aspect of his ordeal would ever come out into the open.

Almost inevitably, however, the news *did* break. The public was at once fascinated and appalled, with Hartwell at the centre of ghoulish interest. Taxi drivers and hospital receptionists backed away from him. He could see in their eyes what they were thinking: 'So *he's* the one. So *that's* what a cannibal looks like.'

Martin Hartwell took the public's reaction hard. Faced with a similar ordeal, he now says, he would, like the fourteen-year-old boy, simply stretch out in the snow and say: 'Shut up, I'm going to die now.'

22 'What if' and survival training

You now know all the principles of survival. The rule 'You'll survive if you think you can' should by now be engraved for ever in your memory cells. You have read about many people who have got themselves out of trouble. You know that it is the initial rush of panic which often accompanies unexpected trouble in unfamiliar surroundings which can do most to prevent your survival.

So it should interest you to know that there is a simple, effective way to sharpen your survival skills and also increase your enjoyment of the outdoors: the 'what if' game. Whether you're driving through snow on a lonely moorland road, or flying a light aircraft over tropical rain forest, or skiing off-piste, or even just riding the underground to work, practising 'what if' will improve your ability to deal with a real emergency, should it ever arise.

What if the car breaks down here in the dark, in a blizzard, in the middle of nowhere?

What if the office block goes up in flames and I'm on the top floor?

What if the lift jams?

It's not alarmist or loony to play this game, just solid good sense – no different from pilots practising in flight simulators, or a company's financial director planning ahead for various contingencies. You will find yourself applying the survival principles and techniques you have learned in this book, and in 'using' them – however hypothetically – you will reinforce them in your memory.

The more you play the 'what if' game, the more proficient, adaptive and safety-conscious you'll become: you'll think about where to install smoke detectors and fire extinguishers in your home, start planning the contents of your survival kit for next year's holiday on the Algarve, make sure you know the emergency exits at your place of work and so on. Even more important, however, is that you will think yourself into the habit of acting rationally, calmly and constructively in an emergency. As you now know, nothing prevents panic better than taking control of a situation. The more you practise taking charge in hypothetical crises, the better you will perform in real ones. What's more, the 'what if' game improves your confidence, and will help you to develop a positive mental attitude and the all-important will to survive.

The bottom line, however, is this: your attitude will be better if you are not only mentally prepared to deal with threats to your life, but physically and emotionally prepared, too. And there can be no better way of doing this than through a bit of real, live, hands-on simulation – a survival training course. A good course will equip you with experience and confidence which, added to the knowledge you have gained in this book, will make you even better able to attack the enemies of survival head-on – and survive.

Human beings are basically creatures of habit. We depend on routine, organization and some degree of discipline – the parameters or boundaries which allow us to be comfortable in our surroundings, which define what might be called our 'comfort zones'. We all live, work and play in our individual zones, and just as individuals are different – unique in our abilities and experience and personalities – so are our personal limits. Everyone establishes their own comfort zones – physical, mental, and emotional. We rarely venture outside them, unless circumstances force us to. It follows, then, that whenever anyone is placed in a situation that stretches them to the outer limits of those individual zones, anxiety, stress and fear will result.

By playing 'what if', you can expand your own mental comfort zone into areas that you're unsure of now. But a survival training course will expand your physical and emotional limits, too. Under the sort of repeated stress which is simulated on such courses, people can learn to make increasingly effective adjustments – in contrast with what happens in the typical emergency situation, when people respond with disorganized and frequently shock-like behaviour: the headless chicken syndrome.

Unknown factors during any emergency will be as numerous as they are variable – factors which fall outside the comfort zones of most people. Rational, positive thinking and action which draws on the experience of simulated survival situations will in most cases be the most effective method of gaining control.

Ultimately, the best way of learning these skills of self-reliance is to get out there and do it for real. There is no substitute for actually employing the techniques that are designed to save your life: discovering that in order to eat, drink, sleep and keep warm in the open, you've got to do it yourself – or face the consequences. Learning at first hand how to cope with fatigue, hunger, thirst, fear and all the other enemies of survival can be a frightening experience. But it's a very salutary one, too. Because you'll come away with the skills and confidence to cope with any survival situation . . . and therefore to cope with almost anything else that life is going to throw at you.

Select bibliography

A full bibliography of background material for this book would occupy many pages. Since all the theory contained in that material has either guided the writing of *Survival* or is directly reflected in it, I recommend for further reading only a few personal accounts.

Steven Callahan, *Adrift*, Houghton Mifflin, New York, 1986.

Chris Cramer and Sim Harris, *Hostage*, John Clare, London, 1982.

Lauren Elder with Shirley Streshinsky, *And I Alone Survived*, Collins, London, 1978.

Dougal Robertson, *Survive the Savage Sea*, Granada, London, 1984.

Elmo Wortman, *Almost Too Late*, George Allen and Unwin, London, 1981.

BAD MONEY

A.M. KABAL

'Midsummer's Eve, the hard men moved . . .'

01.01 hours GMT: in London, Rome, Panama and Gdansk four men are savagely murdered. No one sees the connection. It's a quiet, efficient start to the international crime of the century . . .

But one victim, reporter Tom Wellbeck, leaves behind his ex-wife, fellow-journalist Caro Kilkenny, who is determined to find the truth about his death. And then there's Tom's friend, John Standing – burned-out, alcoholic, but still the one man with the skill and experience to see the case through . . .

They unravel a thread of intrigue that stretches from Warsaw to Washington, from the silent corridors of the Vatican to the murderous jungles of Central America, a vicious thread of bad blood and bad money. And when Standing detects the hand of his old enemy David Medina, he knows their troubles are just beginning . . .

Financial devilry of a high order . . . knowledgeable and sinister
OBSERVER

Also by A M Kabal in Sphere Books:
THE ADVERSARY

0 7221 5232 9   **CRIME/THRILLER**   £3.99

PRECINCT: SIBERIA

Tom Philbin

NINE SQUARE MILES OF SAVAGE NEW YORK STREETS

Siberia: the 53rd Precinct. Where the heaviest criminals hang out; where the most hardened cops are sent.

Detective Joe Lawless: tough, street-smart and ruthless, his battles with the brass have landed him in Siberia. Now he's out to nail a sadistic child-murderer before he kills again . . .

Police Officer Barbara Babalino: sent to Siberia for refusing the advances of her boss, she's out to rescue a young hooker. But the girl's pimp knows something that could destroy Barbara's life . . .

Detective Leo Grady: with five months before retirement and a flask of vodka in his pocket, he thinks he can take it easy. He can forget it. Nothing's easy in PRECINCT: SIBERIA

0 7474 0283 3   CRIME   £3.50

JUNIPER

James Murphy

'Knowing your enemy is not the primary consideration.
You have to know what you are defending first of all.
Then the enemy will show itself.'

Oliver Maitland joined MI5 to defend his country. To
defend freedom and democracy. He's served his time in
the hell of Northern Ireland, battling for a peaceful
solution. Now he's transferred to counter-subversion,
fighting, not the IRA but ordinary men and women.

Phone tapping, mail interception, burglary – it's a dirty
war. And when Maitland finds out the truth behind the
Mountbatten murder he begins to wonder who the
enemy really is.

Operation JUNIPER, brainchild of Maitland's sadistic
boss, 'The Butcher', is the deadliest campaign yet. It's
going to smash the peace movement and sabotage
disarmament talks. Maitland knows the butcher doesn't
care how many British agents have to die to fulfil his
plans. What he doesn't know is that he's top of the
hit-list . . .

Also by James Murphy in Sphere Books:

CEDAR

0 7474 0059 8   ADVENTURE THRILLER   £3.50

LORDS OF THE AIR

GRAHAM MASTERTON

When Herbert Lord was tragically killed in a plane crash in 1931, he left behind an aeronautical empire – and a personal legacy to his sons . . .

JAMES inherits his arrogance, his attraction for women, and the ruthless ambition that will pave his way to the top of the American airline business with scandal – and even murder . . .

RICHARD the stay-at-home, has the dependability to run the British company, the patriotism to adapt it to wartime needs, and the vision to prepare it for the jet age . . .

MICHAEL is endowed with his daredevil flying genius, and the romantic spirit of pioneer flying that will lead him to the lonely skies of Australia's North-West Territory . . .

And to all three, powering across continents through family rivalry and world conflict, glamour and danger, Herbert also left a secret – a secret they cannot learn until they have paid the price . . .

Also by Graham Masterton in Sphere Books don't miss

0 7474 0124 1   GENERAL FICTION   £3.99

WILDTRACK

BERNARD CORNWELL

After the hell of the Falklands War, Nick Sandman, VC, knows what it is to be a hero. Barely able to walk, he's got no money, no job and no prospects. But, defiantly, he clings to the memory of a boat called *Sycorax*, his only possession, his only hope of a life at sea with no rules and no fighting. Until even that dream is shattered . . .

For there is no *Sycorax* to return to – only a beached and battered wreck, torn from its Devon mooring. In its place stands the gleaming ocean racer *Wildtrack*. And into Nick's life comes its menacing owner Tony Bannister, a rich and powerful TV personality. Compelled to make a desperate bargain with the ruthless Bannister, Nick is forced into a deal which may give him a chance to reclaim his dream – but at a price. And in the murky world of deceit and fraud into which Nick is thrown, that price could be his own life . . .

Also by Bernard Cornwell in Sphere Books:
REDCOAT

0 7474 0187 X   GENERAL FICTION   £3.50

All Sphere Books are available at your bookshop or newsagent, or can be ordered from the following address: Sphere Books, Cash Sales Department, P.O. Box 11, Falmouth, Cornwall TR10 9EN.

Please send cheque or postal order (no currency), and allow 60p for postage and packing for the first book plus 25p for the second book and 15p for each additional book ordered up to a maximum charge of £1.90 in U.K.

B.F.P.O. customers please allow 60p for the first book, 25p for the second book plus 15p per copy for the next 7 books, thereafter 9p per book.

Overseas customers, including Eire, please allow £1.25 for postage and packing for the first book, 75p for the second book and 28p for each subsequent title ordered.